United Nations Global Conferences

GW01003689

United Nations Global Conferences discusses the origins, meaning, purposes, trends and controversies concerning the convening and impacts of United Nations global conferences.

It is a particularly propitious time for such a study since there are thirty such conferences to compare, and many argue that they have not been worth the money expended on them. Others, however, suggest that the only effective way to address global problems, such as racism, sexism, over-population, environmental degradation, over-fishing, urbanization, and the proliferation of small arms is through the convening of such conferences. This book, the first comprehensive comparative study of such conferences, provides information essential to the ongoing debate about the pros and cons of multilateralism and includes an examination of:

* the typical structure of a conference
* substantive and institutional outcomes of the conferences
* changes resulting from the conferences
* UN conferences as mechanisms for coping with the problems of the twenty-first century.

This book will be essential reading for students of the United Nations and of international organization and global governance, as well as practitioners from non-governmental organizations.

Michael G. Schechter is Professor of International Relations at James Madison College of Michigan State University, USA. He is the author, co-author, editor or co-editor of fifteen books and has published extensively in the fields of international organization and international relations.

Global Institutions Series

Edited by Thomas G. Weiss
The CUNY Graduate Center, New York, USA

and Rorden Wilkinson
University of Manchester, UK

The "Global Institutions Series" is designed to provide readers with comprehensive, accessible, and informative guides to the history, structure, and activities of key international organizations. Every volume stands on its own as a thorough and insightful treatment of a particular topic, but the series as a whole contributes to a coherent and complementary portrait of the phenomenon of global institutions at the dawn of the millennium.

Each book is written by a recognized expert in the field, conforms to a similar structure, and covers a range of themes and debates common to the series. These areas of shared concern include the general purpose and rationale for organizations, developments over time, membership, structure, decision-making procedures, and key functions. Moreover, the current debates are placed in a historical perspective alongside informed analysis and critique. Each book also contains an annotated bibliography and guide to electronic information as well as any annexes appropriate to the subject matter at hand.

The volumes currently under contract include:

The United Nations and Human Rights (2005)
by Julie Mertus (American University)

UN Global Conferences (2005)
by Michael Schechter (Michigan State University)

The UN Secretary-General and Secretariat (2005)
by Leon Gordenker (Princeton University)

The UN General Assembly (2005)
by M. J. Peterson (University of Massachusetts, Amherst)

The UN Security Council
by Edward C. Luck (Columbia University)

The International Monetary Fund
by James Vreeland (Yale University)

For further information regarding the series, please contact:

Craig Fowlie, Publisher, Politics & International Studies
Taylor & Francis
2 Park Square, Milton Park, Abingdon
Oxon OX14 4RN, UK

+44 (0)207 842 2057 Tel
+44 (0)207 842 2302 Fax

craig.fowlie@tandf.co.uk
www.routledge.com

United Nations Global Conferences

Michael G. Schechter

Routledge
Taylor & Francis Group

LONDON AND NEW YORK

First published 2005
by Routledge
2 Park Square, Milton Park, Abingdon, Oxon OX14 4RN

Simultaneously published in the USA and Canada
by Routledge
270 Madison Ave, New York, NY 10016

Routledge is an imprint of the Taylor & Francis Group

© 2005 Michael G. Schechter

Typeset in Times New Roman by
Taylor & Francis Books
Printed and bound in Great Britain by
TJ International Ltd, Padstow, Cornwall

British Library Cataloguing in Publication Data
A catalogue record for this book is available from the British Library

Library of Congress Cataloging in Publication Data
A catalog record for this title has been requested

ISBN 0–415–34380–1 (hbk)
ISBN 0–415–34381–X (pbk)

Contents

List of boxes

Foreword

This volume is among the first in a new and dynamic series on "global institutions." As the title suggests, we hope that it offers a comprehensive guide to the history, structure, and concrete activities of "UN global conferences." Remarkable as it may seem, there exist few individual works that offer in-depth treatments of prominent global bodies and processes, much less an entire series of concise and complementary volumes. Those that do exist are either out of date, inaccessible to the non-specialist reader, or seek to develop a specialized understanding of particular aspects of an institution or a process rather than offer an overall account of its functioning. Similarly, existing works have often been written in highly technical language or have been crafted "in-house" and are notoriously self-serving and narrow in focus.

The advent of electronic media has helped by making information and resolutions more widely available, but it has also complicated matters further. The growing reliance on the internet and other electronic methods of finding information about key international organizations and processes has served, ironically, to limit the educational materials to which most readers have ready access—namely, books. Public relations documents, raw data, and loosely refereed websites do not intelligent analysis make. Official publications compete with a vast amount of electronically available information, much of which is suspect because of its ideological or self-promoting slant. Paradoxically, a growing range of purportedly independent websites offering analyses of the activities of particular organizations has emerged, but one inadvertent consequence has been to frustrate access to basic, authoritative, critical, and well-researched texts. The market for such has actually been reduced by the ready availability of varying quality electronic materials.

We are delighted that Routledge asked us to edit a series that bucks this trend. They are betting that serious students and professionals will want serious analyses. We have assembled a first-rate line-up of authors. Our intention, then, is to provide one-stop shopping for all readers—students (both undergraduate and postgraduate), interested negotiators, diplomats, practitioners from the non-governmental and intergovernmental communities, and interested parties alike—seeking information about the most prominent institutional aspects of global governance.

UN global conferences

Viewed from the vantage point of the beginning of the twenty-first century, it may be difficult to believe that in the 1960s environmental degradation, population growth, urbanization, and women's rights were not squarely on the international agenda. This changed during the 1970s and the 1990s when the United Nations system launched a series of global conferences on each of these challenges. We asked Michael Schechter—professor at James Madison College of Michigan State University in East Lansing—to undertake the daunting task of making sense of the host of international gatherings that cynics dismiss as "jamborees" but that have changed discourse, priorities, and policies. Public opinion was mobilized. Action was often weak, or certainly inadequate for the magnitude of the challenges identified. But the long-term dynamics have been fundamentally altered.

As this book makes clear, international conferences about economic development are, of course, not exactly new. Conference diplomacy has, since the Congress of Vienna after Napoleon's defeat at Waterloo, been a device for states to address problems. The League of Nations also convened them during the inter-war period.

But, as Michael Schechter clearly demonstrates, the UN institutionalized the conference system as a transmission belt for ideas in order to respond to common, global concerns. His masterful synthesis of a complicated set of meetings and processes builds on much of his own earlier and distinguished work on the topic.[1] Readers will be pleased with his roadmap through the maze of secretariats and leaders, the politics of preparatory committees and conferences themselves, the separate forums by non-governmental organizations, the final declarations and programs of action, and sometimes follow-up and monitoring mechanisms.

During the 1990s, the UN system went back to this method and continued the series begun in the 1970s, but this time as media events for heads of state and government rather than for "mere" ministers. In a new environment marked by the end of the Cold War, the UN convened world summits to promote agendas for the new millennium.

The objective was to mobilize governments and global civil society and to build a consensus and help shape a new agenda for changes that went against orthodoxy.

Toward the end of his term, UN Secretary-General Boutros Boutros-Ghali noted:

> The conferences of the United Nations, and the action programmes and agendas produced by these conferences form, together, an agenda for development committed to by the world community. Through these conferences, development cooperation will be revitalized and reinvented. The United Nations, its Member States, and you, the delegates at the conferences, are deciding development patterns for future generations. You are deciding the form of development cooperation to be adopted by the United Nations; you are setting the standards by which the actions of States, Organizations and individuals will be judged. This is the importance of the international conferences of the United Nations.[2]

Boutros-Ghali was more enthusiastic than Michael Schechter or either of us would be, but this concise volume will permit the readers to make up their own minds. It reaches a broad audience with many useful descriptions, lists of resources, and numerous concrete examples that draw especially on the vital question of how states and global civil society have conversations about pressing problems.

As always, we welcome comments and suggestions from readers.

Thomas G. Weiss, The CUNY Graduate Center, New York, USA
Rorden Wilkinson, University of Manchester, UK
November 2004

Acknowledgements

To a large extent this volume represents the influence of the diverse teachers of international law, international organization, and global governance with whom I have studied. The book, of course, is not the book that any of them would have written, much less are they responsible for it, except as mentors to whom I owe so much. These include those who taught and mentored me while I was a graduate student at Columbia: Robert W. Cox, Lawrence S. Finkelstein, Robert S. Jordan, Oliver J. Lissitzyn, and Donald J. Puchala. And those who subsequently rekindled my interest in the United Nations—Leon Gordenker, Harold K. Jacobson, W. Andy Knight, Charlotte Ku, Gene Lyons, M.J. Peterson, Debbi Schaubman, Edwin Smith and Thomas G. Weiss—and the countless students in my classes on international law, international organization and global governance at James Madison College of Michigan State University.

I also wish to express my appreciation to Michigan State University for granting me a Sabbatical, without which this book could not have been written and to the series editors, Thomas G. Weiss and Rorden Wilkinson, and the series assistant, Effie MacLachlan, for their countless useful suggestions about how to improve this volume.

I have dedicated the book to my parents, Belle and Bernard Schechter, who taught me the love of learning and made it possible for me to attain the formal education that they could not have, and to my wife, Ilene, whose patience, support, love and sacrifices can never be sufficiently acknowledged.

List of abbreviations

ACC	Administrative Committee on Coordination
ADL	Anti-Defamation League
BMS	biennial meeting of states
CBD	Convention on Biological Diversity
CEB	Chief Executives Board for Coordination
CEDAW	Convention on the Elimination of Discrimination Against Women
CIEC	Conference on International Economic Cooperation
CONGO	Conference of Non-Governmental Organizations
CSCE	Conference on Security and Cooperation in Europe
CSD	Commission on Sustainable Development
DAWN	Development Alternatives with Women for a New Era
DDT	dichloro-diphenyl-trichloromethylmethane
DESCON	Consultative Group for Desertification Control
ECA	Economic Commission for Africa
ECE	Economic Commission for Europe
ECLAC	Economic Commission for Latin America and the Caribbean
ECOSOC	Economic and Social Council
EEC	European Economic Community
EPA	Environmental Protection Agency
ESCAP	Economic and Social Commission for Asia and the Pacific
ESCWA	Economic and Social Commission for Western Asia
EU	European Union
FAO	Food and Agriculture Organization
GATT	General Agreement on Tariffs and Trade
GDP	gross domestic product
GEF	Global Environmental Facility

HIV/AIDS	human immunodeficiency virus/acquired immuno-deficiency virus
IAEA	International Atomic Energy Agency
IANSA	International Action Network on Small Arms
IBRD	International Bank for Reconstruction and Development
ICAO	International Civil Aviation Organization
ICJ	International Court of Justice
ICPD	International Conference on Population and Development
ICSID	International Center for Settlement of Investment Disputes
ICSU	International Council of Scientific Unions (now International Council for Science)
IDA	International Development Association
IFAD	International Fund for Agricultural Development
IFC	International Finance Corporation
IFSD	International Fund for Social Development
ILO	International Labour Organization
IMF	International Monetary Fund
IMO	International Maritime Organization
INGO	international non-governmental organization
INSTRAW	International Research and Training Institute for the Advancement of Women
IUCN	International Union for the Conservation of Nature
IUSSP	International Union for the Scientific Study of Population
IWY	International Women's Year
IYPC	International Youth Population Conference
JIU	Joint Inspection Unit
LDC	less developed country
MAD	mutual assured destruction
MCA	Millennium Challenge Account
MDG	Millennium Development Goal
MIGA	Multilateral Investment Guarantee Agency
MSA	most severely affected
NATO	North Atlantic Treaty Organization
NFLS	Nairobi Forward-Looking Strategies for the Advancement of Women
NGLS	Non-Governmental Liaison Service
NGO	non-governmental organization
NIEO	New International Economic Order

NRA	National Rifle Association
OPEC	Organization of Arab Petroleum-Exporting Countries
OAU	Organization of African Unity
ODA	Official Development Assistance
OECD	Organization for Economic Cooperation and Development
PACD	Plan of Action to Combat Desertification
PLO	Palestine Liberation Organization
PrepCom	Preparatory Committee
SDI	Strategic Defense Initiative
SDR	Special Drawing Right
TRIPS	Trade-Related Aspects of Intellectual Property Rights
UN	United Nations
UNCED	United Nations Conference on Human Environment and Development
UNCHE	United Nations Conference on the Human Environment
UNCHS	United Nations Center for Human Settlements
UNCOD	United Nations Conference on Desertification
UNCTAD	United Nations Conference on Trade and Development
UNDP	United Nations Development Program
UNEP	United Nations Environment Program
UNESCO	United Nations Educational, Scientific and Cultural Organization
UNFF	United Nations Forum on Forests
UNFPA	United Nations Fund for Population Activities
UNHCR	United Nations High Commissioner for Refugees
UNICEF	United Nations (International) Children's (Emergency) Fund
UNIDO	United Nations Industrial Development Organization
UNIFEM	United Nations Development Fund for Women
UNITAR	United Nations Institute for Training and Research
UNRRA	United Nations Relief and Rehabilitation Agency
UNSO	United Nations Sudano-Sahelian Office
UPU	Universal Postal Union
USAID	US Agency for International Development
WACLA	World Assembly of Cities and Local Authorities
WCED	World Commission on Environment and Development
WEHAB	water, energy, health, agriculture and biodiversity
WFC	World Food Council
WFP	World Food Program

WFSA	World Forum on the Future of Shooting Activities
WHO	World Health Organization
WIDF	Women's International Democratic Federation
WIPO	World Intellectual Property Organization
WMO	World Meteorological Organization
WPY	World Population Year
WSSD	World Summit for Social Development
WSSD	World Summit on Sustainable Development
WTO	World Tourism Organization
WTO	World Trade Organization

1 Introduction

The United Nations Millennium Summit this week brings to New York City the largest gathering ever of world leaders to address the most serious of global afflictions. It is an occasion calling for hope and perseverance, but most New Yorkers cannot get past the ominous numbers: 91 scheduled protests, at least 175 motorcades, 245 dignitaries requiring Secret Service and police protection, and 3 days of President Clinton stopping traffic in Manhattan. It is no wonder many residents welcome the meeting with the same grousing accorded the West Nile virus.[1]

Those present at the creation of the post-World War II financial institutions in Bretton Woods, New Hampshire, in July 1944 and the creators of the United Nations (UN) in San Francisco from April to June 1945 were Janus-faced. They looked back to the period between World War I and World War II and to the League of Nations and sought to create institutions that built on its strengths, but also succeeded in preventing a world war in the way it had not. And they looked forward to a world where multilateralism would aid in making the world more prosperous and peoples would gain unprecedented human rights, including the right to self-determination. But those planners and policy-makers were not clairvoyant. And the institutions that they created, while impressive in their own right, have proven incapable of coping with an entirely new world, the world of the late twentieth and early twenty-first centuries.[2]

One of the means to try and meet with the demand of this evolving new world order, one with a new distribution of global power, with increased economic stratification, and with a realization of nuclear, health and ecological threats to the very survival of the planet, are UN world conferences and summits, of which the Millennium Summit noted above is sometimes referred to as the "mother of all world conferences." This *ad hoc* institutional response is the subject of this book. As will be seen, the conferences' successes in achieving their goals are variable and often fall way short of the expectations of their conveners. But as will also be seen, the problems that they have addressed are not going away. And while the future form of the world order of the twenty-first century remains very much contested, what is clear is that we are not going back to the world of the mid-1940s and efforts to restructure the UN to accommodate to those changes are not happening quickly.[3] *Ad hoc* institutional responses such as world conferences and summits may not be an adequate institutional solution to the challenges of the day, but they do offer the virtue of flexibility and, as this volume attests, their accomplishments are notable. Their very nature, *ad hoc* as it is, with their tendency to adapt and, at times, to build on and even learn from previous conferences has led them to play an important role in the evolving global governance system of the past thirty-plus years. This book presents that story for the first time.

More specifically, its goal is to discuss the origin, meaning, purposes, trends and controversies concerning the convening and impacts of UN global conferences. This seems a particularly timely undertaking, both because there are now a large number of conferences worthy of comparison and because there are those—including the chairman of one of the most recent of such conferences, Emil Salim of the World Summit for Social Development (WSSD)—who have again suggested that the era of such conferences might be coming to a close.[4] If not that, at least, it has been argued that the value of continuing to convene such conferences needs to be assessed, before additional follow-up UN global conferences are convened, much less new conferences on key issues not heretofore focused on at such conferences, like migration, environmental refugees and sustainable fisheries.[5] This volume is a modest attempt to contribute to such an assessment.

To do this, attention will first be drawn to what such conferences have in common, including the typical "structure" of a conference, and what is distinctive about each of them. To achieve the latter goal, various UN global conferences (most, but not all dealing with aspects of economic and social development) will be described, including their key state and non-state participants and secretariat officials. Descriptions of the conferences will, of necessity, include their major substantive and institutional proposals, including programs of action, declarations, communiqués, treaties, and proposals for global institution-building. The discussions of the various conferences will, of necessity, include an assessment of their success in meeting the challenges for which they were established (e.g. alleviation of human rights abuses, lessening of air pollution or desertification). The assessment of such impacts is, in many ways, the most challenging aspect of the volume. Because conferences rarely result in legally binding outcomes (and thus lack firm compliance requirements); because their subject matter is often broad; because the time since they were convened is, except in rare circumstances, quite limited; because there are so many intervening variables between recommendations made and decisions taken at conferences and the improvement (or worsening) of the problem being addressed (including the actions or inaction of national and local governments and the framing of the Convention's deliberations and accomplishments by the news media); and because there are so many conflicting goals that various parties have set for the conferences as well as multiple unintended impacts, it is very hard to assess conferences' success or failure or their true effectiveness and impacts.[6] And as if these methodological challenges to assessing success or failure were not enough, Michael Glantz contends there are additional challenges to assessing the worth of such conferences:

> Judgments about the relative success or failure of such gatherings in meeting their implicit and explicit goals have varied widely. Often such evaluations have been affected by the existence of cleavages within the international community; cleavages based on political, cultural, ideological, and economic factors. Given the existence of these factors, there are often differing views on what such international conferences might achieve, on who should bear the financial burden of carrying out the suggestions of the conference, and on the nature as well as the causes of the problems being evaluated.[7]

In spite of these methodological challenges to assess whether the conferences have achieved the ostensible purposes for their being convened, attention will also be directed at identifying their other impacts, intended or otherwise, such as their contribution to global networking (legitimizing and igniting national advocacy and transnational social movements) and bureaucratic consequences in member states, including the establishment of new ministries and the empowerment of pre-existing ones.

In spite of the complications of assessing the successes and impact of global conferences, it still happens that such conferences are sometimes discredited even when the causes for their "failures" are totally beyond their control (e.g. because of the timing of elections in a key participating state or the outbreak of war or other higher priority structural events).[8] Often, as will be seen, they "fail" or at least come up short because of the lack of follow-through. But this doesn't preclude some of the very actors responsible for funding and effectuating that follow-through from criticizing them. Peter Willetts's statement on this subject from years ago seems particularly prophetic as scholars and politicians label one conference or another as a failure and thus suffer from conference fatigue, and as a consequence, call for a stop to convening them (or even convening follow-up conferences to assess their success or failures to date and the steps needed to improve the situation):

> As global conferences only arise as a mechanism to deal with issues which would otherwise be of low priority and usually to deal with issues of high contention, they are more likely than institutional meetings to be a "failure." However, a failure in the formal sense of there being no agreed final document, or a document that obscures continuing disagreement, or a commitment to principles without a commitment to action does not mean the conference has failed to have a significant impact in the long run upon the political process. Those trying to promote change may still have shifted the consensus and/or increased the pressure upon their opponents. When priorities on the global agenda are to be changed by raising a new issue, by fundamentally redefining an issue, by giving an issue more attention or by shifting the locus of decision-making, then a global conference can be the mechanism to promote the change in the agenda against the opposition of those who want to maintain the *status quo*.[9]

In addition to describing their goals and operations and addressing the value and limits of the various conferences discussed in this volume, attention will also be drawn to a series of institutional innovations, as conferees sought to learn from what worked or did not work in the past, and recognized the importance of having leadership that is both entrepreneurial and politically savvy, and the necessity to adapt to an ever-changing global environment.[10] The world orders of 1968 and 2005 are quite different in so many respects, including the redistribution of power, the end of colonialism, the end of the Cold War and the increased salience of what were heretofore thought of as issues of "low politics," the increasing influence of non-state actors and the roles of the media and experts in global policy-making. To succeed, conferees needed to be innovative. As will be seen, some of those innovations have succeeded in meeting the challenges of the day. Others have not.

What is a UN global conference?

Conference diplomacy is one of the key features of the UN[11] and the UN has been convening global conferences almost from the beginning.[12] But there is no consensus on a list of such conferences.[13] In part, this is because there is no authoritative definition of what constitutes a UN global conference. Willetts provides us a kind of "bottom line," albeit probably a too-inclusive definition: *"a conference convened on a non-routine basis, under the auspices of the United Nations, with all countries eligible to attend."*[14] The UN Joint Inspection Unit (JIU) accepted the definition of a "special conference" as contained in a 1980 UN Secretary-General report. It is a bit more specific and seemingly includes the key defining elements of such conferences:

> a conference that is not part of the regular recurrent conference programme of a biennium, but that is convened in response to a specific resolution by the General Assembly or the Economic and Social Council, for whose substantive preparation and specific additional budgetary provisions are made and which all States are normally invited to attend. Such a conference usually extends over a period of a minimum of two to a maximum of four to six weeks and requires an intensive level of planning and servicing.[15]

With few exceptions, the conferences discussed in this volume accord with this definition.[16]

It should also be noted that names of conferences can be a bit deceiving. For example, while the first World Population Conference was organized by the UN in 1954, its purpose was to exchange scientific information and it was viewed as an "eminently academic conference." The second World Population Conference was organized in 1965 by the International Union for the Scientific Study of Population (IUSSP) and the UN; most of its participants were experts in the field. It was only the third World Population Conference, held in 1974, that was intergovernmental in nature, i.e., where the representatives from different countries were representatives of those countries' governments.[17] All the UN global conferences discussed in depth in this volume are intergovernmental in nature, although non-governmental ones were often convened at almost the same time in nearby venues.

While the definitions noted above set no substantive parameters, most of the UN's global conferences have focused on various aspects of social, human and economic development,[18] which is to be expected given the key challenges confronting the vast majority of UN members and the bulk of humanity (poverty, environmental degradation and unsustainable development, malnutrition, illiteracy, inadequate housing, unemployment, human rights abuses, gender and racial inequality).

It is also noteworthy that the proliferation of UN global conferences followed the admission of a large number of newly independent African states to the UN and the replacement of Taiwan with the People's Republic of China as a UN member. These countries, most of which were poor and plagued by the sorts of problems that they thought the UN should address more effectively than it had in the past, came to be an increasingly large percentage of the UN General Assembly membership. This enabled them to vote in favor of convening world conferences to supplement the work of the UN's major organs and specialized agencies. The proliferation of UN conferences was also preceded by significant improvements in communications technology and the lowering of international transportation costs, essential for wide coverage by the media and for extensive government and non-government participation.[19] In part, because of its highly publicized nature and the number of attendees (both governmental and non-governmental), the United Nations Conference on the Human Environment (UNCHE; Stockholm, 1972) came to be seen as ushering in the era of so-called mega conferences. That imprecise phrase, however, also implies something about the wide-ranging, often cross-sectoral, substantive focus of such conferences. This can be exemplified by contrasting so-called environmental mega conferences, like the United Nations Conference on Human Environment and Development (UNCED), from other conferences that deal with the environment, such as the United Nations Convention on Climate Change. *Mega* environmental conferences take "a broader overview of the complex of environment and development issues over a longer time frame...they are consequently preceded by years of preparations and negotiations and are held less frequently than single-issue meetings."[20] While this volume does not use the imprecise term mega conferences, all of the conferences discussed herein fit Gill Seyfang's characterization of how they differ from other conferences convened by the UN.

Common characteristics of UN global conferences

In spite of the lack of an authoritative definition or listing of such conferences, it still seems possible and valuable to identify a number of characteristics that such conferences share in common.

Patterns and purposes of UN global conferences

First, there are some common patterns behind and purposes for the convening of UN global conferences. They are often convened as a consequence of the emergence of a new problem, a problem newly recognized as a *global* problem (e.g. urban habitats or race relations), or the heightened politicization of a global problem (e.g. environmental decay or women's rights), or as a consequence of changes in the dimensions of longer-standing problems (e.g. water scarcity or overpopulation). In each instance, however, there need to be people in positions of influence who have become aware of such issues, who are concerned with them, or at least think they should be now attended to, have a "can do" mentality, and who believe that these problems should and perhaps can only be addressed through supranational means. Sometimes those formally initiating the process or given most credit for calling for the conferences are not those who are really responsible.[21] In any event, those calling for UN conferences must believe that there is a lack of adequate or acceptable pre-existing organizations within the UN system to deal with them (i.e. there is no obvious or acceptable pre-existing UN specialized agency[22] and there is little faith in the ability of the UN Economic and Social Council (ECOSOC), or any of its regional[23] or functional commissions[24] to address it effectively).[25] This has led some to suggest that the convening of these conferences underscores the need to change the UN's substantive foci and structure, especially in terms of revitalizing ECOSOC and its various commissions.[26]

Willetts contends that the decline in global conferences in the 1980s (relative to the 1970s and the 1990s) can be explained by the elections of Margaret Thatcher as British Prime Minister and Ronald Reagan as US President. They were both ideologically opposed to powerful supranational institutions, believing that most problems could and should be handled by national (or, in Reagan's case, even sub-national) governments.[27] Accordingly they were not willing to provide substantial funds for such conferences. Such conferences need financial backers, which often means needing the support of the major funders of the UN,[28] but there also needs to be strong support for such conferences in the UN General Assembly and thus all are preceded by months of consultations to obtain that.[29]

As Elisabeth Corell's account of the controversy surrounding the convening of the 1977 United Nations Conference on Desertification (UNCOD) suggests, Thatcher's and Reagan's positions were not unique. Controversy over the convening of UN global conferences is a recurring pattern, even when the need for such a conference seems so obvious to many:

> While the [Great] Sahelian drought [of 1968–1973] served as a catalyst to elevate desertification to the status of a "global" problem, there were nevertheless differing views on the desirability of holding an international conference on the subject. Developing countries maintained that desertification could not be solved nationally or regionally but must be approached through a global strategy. They also argued that such a strategy was appropriate since the most affected states lacked the financial and technical resources needed to effectively combat desertification. Industrialized states, on the other hand, did not agree that an international conference was needed or would be effective—even if some did agree on the need for a world strategy for desertification. They argued that creating a new institution would not solve the problem and that the UN system already had adequate capacity to consider all aspects of desertification.
>
> However, the Sahelian drought had galvanized world opinion in favor of the need to "fight" desertification and a "global desertification movement" demanded a fully fledged UN conference to bring political weight to addressing the problem.[30]

Paul Taylor divides up conferences between those intended to defend and uphold standards of behavior for governments and individuals (e.g. those relating to race relations, women's rights, arms control) and those intended to lead directly to a range of practical activities, frequently including the establishment of new or the reform of preexisting organizations, and the allocation of new resources (e.g. those relating to population, food and the environment).[31] Volker Rittberger's "rule-making conferences" and "action-oriented conferences" would both seem to be a subset of Taylor's latter rubric.[32] Thus it seems appropriate to think of such conferences as change agents or even agents aimed at bringing the moral force of the UN to bear on particular issues, whereas pre-existing UN organs (and other intergovernmental organizations) might be characterized as defenders of the status quo or at least as committed to slower changes.[33] Framing UN conferences in these terms further explains why their existence has often been controversial and, in part, why there have been recurrent patterns of conference proliferation followed by periods of conference fatigue.

What is clear, however, is that all UN global conferences seek to raise global consciousness about a particular problem, hoping to change the dominant attitudes surrounding the definition of the issue or, stated differently, to treat as global challenges issues heretofore treated only as local or regional problems.[34] Hard as it might be to imagine today, this is true even of issues like the environment, but also human rights issues related to race, gender and human settlements. Such conferences also aim to mobilize national and local governments and non-governmental organizations (NGOs) to take action; to establish or endorse international standards, principles and guidelines (i.e. legally binding conventions are the exception rather than the rule); to serve as forums for communication, supplementing diplomatic methods, where new proposals can be debated and consensus sought; to build institutional capacity both within member states and at the global level; to further legitimize global governance by making the governance process more inclusive; and to set in motion a process whereby governments make commitments and can be held accountable.[35] While not initially one of the explicit purposes of such conferences, over time they have been found to be essential to the building, legitimizing and reinvigorating of global social networks, a phenomenon particularly true in terms of the various women's conferences.[36]

There is also a fairly common pattern that describes how most of the conferences operate. A country or coalition of countries calls for a conference, sometimes at the urging of interested non-governmental actors. ECOSOC or the UN General Assembly, or both, vote on a draft resolution calling for such a conference, noting the country that has offered to play conference host, setting up Preparatory Committees (PrepComs), either comprised of governments appointed by the President of the UN General Assembly or relying on a pre-existing intergovernmental organization, like a functional ECOSOC Commission,[37] a timetable for PrepComs and the conference itself.[38] The resolution also sets out a conference budget as well. Then the UN Secretary-General appoints a Secretary-General (or Rapporteur-General) for the conference, frequently either a figure of international standing from outside the UN or the head of some relevant program or department from within the UN secretariat (see Appendix I for a list of the major conference officers). As the cases will make clear, this is a more important task than it might first appear: the conference Secretary-General makes all of the administrative arrangements and provides the political leadership for the conference. Those administrative arrangements include establishing working committees, the composition of which is key to the final action plan, resolutions and any communiqués. One of the few systematic UN reports on such conferences argues that the conference Secretary-General "should be a person of stature, capability and skill who can maximize the impact of the conference on governments and world opinion, and ensure a satisfactory outcome through a sound and acceptable plan of action."[39]

The PrepComs are responsible for overseeing the work of the conference secretariat and any expert and regional meetings.[40] They also determine the draft agenda, rules of procedures, organizational arrangements, a comprehensive preparatory timetable, procedures and patterns for interaction with the UN system and other participants, and documentation requirements. All of the PrepComs' recommendations become a part of subsequent General Assembly resolutions. "Most importantly, the preparatory process needs to be designed in such a way as to mobilize the support of national delegations for the emergence of an international consensus on major themes and issues." This is particularly important because of the tradition of consensus decision-making at UN global conferences whereby any single delegation might block an agreement or an aspect of a program of action that all of the other delegates support.

> More often, consensus is arrived at through negotiations among a bewildering variety of regional, political, economic and other interested groups; and the countries which still do not support the consensus text, or parts thereof, may choose to state their reservations for the record.[41]

In the most extreme cases, delegates walk out of conferences.

Prior to the conference itself, there are usually regional intergovernmental meetings, which correspond to ECOSOC's regional commissions, which often service or assist in servicing the conference. Not simply does this provide a good tie-in to the UN, but it can provide divergent views, possibly contributing to better policy decisions, and the sort of support that is necessary for subsequent policy implementation. The conference plenary sessions themselves have basically three purposes: (1) to open the meeting with a group of speakers designed to attract media attention and to establish the procedure for the rest of the conference; (2) to provide a platform for parties to enunciate their public positions; and (3) to approve, in a pro forma fashion, the work that had been accomplished by working committees.[42] The Conference of Non-Governmental Organizations in Consultative Status with the United Nations (CONGO) is responsible for ensuring NGO participation in the process, especially at the PrepComs, and for working with the conference secretariat on access to conference documents.[43] Over time, NGO access to materials and participation at such conferences has increased, but this has not been without setbacks (i.e. in some conferences, like Vienna, the roles of NGOs have been more restricted than in others). Moreover, beginning with the Stockholm conference on the Human Environment, almost all UN global conferences are accompanied by parallel NGO and other civil society conferences. The size and intensity of interaction between the non-governmental and the intergovernmental (official) conferences vary considerably, but in just about all instances, the existence of NGO parallel conferences provides a vivid contrast to other large UN meetings (e.g. meetings of UNCTAD) where they are non-existent.

More recently, some conferences—often called world summits—have a couple of days reserved for participation by heads of state and government. Their participation at some is quite high (e.g. whereas two heads of state attended the Stockholm conference, 102 attended the Millennium Summit). Overall oversight of the conferences—including their priorities and goals—is traditionally handled by the Administrative Committee on Coordination (ACC) or its successor organization, the Chief Executives Board for Coordination (CEB).

Almost all conferences use their action plans to assign responsibility for policy implementation.[44] Increasingly, civil society has been turned to by UN conferees for assisting governments in policy implementation, usually however contingent on government funding.[45] Action plans, until recently, have oftentimes also called for follow-up conferences. In June 2003, however, the UN General Assembly voted to end what had become a practice of automatic five-year reviews of UN conferences, moving instead to a system in which both the format and timing of any follow-up conferences would be decided on a case-by-case basis. The rationale is that the follow-up conferences, which themselves had become large and costly, should be more strategic and less routine. It was also hoped by some that this would make the conferences themselves more efficient and effective.[46]

Common critiques and praise for UN global conferences

The existing literature, journalistic and academic, and the speeches of policy influentials around the world, both criticize and praise UN global conferences, often glossing over distinctions between the conferences, something the approach taken in this book hopes to correct.

Criticisms of UN global conferences (see Box 1.1) come from across the ideological spectrum and some are in tension with one another. Moreover, the media have an additional specific gripe, namely that the conferences' procedures and their substantive discussions are too nuanced for the sort of "sound bites" that capture their audience's attention.[47]

Defenders of UN global conferences are found both within the UN and outside of it. Obviously, as will be seen in subsequent chapters, there are, even among the supporters of UN conferences in general, opponents of *specific* conferences, not to mention particular decisions taken at the various conferences. Supporters of conferences, in the aggregate, however, find them praiseworthy for a variety of reasons, some (as seen in Box 1.2) not entirely consistent with each other nor obviously with the critiques.

Through a detailed analysis of thirty years of experience with UN conferencing, we should be able to shed some light on these frequently asserted but less often documented generalizations, some of which will be found wanting. And, as importantly, this volume will lead to new and important conclusions as well.

Organization of the book

Chapter 2 focuses on the first two global conferences, which both set patterns for conferences to follow and, especially the Stockholm conference, which raised expectations as to their possibilities. Chapter 3 discusses the conferences of the 1970s that followed the post-Stockholm euphoria. The substantive foci of those conferences reflected the growth and changed composition of UN membership resulting from decolonization: by 1965 the UN's membership stood at 118, more than twice as many as at its founding and a majority of which were economically less developed countries. But the discussions of the conferences of the 1970s also evidence the clear limits as to what can be accomplished in an era plagued by ongoing tensions between the then two superpowers, the USA and the Soviet Union, and between the North and South, the rich and poor, tensions exacerbated by the oil boycott and sudden increase in oil prices effectuated by OPEC (the

Box 1.1 Critiques of UN global conferences

- Too expensive and *a waste of money* that could be better spent dealing with problems already identified rather than just talking about the problems.[1]
- *Duplicative* (i.e. that most focus on some aspect of issues related to development, issues presumably falling within the purview of pre-existing UN and other intergovernmental organs).[2]
- *Repetitive and overlapping* (as with multiple conferences dealing with the environment or with multiple conferences dealing with the rights of women, an issue also discussed at environment and human rights conferences).
- *Divert attention from other serious issues*, as the media presses governments and NGOs to focus on the particular topic of the conference almost to the exclusion of others or at least relegating others to less prominent places on national agendas.
- *Concentrate scarce human resources*, especially of economically less developed countries, *on a single issue*, which may not be the most pressing problem facing that country at the time.[3]
- Pervaded by a *primacy of politics* that "eventually leads to debates driven less by the need to make substantive progress than to reach agreements on ambiguous texts lending themselves to conflicting interpretations."[4]
- Seek to *pre-empt more radical solutions* to key problems by having states rather than NGOs deal with them and by controlling the selection of NGOs that participate and controlling the participation of the NGOs that do participate.
- Likely to *result in compromises* rather than commitments to real change or a tendency to compromise issues to a point of inaction.
- *"Unrealistic"* in terms of what they are trying to accomplish in such a short period of time, i.e., trying to influence the course of economic and social development on a global scale.
- *Not focused on the root causes* of the problems they address and thus propose only superficial or temporary relief, relying on measures that must be designed in such a way that there

need to be no change of fundamental structures, seemingly acting as if the "present forms of social economic organizations are fixed, permanent or somehow rooted in nature."[5]

- Provide opportunities for *inflammatory rhetoric* and distortions of issues for the purposes of propaganda.
- Likely to involve *commitments by governments that they are unlikely to honor.*[6]
- Likely to result in *too much global regulation*, including interference with market forces.
- *Threaten national sovereignty* as they set specific goals and demand increased funding for specific activities.
- Focused on women's rights, environmental protection and democratization, which some see as a thinly disguised *effort to impose a new world order favoring the values of a few powerful countries.*[7]

Notes

1 Former US Secretary of State Warren Christopher at the September 25, 1995, meeting of the 50th Session of the UN General Assembly articulated a variant of this critique: "And we should adopt a moratorium on big UN conferences once the present series is completed, concentrating instead on meeting the commitments of those we have held." http://dosfan.lib/uic/edu/ERC/briefing/dossec/1995/9509/9509 25dosses.html. The Clinton Administration eventually adopted a moratorium on the funding of mega conferences, excepting the race conference. Christopher's, however, was only one of the reasons. See, for example, Conference report on 3194, Consolidated Appropriations Act, 2000 (US House of Representatives, November 17, 1999) and Foreign Affairs Reform and Restructuring Act of 1997 (Senate, June 16, 1997), s. 903, p. S5655.

2 In some instances, at least, these appear to be bureaucratic "turf" arguments (i.e. pre-existing institutions sensing a new problem to which countries might contribute resources make a claim for already dealing with the problem or being eager to deal with it rather than have funds expended on a conference, much

less a new follow-up mechanism). See, for example, Thomas G. Weiss and Robert S. Jordan, *The World Food Conference and Global Problem Solving* (New York: Praeger Publishers, 1976), p. 14 and Paul Taylor, "Population: Coming to Terms with People," in Taylor and Groom, *Global Issues*, p. 156.

3 Weiss and Jordan's discussion of the first World Food Conference also shows how such conferences can squeeze out other activities by involved intergovernmental organizations. *World Food Conference*, pp. 97–98.

4 Jacques Fomerand, "UN Conferences: Media Events or Genuine Diplomacy?" 2 *Global Governance* September– December (1996): p. 362.

5 Diego de Gaspar, "Beyond Conference Ritual," *Development Forum*, vol. 4, July–August (1976): p. 2. Gaspar opines that the pressures of population might finally overcome these inertial tendencies. Lamont C. Hempel, *Environmental Governance: The Global Challenge* (Washington, DC: Island Press, 1996), p. 51.

6 Lynton Keith Caldwell, with Paul Stanley Weiland, *International Environmental Policy: From the Twentieth to the Twenty-First Century*, 3rd edn., rev. (Durham, NC: Duke University Press, 1996), p. 63.

7 United Nations, *World Conferences*, p. 2.

Organization of Arab Petroleum-Exporting Countries) in the aftermath of the 1973 Arab–Israeli war. The lull in UN conferences during the 1980s is the focus of Chapter 4. In part, this is a consequence of the letdown in terms of the limited accomplishments in the conferences that preceded them. But the slowdown in convening conferences was also a consequence of domestic political changes, especially within the USA, and the world's focus on the collapse of communism in the former Soviet bloc. The USA's turn away from the UN including its loss of interest in global conferences is often described as the crisis of multilateralism; and the collapse of the Soviet bloc clearly distracted the world's rich from the problems of the South. An upsurge in conferences and summits followed in the early post-Cold War era. They are the subject of the volume's fifth chapter. Many of these conferences were renewed attempts to deal with the problems not "fixed" the first (or

Box 1.2 Contributions of UN global conferences

- *Mobilize national and local governments and NGOs* to take action on major global problems that the UN and many member states were heretofore not organized or ready to deal with.
- *Establish international standards and guidelines* for national policy and, less often, binding treaties.
- Serve as *forums where new proposals can be debated* and consensus sought on important and contentious issues of regional and sometimes global concern.
- Set in motion a *process whereby governments can make commitments* and report back regularly to the UN.
- Attempt to *counter the hierarchy of most of the UN system* and the bureaucratic inertia that is seen to plague it and other intergovernmental organizations.
- Contribute to the *creation, sharing and dissemination of information* on vital global issues.[1]
- Assist in the *establishment of mechanisms for monitoring states'* progress in meeting particular global challenges.
- Provide vital *early warning functions* (as in the case of famines, HIV/AIDS, the proliferation of small arms trafficking, or overpopulation) in a state-centric world where that is not very easy to do.
- Offer opportunities to think globally and operate along functionalist lines, *forging necessary cross-sectoral linkages among issues* that might otherwise be separated owing to the UN structure.
- Serve a set of explicitly *normative functions* (e.g. stopping the abuse of women).
- Provide a boost to the growth of a still incipient *global civil society*.
- Serve, especially in the eyes of leaders of economically less developed countries because of their voting procedures, "as a means to obtain favorable decisions ... [and as offering] a valuable *strategy for the attainment of goals that cannot be realized through* well-meaning non-binding resolutions passed by *the UN General Assembly and other UN bodies* [which may have less hospitable decision rules]."[2]
- Provide a *way to sidestep the UN system's power distribution* that is seen by many to be largely out of synch with the time

and thus contributing to the UN's delegitimacy in the eyes of the bulk of humanity.

- Provide a way to try and work with NGOs and businesses in terms of policy implementation, including NGOs and multinational corporations that are often better funded, more technologically advanced and better connected to other elements in civil society than the UN itself.[3]
- Offer forums for learning by policy makers, including about new linkages between issues heretofore treated separately.

Notes

1 Such an argument takes into account technological developments with the contention that "even in the Internet era, critical ideas are most effectively delivered in person." A.B. Meyerson, "Burning the Bridge to the 21st Century: The End of the Era of Integrated Conferences?" *ESCAP Report*, vol. 9 (2003): p. 9. McDougall's study of the 2001 World Conference against Racism, Racial Discrimination, Xenophobia and Related Intolerance (WCAR, Durban, South Africa) shows that merely agreeing to convene the conference can serve this purpose: "Before the General Assembly convened the World Conference [on racism] process, for example, there was very little data or analyses of ethnic conflict as an issue of racial discrimination in Africa." Gay McDougall, "The World Conference against Racism: Through a Wider Lens," *Fletcher Forum on World Affairs*, vol. 26, Summer/Fall (2002): p. 141.

2 Werner Feld and Robert S. Jordan with Leon Hurwitz, *International Organizations: A Comparative Approach*, 3rd edn. (Westport, CT: Praeger, 1994), pp. 140 and 143.

3 Muldoon is particularly expansive regarding the 1992 United Nations Conference on Environment and Development (UNCED): "The access and participation of civil society organizations before, during, and after the conference were a breakthrough for NGOs." James P. Muldoon, Jr., *The Architecture of Global Governance: An Introduction to the Study of International Organizations* (Boulder, CO: Westview Press, 2004), pp. 240–241.

second or third) time around. But there was also an attempt to deal with issues in a much more holistic and integrated way than at earlier conferences. However, the achievements of the conferences of the 1990s were clearly constrained by the unwillingness or inability of governments to expend large resources to fulfill the conferees' goals. Partly as a consequence, the twenty-first century began with the "mother of all conferences," in which the UN Secretary-General sought to refocus the world's attention on the needs of economically less developed countries, setting concrete and specific goals to be achieved later in the twenty-first century. In addition to discussing the Millennium Summit, the sixth chapter discusses other recent UN conferences, including the first explicitly focused on the issue of military security. It, like others that succeeded it, were partly overshadowed by the tragic events of September 11, 2001. The concluding chapter seeks to draw together the lessons of more than thirty years of global conferences, including the degree to which such institutions are an effective way to meet the challenges of the evolving world order.

2 Setting the pattern, 1968–1972

- **International Conference on Human Rights**
- **United Nations Conference on the Human Environment (UNCHE)**

As noted in Chapter 1, the first large UN conference was the 1946–1948 UN Conference on Trade and Employment. It, of course, was followed by UN conferences almost every year and more than a dozen in some years. Most of those, however, like the United Nations Conference on Trade and Development (UNCTAD) do not meet the criteria set out in the first chapter. Rather, they are recurrent, regularly scheduled conferences not specially convened by the UN General Assembly or ECOSOC to deal with a particularly pressing global problem. Thus, while the conferences discussed in this chapter have countless precedents, they differ from what preceded them and many that followed them in a number of important ways.

Most commentators on UN global conferences begin their studies in 1972 with the United Nations Conference on the Human Environment (UNCHE). They do so because it is taken as a major turning point in UN conference diplomacy, both because of its massive attendance and the existence of a parallel NGO conference. But this volume's discussion of global conferences starts with the 1968 International Conference on Human Rights, a conference often relegated to footnotes when discussing more recent human rights conferences, or to a passing comment about the irony of holding a human rights conference in Tehran (just as some found irony in the UN convening a major women's conference in Beijing; others saw it as a useful lever to encourage the Chinese government to take more seriously the rights of women as some might have argued in 1968 that having a human rights conference in Tehran could have encouraged the Shah of Iran to allow more freedom in Iran).[1] But, as will become clear shortly, the 1968 human rights conference sheds light on a number of themes about the impact of global events on global conferences as well as about the ways in which their documents can be used to affect such events. Moreover, as we will soon see, many of the key substantive debates at the conference will sound depressingly familiar to anyone familiar with Middle Eastern events of the early twenty-first century.[2]

While both of these conferences were convened during the Cold War (i.e. serious conflict and rivalry, but short of all-out direct military conflict) between the USA and the Soviet Union, they evolved during a period of lessened tension in that conflict. While this is particularly true in the case of the Stockholm conference, coming in an era some described as one of détente (i.e. lessened tensions in international relations), even in 1968, during the Vietnam War, US President Lyndon B. Johnson had reached out to the Soviets to negotiate an end to their arms rivalry. While ultimately an abortive effort at arms negotiations, it eased the tensions enough so the UN global conferences could begin in earnest.

International Conference on Human Rights

The International Conference on Human Rights was held from April 22 to May 13, 1968, in accordance with UN General Assembly Resolution 2081 (XX) of December 20, 1965. It was seen as the major event of the International Year of Human Rights (1968), selected to celebrate the twentieth anniversary of the Universal Declaration of Human Rights.[3] Although not legally binding when first articulated in 1948 and criticized subsequently for being an enumeration of "Western" human rights values masquerading as universal values (a refrain heard again in Vienna in 1993 and not resolved then or since),[4] the Universal Declaration remains the keystone UN document in the human rights field and, over time, many of its provisions have become binding customary international law (i.e. binding on governments because those provisions have been widely accepted as if they are legally binding) or treated as an authoritative interpretation of the UN Charter and thus legally binding.[5]

The aims of the conference were as follows:

1   Review the progress which had been made in the field of human rights since the adoption of the Universal Declaration of Human Rights.

2   Evaluate the effectiveness of the methods used by the UN in the field of human rights, especially with regard to the elimination of

all forms of racial discrimination and the practice of the policy of *apartheid*.

3   Formulate and prepare a program of further measures to be taken subsequent to the celebrations of the International Year for Human Rights.[6]

The hope was that the conference would be well attended by prominent people committed not simply to reviewing the UN's past human rights record, but also setting forth new areas for work. Indeed, UN Secretary-General U Thant's rationale for convening such a conference foreshadows rationales for other global UN conferences:

> It was undoubtedly useful to depart from the routine succession of United Nations meetings on human rights for the purpose of a detached stock-taking and long-term planning. It was important to call on governments to send specially qualified persons, including some of those who have participated in United Nations activities, as well as many who were active in the field of human rights outside of the United Nations framework, in a great confrontation of cultures, historical traditions, political conceptions, religious and philosophical outlooks.[7]

Because the conference was taking place during the Vietnam War, a hot war coincident with the ongoing Cold War between the USA and the Soviet Union, there was concern by some that conferees could become bogged down in propagandistic speeches, concern presumably generated from experience at the UN where often vituperative discussions of human rights focused on South Africa and Israel.[8] Accordingly, the PrepCom for the conference, which was set up to make proposals to the General Assembly relating to the agenda, duration, venue and means for defraying the costs of the conference, and to organize and direct any necessary documentation, including evaluative studies,[9] "stressed the need for moderation, restraint and objectivity and an atmosphere as free as possible from political recrimination."[10]

As befits what was to become common practice, the host country, Iran, offered to pay part of the conference's estimated $500,000 bill.[11] Also as would become a common practice (i.e. expressing appreciation to the host country through honorific roles), Princess Ashraf Pahlevi, the Shah of Iran's sister, was elected as the President of the conference. She was a leading campaigner for human rights in the UN, including in ECOSOC. It also elected eighteen vice-presidents and established three sessional committees. In accordance with the General Assembly's wishes that the conference Executive Secretary should come from within the UN Secretariat, the UN Secretary-General appointed the Director of the Division of Human Rights to fulfill that role.

More than 2,000 delegates, representing eighty-four governments and sixty-one international organizations, attended the conference. These included, as *official* observers, representatives from three UN bodies (the Special Committee on the Situation with regard to the Implementation of the Declaration on the Granting of Independence to Colonial Countries and Peoples, the United Nations High Commissioner for Refugees, and the United Nations Children Fund), at the invitation of UN General Assembly representatives from four UN Specialized Agencies (the ILO, UNESCO, WHO and the FAO) and four regional organizations (the Council of Europe, the League of Arab States, the OAU, and the Organization of American States), but not representatives from NGOs.

But (especially human rights) NGOs were obviously aware of the upcoming conference. In anticipation of the conference and in light of what he saw as the spreading human rights atrocities in Vietnam, the Congo and Southern Africa, Sean MacBride, co-founder and chairman of Amnesty International, spearheaded the organization of a coalition of human rights NGOs. In those years Amnesty International did not want much from the UN and the UN did not want much from it— Amnesty International's advocacy focused on the power of international public opinion in general and specifically on individual prisoner-of-conscience releases. It relied mainly on correspondence between Amnesty International members and the relevant national governments. Thus, MacBride chose to organize a coalition, comprised of mass membership religious organizations with large congregations in many countries as well as human rights NGOs such as Amnesty International. It became a permanent subcommittee of the 300-member Conference of Non-Governmental Organizations in Consultative Status with the United Nations (CONGO), which coordinated UN–NGO procedural relations, thus laying the foundation for greater influence in the future, including at future UN global conferences. MacBride also co-chaired a Geneva meeting of seventy-six UN human rights NGOs and of fifty experts sitting as the Montreal Assembly of Human Rights. Both of these gatherings generated recommendations for the Tehran Conference, including MacBride's personal priorities, namely heightened protection for victims of armed conflict and the appointment of a UN High Commissioner for Human Rights. Because they were not formal observers at the conference, NGO representatives could not speak, but they drafted and promoted resolutions.[12]

While the UN General Assembly had determined who could participate at the conference, this did prevent a sharp credentials debate before any substantive discussions even began. On April 22, a number of Arab and other states challenged Israel's participation in the conference, claiming that Israel was violating the human rights of those living in the occupied Arab territories. In response to Mustafa Medani of Sudan's accusations of Israeli "atrocities in the Israeli occupied territories," the Israeli spokesman asked: "How many Sudanese Negroes have been slaughtered in the last few years, 100,000, 200,000, half a million?"[13]

In his opening address, UN Secretary-General U Thant focused attention on the other hotbed of human rights debate, by calling for the eradication of South Africa's policy of apartheid. Although abandoning absolute neutrality can cost a UN Secretary-General support amongst key constituents—as did Trygve Lie's stand on the North Korean invasion of South Korea, Dag Hammarskjöld's in the Congo Crisis and U Thant's own on the Vietnam War—U Thant's decision not to remain neutral on this particular issue cost him "little" and may even have "add[ed] something to the moral posture of the Office [of Secretary-General] and illegitimacy of racial discrimination." In part, of course, this was because U Thant's position on apartheid coincided with that of most of the UN's members.[14] That was partly because of the changing membership of the UN; indeed it is not entirely a coincidence that U Thant, the first Secretary-General from the "third world" took office not long after the "third world" had achieved a majority in the General Assembly. Moreover, U Thant's "style, tone, and the nature of his work" came to express the interests of "third world" countries, including in the areas of economic development, anti-colonialism and human rights.[15]

Given the global context (East–West competition over winning the hearts and minds of those in recently independent countries), the theme of Soviet Premier Alekesi N. Kosygin's message, that was read to the conference, was not unexpected either. In it, he asserted that "Peoples of the world are greatly concerned about the policy of imperialist aggression, which is causing death and suffering to millions of people." He continued by noting that the Soviet Union would "fight against imperialist aggression, colonialism, racism and neo-Nazism and will render every assistance and strong support to the peoples fighting for freedom and independence." US President Johnson's message to the conference noted that "We in the United States are committed by word and will to give realities to the rights embedded in our laws." Johnson, known in the USA for his successful struggle for landmark civil rights legislation, continued by noting that Americans "are struggling hourly to translate these laws into better, fuller lives."[16]

On May 5, the conferees approved an African resolution condemning racial discrimination by white minorities in southern Africa. Twenty-one countries, including the United States, abstained on the resolution, which referred to South African apartheid as a "crime against humanity" and a "threat to international peace and security." The latter is the language which would allow the UN Security Council to authorize the use of force against the South African regime. Nazism, neo-Nazism, racism and other ideologies based on terrorism and racial intolerance were also condemned.[17] On May 7, the conference passed a resolution, without reference to any of the three committees, that called on Israel to respect the rights of Arabs in territories occupied during the 1967 War, including desisting "from acts of destroying homes of the Arab civilian population inhabiting areas occupied by Israel." It also affirmed "the inalienable right of all inhabitants who have left their homes as a result of the outbreak of hostilities in the Middle East to return, resume normal life, recover their property and homes, and rejoin their families."[18] The conference President forwarded the text of the resolution to the President of the UN General Assembly, Cornellu Manescu of Romania. It is noteworthy that it also called for the establishment of a special General Assembly committee to investigate violations of human rights in the occupied territories and called on Israel to "desist forthwith from acts destroying the homes of the Arab civilian population."[19] Other contentious resolutions condemned the North Atlantic Treaty Organization (NATO) for its supply of arms and ammunition "which were used to suppress the indigenous people under Portuguese domination" and called upon the United Kingdom to use "all the necessary measures, including the use of force, to put an end to the illegal minority racist régime of Rhodesia, as well as to grant independence to the people of Rhodesia based on the principle of majority rule."[20] "Of particular interest" to Amnesty International, even though it was not directly or exclusively related to prisoners of conscience, was the resolution introduced by the governments of India, Czechoslovakia, Jamaica, Uganda and the United Arab Republic. It noted that

> minority racist or colonial regimes which refuse to comply with the decisions of the United Nations and the principles of the Universal Declaration of Human Rights frequently resort to executions and inhuman treatment of those who struggle against such regimes;

and considered that such persons should be protected against inhuman or brutal treatment and also that such persons if detained should be treated as prisoners-of-war or political prisoners under international law.[21]

On May 13, the conference unanimously approved the Proclamation of Tehran. It condemned apartheid as a "crime against humanity," which "continues seriously to disturb international peace and security." Thus, it was deemed "imperative for the international community to use every possible means to eradicate this evil"; the struggle against apartheid was thus recognized as a legitimate one.[22] Further, in keeping with the UN's ideology of the time—deemed developmentalism by Robert W. Cox[23]—the widening gap between economically developed and economically less developed countries was portrayed as impeding the realization of human rights. Thus, a "maximum possible effort" had to be made to close that gap, something that had not even begun to happen during the UN's First Development Decade.[24] While not explicitly taking a position on whether so-called second-generation human rights (economic, social and cultural rights) should precede or follow "first-generation" human rights (civil and political rights), the Proclamation stated that the "full realization of civil and political rights was impossible without the enjoyment of economic, social and cultural rights," a position seemingly splitting the difference between the USA's emphasis on first-generation rights and the Soviet emphasis on second-generation rights. The Proclamation more clearly toed the Soviet line in noting that "general and complete disarmament was one of the highest aspirations of all peoples" and that "disarmament would release immense human and material resources which should be used for the promotion of human rights and fundamental freedoms." The USA saw the Soviet embrace of "general and complete disarmament" as a propaganda ploy to win support of developing countries, knowing that it was at odds with the US strategic doctrine of the time, Mutual Assured Destruction (MAD). Although not elaborated upon in detail, the Proclamation also called for the elimination of racism and of discrimination against women.[25] Resolution XVIII also appeared to "split the difference" in terms of overpopulation and family planning. Although observing that

the present rapid rate of population growth in some areas of the world hampers the struggle against hunger and poverty, and in particular reduces the possibilities of rapidly achieving adequate standards of living, including food, clothing, housing, medical care, social security, education and social services, thereby impairing the full realizing of human rights

conferees also noted that "couples have a basic human right to decide freely and responsibly on the number of and spacing of their children." Accordingly, conferees merely urged concerned member states, and UN bodies and specialized agencies "to give close attention to the implications for the exercise of human rights of the present rapid rate of increase in world population."[26]

Implementation and conference follow-up were quite modest. In part, this might be because the calls for implementation and follow-up in the Secretary-General's opening address and in the closing Proclamation were modest. Most surprising is that there was no real push for ratification of the International Covenants on Civil and Political and Economic, Social and Cultural Rights, even though they had just been approved in 1966, after a major push by the UN's General Assembly. Indeed, the UN Secretary-General's final report (delivered in 1969, pursuant to a request by the General Assembly in the preceding year) on measures and activities taken in connection with the International Year of Human Rights (1968) is hardly impressive. According to his report, seventy-one UN member states reported on measures and activities undertaken by them in connection with the International Year. Twenty-seven states reported that they had proclaimed 1968 as the International Year of Human Rights. "Several" heads of state or government had issued special measures and eight parliaments or national assemblies had held special meetings to commemorate the twentieth anniversary of the Universal Declaration. Various human rights documents were discussed in education institutions throughout the world. A number of countries had set up special bodies to study the question of ratifying various human rights conventions and, in "several" countries, new or amended national legislation was passed to bring the laws into conformity with the Universal Declaration and other UN human rights instruments.

Even the General Assembly's Resolution 2588A (XXIV), pursuant to the Secretary-General's report, was limited in its scope. It "invited" governments, the UN and other bodies "to give effect, as appropriate" to the conference's recommendations. Somewhat more controversially, on December 15, 1969, the General Assembly, by a vote of 82–1–29 adopted Resolution 2588B (XXIV), which reaffirmed the right of all peoples under colonial and foreign rule to liberation and self-determination and supported the liberation movements in southern Africa and elsewhere "in their legitimate struggle for freedom and independence."[27]

The International Covenants did not enter into force until 1976, although before then many of their provisions had become binding as customary international law or because national governments and regional organizations had introduced legislation or adopted legally binding treaties relating to them.

Thus, the immediate substantive impacts of the Tehran Conference were quite modest, consistent with the organizers' stated intentions. But, as noted, the conference format set a pattern followed quite closely by many subsequent conferences. Moreover, the conference's long-term, albeit indirect and perhaps unintended, impact on Amnesty International should not be overlooked. While it would literally be decades before Amnesty International would succeed in getting UN human rights conferees to agree on the establishment of a UN High Commissioner for Human Rights, the Tehran Conference included the opening of political space for NGO input on issues such as those.

United Nations Conference on the Human Environment (UNCHE)

Along with decolonization, the environment is one of the global policy areas in which the UN is often given most credit for its activities, and one of the few in which it is portrayed as playing a leading role. Its first global conference on the environment, the United Nations Conference on Human Environment (Stockholm, June 1972), has been described as a milestone in conference diplomacy for increasing international awareness of the problem of environmental degradation, its international scope, and its relations to other issues, including economic development. UNCHE conferees also agreed to establish the first UN body to serve as a focal point for global environmental policy, what came to be the United Nations Environment Program (UNEP).

Prior to the 1960s, little international attention had been paid to the challenges of the global environment, although the United Nations Educational, Scientific and Cultural Organization (UNESCO) had established the International Union for the Protection of Nature as long ago as 1947 and a number of other conservation activities had been undertaken by other UN specialized agencies, including the FAO and WHO. There was also some national legislation and various regional organizations, including the century-old Danube Commission and the United Nations Economic Commission for Europe that had done some innovative work, especially in the areas of transnational water and air pollution.[28] But it was only in the late 1960s that talk about the necessity to take *global* action became pervasive.

Central to this seeming abandonment of what the economist Kenneth Boulding called "frontier economics," the then dominant paradigm that economic growth and material prosperity were limitless,[29] was the publication of Rachel Carson's seminal book, *Silent Spring* (first serialized in *The New Yorker*), which warned in 1962 of the hazards of the pesticide dichloro-diphenyl-trichloromethylmethane (DDT).[30] In the book, Carson meticulously described how DDT entered the food chain and accumulated in the fatty tissues of animals, including human beings, and contributed to cancer and genetic damage. She argued that a single application of DDT on crops killed insects, not simply those targeted and not simply those initially killed. Its impacts lasted weeks and months, even after it was diluted by rainwater. The chemical industry in the USA reacted swiftly to Carson's arguments, not simply because of her attack on DDT but also because she had gone on to suggest that, at times, technological progress was so at odds with natural processes that it had to be curtailed. Carson's arguments against DDT, however, were picked up by the US government as well as the general public and thus the debate shifted from whether pesticides were dangerous to deciding which ones were.

Carson's broader questions about technology were picked up and built on by the so-called Club of Rome, an NGO that brings together scientists, economists, business executives and high-ranking public servants. Its various publications, including *The Limits to Growth*, published in 1972, warned that if then current growth trends in world population, industrialization, pollution, food production, and resource depletion continued unchanged, the limits to growth on the planet would be reached some time within a hundred years. They predicted that the most problematic result would be a rather sudden and uncontrollable decline in both population and industrial capacity. While the Club's studies were criticized for underestimating the possibilities of positive technological innovation, the power of the market and governmental regulation, they provided part of the context for the Stockholm conference.

Also part of that context were Paul Ehrlich's widely read 1968 book, *The Population Bomb*, which raised the specter of economically less developed countries suffering from irredeemable Malthusian misery, and a series of studies funded by the UN and undertaken by the UN Secretary-General in accordance with UN General Assembly Resolution 2398 (XXII) in 1968. The so-called "U Thant Report" or "Man and His Environment" (published in May 1969) contended that the world had about a decade to begin to seriously address issues related to air and water pollution, soil erosion, and waste of natural resources. The report, which was widely publicized and has been credited with being a turning point in publicity of ecological problems, contended that action had to be taken at the local, national *and* global level.

It was the Swedish government which pushed for the idea of a global UN environmental conference. Sverker Åström, Sweden's Permanent Representative to the UN, placed the idea on the General Assembly's agenda in 1968, proposing that such a conference be convened in 1972. The General Assembly's endorsement of the idea [Resolution 2398 (XXIII)] followed an ECOSOC resolution on the subject [1346 (XLV)], in which ECOSOC underlined the need to limit and, where possible, to eliminate the impairment of the human environment. The General Assembly's resolution requested a report from the UN Secretary-General, in consultation with the Advisory Committee on the Application of Science and Technology to Development, which would cover the main problems that such a conference should consider and the preparatory process that should be used. The Secretary-General was also advised to consult with member states, representatives of the UN specialized agencies and the International Atomic Energy Agency (IAEA), and to draw on appropriate contributions from other intergovernmental and non-governmental organizations. The Secretary-General, in turn, called for a broad, action-oriented conference, a theme accepted and elaborated upon by ECOSOC in subsequent resolutions, in which it underscored the necessity for developing guidelines for action. ECOSOC also entrusted the UN Secretary-General with setting up a conference secretariat, naming a conference Secretary-General and accepted the Swedish offer to host the conference.

The General Assembly established a PrepCom, which subsequently held four sessions. NGOs attended all of them as observers. The first PrepCom was held in New York City, March 10–20, 1970. It worked on the topics for the conference. It was greeted by a written statement from U Thant in which he declared that: "Never in the twenty-five-year history of the United Nations has there been a problem of more relevance to all nations than the present environmental crisis." He went on, in a statement that seemed to resonate with Carson's writings: "the aims and methods of the industrial revolution, which has brought such immense prosperity to some area of the earth, must come under review before it has even reached the entirety of the globe."[31] A second PrepCom session was held in Geneva, February 8–19, 1971, and prepared a provisional agenda for the conference, discussed the possible form and content of a declaration on the human environment, and recommended the establishment of an intergovernmental working group on the declaration. Representatives of the International Union for the Conservation of Nature (IUCN) and the International Society of Soil Science participated in the working group, underscoring the increased involvement of NGOs in UN global conference proceedings. The third and fourth PrepCom sessions were held in New York (September 13–24, 1971, and March 6–17, 1972), dealing with the draft declaration and organizational and financial implications of the various recommendations. This self-same pattern of PrepCom activity frequently repeated itself in subsequent conferences.

Another major innovation for NGOs occurred in May 1971 when conference Secretary-General Maurice Strong commissioned Dr René Dubos of the Rockefeller Institute for Medical Research to chair a group of experts, some of whom had connections with NGOs. The group, which was to be managed by an NGO, the International Institute for Environmental Affairs (subsequently called the International Institute for Environment and Development), was charged with preparing a background report and

> [to] reach out for the best advice available from the world's intellectual leaders in providing a conceptual framework for participants in the United Nations Conference and general public as well ... The only restraint on those who prepared the report was a request that they should not prejudge the work of governments at the United Nations Conference by proposing specific international agreements or actions—its main purpose being to provide background information relevant to official policy decisions.[32]

While the "restraint" resonates with the state-centric times in which the Stockholm conference was being convened, there were a number of additional precedent-setting innovations regarding NGOs at the conference. For example, the rules of procedure adopted at the conference allowed NGOs to observe and speak at open plenary or committee sessions. Invitations were issued both to NGOs that already had consultative status with ECOSOC and those that did not. The latter included NGOs of a "genuinely international character" which, in the judgment of the conference Secretary-General, were "directly concerned with the subject matter of the conference and could contribute to its objectives."[33] There are some who believe that Strong's invitations showed a pro-business bias. In this context, it is probably worth noting that Strong's opening address to the conferees argued that while a no-growth policy was unrealistic, governments would need to re-examine the basic purposes and processes of such growth.

Perhaps the most innovative, precedent-setting and potentially important of the innovations, however, were the "alternative proceedings" arranged by the Swedish United Nations Association and the National Council of Swedish Youth. Over 200 groups participated in the Environment Forum, which provided another potential route by which NGOs could influence the intergovernmental conference. Also noteworthy was the emergence of the Friends of the Earth as a powerful environmental NGO. Perhaps it was not surprising that Friends of the Earth, and other more politicized NGOs, came into conflict with older NGOs, like the IUCN.[34] That, of course, compounded the challenges confronting NGOs in trying to influence the policy-making process, as did the fact that many INGOs thought their national affiliates should be doing the lobbying of national delegations, something that worked much better with some country delegations than with others.[35] There were other alternative proceedings, including the Life Forum, and counter-conferences, such as the Hog Farm Commune's night rally that Strong attended and which drew attention to the call for a commercial whaling moratorium. A further, precedent-setting innovation was the daily delivery of the *Ecologist* to conferees and NGO delegates.

Although the intergovernmental process appears to have gone well, there were quite a few controversies and challenges to overcome. Given the context—calls for limiting growth and what that implied for economically less developed countries—it should come as no surprise that many economically less developed countries were unenthusiastic about the UNCHE, at least when the preparatory process was launched. Moreover, the developed countries' focus on pollution, recycling, climate change, low-waste technology and environmental assessment led some from economically less developed countries to question whether they should even attend the conference. According to Gosóvic:

> In order to secure greater interest and participation by the developing countries and in light what had been learned during the initial preparatory process, the Secretary General of the Conference [Maurice Strong] made a fresh attempt to define the conceptual framework. For this purpose he convened a panel of [twenty-seven] experts [June 4–12, 1971] at Founex, in

Switzerland, to clarify and define the relationship between development and environment. This was one of the milestones in the history of environment as an issue on the international agenda. It marked the beginning of a protracted effort to secure the interest and participation of the developing countries to overcome the limitations of the initial North-based formulae, and to seek more universally appealing development. The Founex report affected the orientation of the Conference and, ultimately, the direction and scope of international environmental action in the post-Conference period.[36]

The Founex Report, which became the focus of discussion at a series of regional seminars convened by the Economic Commission for Africa (ECA), the Economic Commission for Asia and the Far East, the Economic and Social Office for Western Asia, and the Economic Commission for Latin America and the Caribbean (ECLAC), argued that "environmental concerns are part and parcel of the development process. The experts considered that environment was not simply the biophysical sphere; it was also socio-economic structures; the two formed an interdependent and inextricable web." Environmental damage "was due to the very same socio-economic forces and causes that were at the root of poverty, underdevelopment, economic growth, and social change."[37] While the Founex Report has been widely praised, it did not answer all of the qualms of economically less developed countries. For example, the Brazilian and Indian governments continued to stress that the environmental concerns of the North should not be used as an excuse to impose development restrictions on the South, which should be allowed to enjoy the same rights to develop as countries in the North had earlier enjoyed.[38] More specifically, economically less developed countries wanted to be sure that any money spent by the North on environmental challenges in the South should be in addition to those resources already identified for meeting the UNCTAD I official development assistance (ODA) target of 0.7 percent of GNP.[39] This so-called "additionality" demand is one that was not well received by the United States in particular. This was in spite of the fact that there was additional behind-the-scenes work by Strong to ensure that the Founex meeting would have a good chance of succeeding. In late 1971, Strong had gone to visit the President of the World Bank, Robert McNamara, to have the Bank make the case to economically less developed countries as to why the conference was in their interest. Strong reasoned that the Bank was particularly close to such countries and thus they were likely to listen to the World Bank

President. McNamara assigned the task to his environmental advisor James Lee, and to Mahbub ul Haq. Ul Haq and others on the Bank staff proved to be quite important at the Founex meetings.[40]

Moreover, as the economically less developed countries became engaged in the conference proceedings and more organized, which they were not initially or at least not relative to conferees from economically developed countries, they issued a call for a focus on drought, desertification, the effects of pesticides and pest control, soil and water, water-borne diseases and health, human settlements, wildlife, economics and trade, industrial location, transfer of technology, and technical assistance and training. This was obviously a departure from the developed countries' agenda, presenting Strong with yet another challenge.

But the challenges confronting Strong and his colleagues were not limited to the demands made by the economically less developed countries. While most Western European countries backed the proposed conference, France and Britain were "openly skeptical." They argued that there was no great need for UN political action on the environment and that a conference would be too expensive for the UN system relative to its usefulness:

> Some French and British representatives also expressed fears that environmental issues would be used by developing countries to extract financial support, in particular from former colonial powers such as France and the United Kingdom. Both countries, however, gradually adopted a more positive stand and came to support the general idea of a conference as conference preparations proceeded.[41]

There is also evidence, only recently uncovered, that suggests that there was an even wider group—the so-called Brussels Group (Britain, France, the USA, West Germany, Italy, Belgium, and the Netherlands)—that began meeting in 1971 in an attempt to limit any proposed institutional follow-up mechanism to a minor coordinating role. The group was clearly concerned about environmental regulations that might affect international trade. They appear to have been unconcerned about the environmental consequences of global industrialization.[42]

Although preparations for the Stockholm conference coincided with the *Ostpolitik* (West Germany's policy of *rapprochement* with the Eastern bloc) and the emergence of what came to be known as the policies of détente, the Cold War and the Vietnam War were still in process. Thus, it seemed a pleasant surprise when Soviet and US representatives to the UN both endorsed the notion of East–West cooperation on environmental issues. But the promised cooperation was short-lived or at least operated within limits. The chief stumbling block focused on the possible conference participation of a Soviet bloc member, the German Democratic Republic (East Germany). The East Germans and their allies argued that environmental issues were transnational and thus global participation at the conference was called for. Western countries insisted on applying the so-called Vienna formula, under which UN meetings were open only to members of the UN or any of its specialized agencies.[43] Since the West's ally, the Federal Republic of Germany (West Germany) was a member of UNESCO and the WHO, but East Germany was not, only West Germany would be able to participate. In December 1971, the UN General Assembly voted to apply to the "Vienna formula." As a consequence, the Soviet Union and most of the Soviet bloc boycotted the conference. Throughout the conference, however, Strong kept in close touch with the Soviets.

A total of 113 UN members convened in Stockholm on June 5, 1972, for the two-week conference. Three main committees were set up to examine the main substantive issues on the conference agenda. The First Committee discussed human settlements and the non-economic aspects of environmental issues. The Second Committee addressed natural resource management and its relation to development. The Third Committee studied issues relating to pollution and an appropriate institutional response to environmental questions. The conference also set up a Working Group on the Declaration on the Human Environment.

On the final day of the conference, June 16, 1972, conferees adopted a Declaration on the Human Environment, comprised of twenty-six principles. It declared that governments should strive to protect the environment through conservation and anti-pollution measures, to provide assistance to economically less developed countries to guard against natural disasters, to promote stable prices for commodities, to promote rational and planned development of human settlements and housing, to encourage the rational management of resources, to pursue environmental education and scientific research, to encourage just compensation to victims of pollution or environmental damage, and to seek the elimination of nuclear weapons. The text of the Declaration was adopted by acclamation, although a number of countries expressed reservations and made other observations concerning various provisions, even though they knew they were not legally binding. Among the most significant aspects of the Declaration is Principle 21, which many now understand to be binding customary international law (i.e. underscoring how UN global conferences can contribute to norm creation):

> States have, in accordance with the Charter of the United Nations and the principles of international law, the sovereign right to exploit their own resources pursuant to their own environmental policies, and the responsibility to ensure that activities within their jurisdiction or control do not cause damage to the environment of other States or of areas beyond the limits of national jurisdiction.

Conferees also made a total of 109 recommendations in its Action Plan, including in the areas of human settlements, natural resource management, pollution measurement and control, the relationship of environment and development to trade policy, and the pursuit of environmental education. Interestingly the Action Plan makes recommendations to governments and intergovernmental organizations (UN and regional bodies), but not to NGOs. It is also significant that some of these recommendations passed in spite of opposition from key actors at the conference. For example, the United States did not accept the notion that when environmental regulations restricted trade with economically less developed countries, compensation should be paid. The United States, Canada, Japan, and several West European countries opposed the creation of a separate financial mechanism for human settlements. Japan voiced its opposition to a recommendation calling for a ten-year moratorium on whaling. China, France and Gabon voiced opposition to the conference's condemnation of nuclear tests, especially above-ground testing (twenty-nine other countries abstained on the vote). National interests clearly were in play at Stockholm.[44]

Significantly, conferees also voted to create a governing council for environmental programs, and to establish a small secretariat to carry out the governing council's recommendations and a voluntary fund to support environmental projects. Moreover, it called on the UN General Assembly to establish June 5 each year as World Environment Day.

On December 15, 1972, the UN General Assembly, by overwhelming majorities, approved resolutions that established World Environment Day and created the UNEP, with a secretariat, a governing council, a voluntary environment fund, and Earthwatch, an international environment information network. The General Assembly resolution also called upon the UN to collaborate with

NGOs in effectuating the recommended changes. This, and especially the establishment of UNEP, addressed the institutional follow-up question that confronted the conference. The particular outcome, a compromised coordinating and stimulating program that was under ECOSOC rather than a more bureaucratically powerful specialized agency, resulted chiefly from two factors. Major UN specialized agencies contended that there was no need to create a separate UN agency for the environment, as they had already staked out claims to environmental aspects within their own fields of concern and thus collectively they could do a satisfactory job, and few governments were strong advocates of a major new international agency because they were uncertain as to the optimal institutional approach to the question and the environment remained relatively low on countries' priorities. There is some evidence that scientists and NGOs were among the strongest proponents of a powerful new institution, but government representatives were in charge at Stockholm.[45] In the end, as Branislav Gosóvic suggests:

> [UNEP's] coordinating but non-operational mandate ... contained the risk of impotence and frustration. This was compounded by the provision of a "small" secretariat, which represented an important concession to the specialized agencies. They felt that anything "small" was less likely to interfere in their work, could not duplicate their activities, and could not undertake environment-related actions on its own.[46]

John McCormick's summary judgment is more positive. He focuses on the fact that UNEP offered "NGOs and INGOs (international nongovernmental organizations) a new forum in which they could attempt to influence public policy."[47] Even Gosóvic found the setting up of a fund to pay for UNEP's operations "somewhat remarkable" and "out of character with what developed countries liked to do." He opined that this probably showed their concern for the issue and their desire to influence policy decisions.[48] Also remarkable, indeed unique, was the fact that UNEP was sited in Nairobi, Kenya, the first UN organ to be sited in the "third world." During the discussions about the establishment of UNCTAD and UNIDO (the UN Industrial Development Organization), economically less developed countries had proposed that UNEP be sited in the "third world." There had been a lot of discussions at various regional meetings about Nairobi as the site, and the G-77 had taken a collective stand calling for Nairobi. When the UN General Assembly voted on it, industrialized countries abstained from the vote, calling instead for a comparative study of different venues. Indeed, industrialized countries thought of UNEP as their organization and thus felt it should be located in their midst. They even argued that the institutional design agreed to at the conference was devised with Geneva in mind. Governments of economically less developed countries held firm, believing that an organization sited in the South would be less subject to domination by industrialized countries and NGOs dominated by the North.[49] In spite of its compromised charge and its location, some were quite hopeful about UNEP's founding, especially when contrasted with UNCTAD and UNIDO that had preceded it. They had only been established after very bitter fights.[50]

Perhaps as important in the long run as the accord on UNEP were the institutional consequences in national capitals. Both in anticipation of the Stockholm conference and in its aftermath, numerous governments and intergovernmental organizations established ministries and departments focused on meeting environmental challenges. For example, the convening of the conference—and the necessity that its President would have to speak at the conference—forced the World Bank to think about what he would say when made "to stand up and explain what the Bank had been doing to protect the environment" (i.e. the mere convening of the conference had significant, if immeasurable, impacts on the lead agency in development work). It should be added, however, that the Bank President at the time, Robert McNamara, was "sympathetic to environmental concerns" and thus his speech at the Stockholm conference was spoken with personal conviction and passion: "The evidence is now overwhelming that roughly a century of rapid economic expansion has gradually contributed to a *cumulatively monstrous assault on the quality of life* in the developed countries." McNamara credits Barbara Ward, who was a leading figure in preparing for the conference and in the process of writing what was to become an influential book on development and environment, *Only One Earth: The Care and Maintenance of a Small Planet*, with convincing him to think about environmental problems as an important consideration for poor countries. "With the Stockholm conference in prospect, McNamara [also] established the position of environmental adviser, to which he appointed James Lee," an American expert in public health and epidemiology. The main theme of the Bank's early environmental work was disease prevention, including those related to Bank-funded hydroelectric and irrigation projects.[51]

Moreover, "[w]hen Brazil's delegate to the [Stockholm] conference (Henrique Brandão Cavalcanti) returned home, he convinced his government to create a Secretariat of the Environment—an action that permanently improved the prospects for protection of Brazil's vast biological resources."[52] Similarly, Enrique Iglesias, who was Executive Secretary of ECLAC and had been involved in the UNCHE's preparation, "was inspired to follow up the commitments adopted by giving them a Latin American and Caribbean dimension. Thus in the mid-1970s, ECLAC for the first time seriously introduced the environmental dimension to its activities."[53]

When all was said and done, close observers deemed Stockholm a success, both in absolute and relative terms: "Rhetoric flourished at Stockholm, but the United Nations Conference on Human Environment differed from other United Nations conferences in its initiation of positive measures that have translated published resolutions into actual accomplishments."[54] Moreover, the unprecedented participation of NGOs in the global environmental policy-making process was seen to draw "new public and political attention to their work and encouraged them to be more persistent in their efforts to work with each other and to influence public policy" (i.e. they were legitimized and global environmental networks were energized). Further, the presence and active participation of newly independent countries at the conference "encouraged the industrial countries—for the first time—to acknowledge that poorer emerging countries had a different set of priorities and that underdevelopment was as much a cause of environmental problems as overdevelopment,"[55] exemplifying how UN global conferences affect global policy-makers' mind sets.

In sum, the factors explaining the success in Stockholm include the following, not all of which were evident in subsequent UN conferences:

- Preparatory stages of the conference were "action-oriented; it was intended by its managers to lead to positive results and not merely to statements of principles." The conference hosts also wanted more than rhetoric.
- Preparations were extensive and thorough, with sufficient time being allowed to conduct necessary research, obtain agreements and to resolve or manage "more unpalatable political differences."
- Popular interest and support reinforced the sense of necessity for the conference and its action orientation, even though civil society's direct influence on delegates was limited.
- Skillful management before, during and after the conference, with considerable credit being given to Maurice Strong. Note, for example, his behind-the-scenes work with the World Bank and

with the Soviet Union. Indeed, some have suggested that Stockholm illustrated "the importance of naming a strong personality like Maurice Strong to head the effort and of choosing a sympathetic host like Sweden."[56]

• The presence of a large number of NGOs and newly independent African and Asian states.[57]

Auspicious as all of this was, the 1970s witnessed a significant decline in public interest in environmental issues, owing to the oil crises, retreat of US leadership in multilateral environmental issues, economic stagnation, ongoing reservations by economically less developed countries (including important ones like India and Brazil), and high unemployment rates. Moreover, the doom scenarios that were so popular in the 1960s came under increased attack in the 1970s.[58]Further, UNEP, with its limited funding base, narrow mission and location in the South had only limited success in keeping environmental issues high on member states' agendas. Even the World Bank, under McNamara, quickly "downplayed" environmental issues:

> Only three months after the Stockholm conference, McNamara made no mention of environmental issues in his annual report to the Board of Governors, neither in his review of Bank activities during the previous year nor in his outline of the program for the next five years. His report the following year was also silent on the issue except for a passing mention of the Office of Environmental Affairs as one of a number of new offices. The *Annual Report* for 1973 did have a short and anodyne section on "environmental impact;" but six years elapsed before another environmental heading appeared (in 1979) and another six years before the next one appeared (in 1985).[59]

Although personally committed to minimizing the environmental damage caused by Bank projects, McNamara thought that the Bank could do what was needed with a minor initiative. He was surely not alone then in underestimating the environmental implications of Bank and Bank-like projects. Moreover, many on the Bank staff were skeptical of subjecting Bank projects to the scrutiny of "environmental specialists" using different standards from their own. (It would be a long time before non-economists had respect within the Bank, a challenge that has yet to be overcome by the IMF.) Moreover, NGOs seemed to ignore the Bank and its environmental record in the 1970s— something even apparent years later with the "Fifty Years is Enough" movement[60]—and indeed there was something of a backlash against the Bank's apparent deviation from its traditional focus on rapid development. As a sign of the times, some commentators went further, portraying "deep ecologists" as socialists and/or anti-growth.[61]

Thus, while the UNCHE had ended on a relatively upbeat note and was viewed as such an institutional success that governments were willing and anxious to try to replicate it in other issue areas, it would be years before the value of its proceedings would begin to yield concrete results. That was as true of the slow acceptance of the Stockholm principles as customary international law and UNEP's ability to exert an impact on global environmental consciousness and policy-making as it was the limited influence exerted by the multiple environmental NGOs stirred to action by the conference's convening. In the near term, the UNCHE was overtaken by an inauspicious global economy, bureaucratic inertia (especially in the World Bank) and a lack of leadership by the global hegemon, with no one stepping up to fill the vacuum. And things did not fare that much better in the longer term, as was evidenced by the convening of and discussions at the second major global UN environmental conference, held in Rio in 1992.

3   The first rush of UN global conferences, 1974–1979

- **(Third) World Population Conference**
- **World Food Conference**
- **World Conference on Women**
- **United Nations Conference on Human Settlements (Habitat I)**
- **United Nations Water Conference**
- **United Nations Conference on Desertification (UNCOD)**
- **World Conference Against Racism**
- **United Nations Conference on Science and Technology for Development**

The focus of most of the conferences of the latter half of the 1970s was on problems of economically less developed countries. This was a reflection of the fact that during the 1970s the UN had increasingly become

> a global political forum for the Third World and a centre of debate and negotiations on economic and social issues. Their three-fourths majority gave the countries of the South decisive influence on topics discussed and procedures in the General Assembly and in many United Nations bodies and specialized agencies.

But despite this new emphasis, the outcomes for the economically less developed countries were "disappointing."[1]

The afterglow of the Stockholm conference and the expectations surrounding Soviet–American détente had provided much of the heightened anticipation and initial excitement surrounding the conferences in the remainder of the decade of the 1970s. But all of this would prove short-lived, not simply because, as noted above, the afterglow of the Stockholm conference didn't last very long. By the time the conferees met in Bucharest (to discuss issues of overpopulation) and Rome (to discuss food problems), tensions between the Soviet Union and the United States were on the horizon. The US government seemed unprepared for the fact that the Soviets were not ready to concede the Middle East as outside their sphere of influence and were totally shocked when the Soviets assisted Cuban troops in being deployed in Africa. Compounding the difficult geo-strategic context of the conferences of the 1970s were ongoing tensions between China and the Soviet Union and so-called North–South divisions, i.e. tensions between the rich and poor. Those last tensions, which played out in a variety of ways in the conferences discussed in this chapter, were exacerbated by the success of OPEC in raising oil prices and the (short-lived) fear of rich countries that other commodity-exporting countries might replicate that experience.

(Third) World Population Conference

The World Population Conference held in Bucharest, Romania, August 19–30, 1974 was actually the third such conference sponsored by the UN, but the first that meets the criteria adopted herein (and elsewhere) as a UN global conference. The first two UN-sponsored conferences— convened in 1954 (in Rome) and 1965 (in Belgrade), in collaboration with the IUSSP—brought together experts from UN member states to discuss scientific ideas as well as more general problems relating to population. Significantly, these experts were not selected by their governments "and their remarks were not intended to reflect the position of their home countries." So, although "some of the ideas generated at these conferences may have influenced the ideas of political leaders, [since] the ostensible purpose of the conferences was not to formulate population policies,"[2] it seems appropriate to start with the Bucharest conference.

Although public concern with rapid population growth (e.g. in Egypt, India and Pakistan) goes back almost to the origins of the UN, the notion that "rapid population growth was a hindrance to development, and, more important, contraceptive technologies were available that could enable couples to limit their fertility if they wished" was not pervasive until later (by 1970) and provides an important element in the context of the origins of a (Third) World Population Conference, one which involved a shift from scientific inquiry to population policy. Also key to that context were the changed positions of the United States, from President Eisenhower to President Kennedy, and of the Soviet Union, whose opposition was based on Marxist principles. The view that economic growth of and by itself would "solve" the problems of population[3] was tempered perhaps because of India's strong support for UN technical assistance for population programs, and of the UN itself, a change prompted by a multimillion-dollar US contribution to the United Nations Fund for Population Activities (UNFPA, now called the United Nations Population Fund, but retaining its original abbreviation).[4] The widely accepted view of the Stockholm conference as a success also appears to have contributed to the decision to convene the first intergovern-mental conference relating to population issues.[5] In more global structural terms, the conference was convened in a period of East–West détente and in the aftermath of the May 1974 UN General Assembly's adoption of the Declaration and Programme of Action on the Establishment of a New International Economic Order (NIEO), calling upon the advanced industrialized capitalist Northern states to take various actions to correct the economic imbalance in the world, including increased financial and technical assistance.[6] The displace-ment of an East–West with a North–South split in UN affairs, symbolized by the NIEO demands, is also critical to understanding what happened at Bucharest.

As was true at Stockholm, a parallel civil society conference—called the Population Tribune—met and, as was true in Tehran, the Bucharest conference was seen to be the focal point of a UN-declared year. "Both the conference and the Tribune placed an overwhelming focus on socioeconomic development, with population relegated to the lesser role of a contributing factor in the development process."[7] This emphasis was also reflected in the World Population Plan of Action. The Tribune, which was physically separated from the intergovern-mental conference, attracted 1,350 people, 300 of whom were official observers. About half were women; 22 percent were from economically less developed countries. Following precedent, the Tribune was respon-sible for a newspaper, the *PLANET*. It was published in Bucharest by the International Planned Parenthood Federation. Its ten issues were a major source of news during the conference. Also following precedent, there were additional alternative conferences, including the Encounter for Journalists on Population, which included fifty journalists from the "third world" and the International Youth Population Conference (IYPC). The latter, attended by over 200 people under the age of 30, was marked by "procedural and substantive disagreements" and "deep political and ideological divisions." Its final statement, which "embraced views acceptable to the majority of the delegates," charac-terized the contemporary world as suffering from "abject poverty, malnutrition, widespread disease, massive unemployment and shameful inequality and injustice." Significantly, it went on to suggest that "[t]he primary causes of these conditions are the exploitative and repressive social, economic and political structures and institutions, often the legacy of prolonged colonial oppression," rather than overpopulation. The consensual statement did note, however, that

> a high rate of population growth in some countries adds to their existing social and economic problems. Measures to reduce a high rate of population growth ... [however] will only be effective when they are part of a comprehensive and integrated strategy for rapid social and economic development.

The IYPC also seemed to support the principle of family planning, endorsing the notion that people should "freely choose the number and spacing of their children."[8]

The recommendation for convening the intergovernmental conference originated with ECOSOC's Population Commission[9] and was approved by ECOSOC itself in April 1970. In December of that year, the UN General Assembly designated 1974 as World Population Year (WPY) and requested that the UN Secretary-General prepare a set of UN activities for the year. In June 1972, the Population Commission was designated as the intergovernmental preparatory committee for the Conference (as well as WPY). In the same year a Mexican, Antonio Carrillo-Flores, was appointed conference Secretary-General. Prior to the conference, four symposia were convened: Population and Development (Cairo, June 1973); Population and the Family (Honolulu, August 1973); Population, Natural Resources and Environment (Stockholm, September–October 1973); and Population and Human Rights (Amsterdam, January 1974). Reports resulted from each of these symposia, which along with the World Population Plan of Action, the central document of the conference, were the conference's major documentary outcomes.

Preparations for the conference were well underway before the UN General Assembly had designated 1975 as International Women's Year (IWY). But once that year was designated and the first female UN Assistant Secretary-General, Helvi Sipilä, had been named, attention was drawn to the fact that Population Conference's preparatory committee had devoted no particular attention to women's roles in population questions. These concerns were the focal point of an unofficial preparatory meeting, the International Forum on the Role of Women in Population and Development, organized in early 1974 by NGOs together with the Assistant Secretary-General's Center for Social Development and Humanitarian Affairs. The unofficial preparatory conference was attended by "a prominent female personality" from each of 116 countries. This meeting proved to be a seminal event, after which some have argued that it was no longer possible to ignore the link between women and population. Indeed, many of the women who had participated at the informal conference were later part of their countries' delegations at the Bucharest conference. "Thanks in no small measure to their efforts, the World Population Plan of Action gave appropriate recognition to the importance of population policies to women and to the role women had to play in these issues."[10] Conference Resolutions IV, XII and XVII urged all countries to eliminate social practices and legislative measures that discriminated on the grounds of sex. Further, the UN and its specialized agencies were asked to give consideration to the impacts of development efforts and programs on improving the status of women. It was also recommended that individuals be allowed full freedom to choose, in a responsible manner, the number and spacing of their children.

The opening days of the official conference were spent on procedural matters, including the election of George Macovescu, the Romanian Foreign Minister, as the conference President. Although the credentials of the 136 participating governments were approved, that was not without controversy as had become typical during the Cold and Vietnam Wars.[11] Also attending were representatives of five specialized agencies, other UN bodies, eleven intergovernmental organizations, and 109 NGOs. The latter two groups simply had the rights of observers.

Early on, even in the committee sessions, two opposing perspectives emerged. Underlying the views articulated by the majority of "third world" delegates "was the belief that demographic variables are wholly derivative effects of general social and economic development." Advocates of this view, and perhaps significantly led by Algeria, one of the forces behind the NIEO, "made frequent reference to the new international order as *the* fundamental solution to population problems." Some simply suggested that the discussion of population problems diverted attention from more important issues. "The possible reflexive effects of demographic variables upon social and economic development were perceived to be absent or inconsequential." The experience of Europe was used to show that demographic growth does not affect development negatively and that fertility declines are a natural concomitant of social and economic transformation. As the leader of the Indian delegation put it, "development is the best contraceptive." What is perhaps of more interest, at least in retrospect, is how surprised Western delegates and the UN Secretariat were to find the rejection of the premise that rapid population growth was a major cause of underdevelopment rather than its consequence. Jason Finkle and C. Alison McIntosh conclude that the element of surprise was due to

> the dominant role played by population experts and family planning advocates in the [conference's] preparatory process and the partial exclusion of those parts of the UN system and the donor agencies that might have been expected to be better attuned to broader political issues.[12]

The minority view at the conference—held by government representatives from most of Asia, Western Europe, North America and some of Latin America—was that "demographic variables are integral parts of economic development, both affecting it and affected by it. Under this construction even strenuous efforts at social and economic development may fail unless attention is paid simultaneously to demographic factors."[13]

In light of these disagreements, the World Population Plan of Action was necessarily a compromised document, especially as it was adopted by consensus by the 136 participating governments. Still the Holy See asked that it be disassociated from certain sections of it.[14] The Plan looks at population variables in the context of socioeconomic development, stressing the interconnections between population growth and social and economic development. It does not set "targets" for population growth, life expectancy or family size; however, it invites countries that consider their birth rates detrimental to their national purposes to consider setting quantitative goals and implementing policies to meet those goals by 1985. The Plan also recommends all governments encourage the dissemination of information on responsible parenting and to make contraceptives available to those who want them. Conferees also agreed that considerable expansion of international assistance in the population field was necessary to implement the Plan; they specifically called upon the UNFPA to take the leadership role in producing a guide for international assistance in population matters to be made available to requesting governments and institutions.[15] But the empowerment of the UNFPA should not be mistaken, however, for a relinquishment by governments of their national sovereignty, especially by economically less developed countries, in so highly politicized an issue as population policy. Paul Taylor's conclusion on this point seems right on target:

> The conclusion is hard to avoid that the Bucharest Conference was the scene of a collision between, on the one hand, an activist and managerial approach towards population policy, which suggested a preference for a co-ordinated program at the international level, which tended toward supranationalism, and which reflected Western values; and, on the other hand, a "statist" view, seeking to keep the hands of national governments relatively untrammeled in pursuing population policies, and, indeed, seeing the population area as one in which national autonomy could be further developed, and preferring the approach of the harmonization of individual national actions.[16]

In this context, Jyoti Singh contends that three agreements from Bucharest were particularly significant: (1) "Population and development have an integral and mutually reinforcing relationship"; (2) the formulation and implementation of population policies are the sovereign right of each government; and (3) the sovereignty issue was closely linked to basic human rights (e.g. in adopting population policies, countries were to recognize the basic right of all couples to decide freely and responsibly as to the spacing of their children and have access to information and education to make those choices responsibly).[17]

Critics contended that there was no sense of urgency in the Plan apparently because many delegates thought other issues, such as the structure of world trade, resources for international assistance, pollution, education, women's rights, and socioeconomic development, were more salient to their countries' goals than were population issues.[18]

In any event, the conference clearly succeeded in two of the main objectives of all such conferences: extending the population debate beyond the confines of academic, journalistic, and narrowly defined programmatic concerns and moving it to the center of the political arena; and educating the public about the necessity to see population problems and possible solutions in the overall economic and social context. On the other hand, there were some surprising lacunae at the conference: there was no sustained discussion of successful family planning programs; the "limits to growth" arguments were not discussed, nor were the views of advocates of zero population growth expressed. Moreover, conferees did not address how quickly to increase education for women, nor how to improve job opportunities for women in economically less developed countries.[19] Clearly, the timing of the conference—in the aftermath of the Sixth Special Session of the UN General Assembly where the NIEO was most dramatically asserted—affected the atmospherics and thus the debates and outcomes of the World Population Conference. Timing and global structural factors are critical factors in explaining conference debates and, ultimately, their success in meeting the challenges that led to their convening in the first place. Of course, the artificial separation of global discussions of the population and food issues, "necessitated" by political considerations, also affected the discussions in Bucharest and the recommendations resulting from the conference.

World Food Conference

Even though the notion that governments had to cooperate concerning matters of food production predated the establishment of the UN— the FAO's origins can be traced to a 1943 conference of WWII allies at Hot Springs, Virginia[20]—the context for the November 5–16, 1974 World Food Conference was one of crisis: a drop in global food production in 1972; a deterioration in the trade position of economically less developed countries; galloping worldwide inflation and a four-fold increase in the price of petroleum and fertilizers, owing to the 1973 Arab–Israeli war and the consequent OPEC oil embargo; poor weather and unprecedented US grain sales to the Soviet Union that significantly tightened the wheat market, prompting "apocalyptic predictions of mass starvation and famine."[21] In this crisis environment, conferees at the Fourth Conference of Heads of State of Non-Aligned Nations meeting in Algiers on September 5–9, 1973, urged that a joint, emergency conference of the FAO and UNCTAD be convened at the ministerial level. On September 24 of the same year, US Secretary of State Henry Kissinger proposed that a world food conference be convened under UN auspices, as soon as possible. Kissinger's call was seen as remarkable, given that for twenty-five years the USA had opposed proposals for international food aid policy,[22] but it could also be seen as an indirect criticism of existing institutions and was so seen by the FAO. (The US neglect of UNCTAD was unremarkable, given long-standing US opposition to an organization that it saw as "third world"-biased, including in its studies, recommendations and secretariat.) Indeed, one of the presumably unintended consequences of convening the conference was re-energizing the FAO, perhaps out of fear or defensiveness.

On October 4, the USA called for the conference to be added to the agenda of the UN General Assembly. On December 17, the General

Assembly agreed [Resolution 3180 (XXVIII)] to convene such a conference to study the world food situation. It subsequently appeared on the ECOSOC agenda (on May 15, 1974), which recommended that a conference be held in 1974 [Resolution 1840 (LVI) of May 15]. The FAO welcomed the proposal and offered up to $500,000 in conference expenses. ECOSOC recommended that it be held in Rome, where the FAO had its headquarters. Invitations were issued to all states, representatives of the liberation movements recognized by the OAU and the Arab League (but without the right to vote), all interested UN organs, UN specialized agencies, the IAEA, the General Agreements on Tariffs and Trade (GATT), other interested intergovernmental organizations (as observers), NGOs with consultative status with ECOSOC or the FAO (as observers) as well as other NGOs that might contribute to the conference (as observers). It was to be held in Rome, but under UN rather than FAO auspices, which can be viewed as a compromise. Economically less developed countries preferred that the conference be convened under UNCTAD auspices and they had clear reservations about the FAO, which they thought had not been particularly responsive to their needs.[23] Holding it outside of the FAO (but within the UN orbit) was also seen as necessary in order to insure that there would be a conference open to all; attendance by the USSR, not a member of the FAO, was particularly important.[24] The FAO secretariat understood this, but it expected that any recommendations made by the conference would be implemented through pre-existing institutional machinery. Indeed, the FAO's offer of $500,000 toward the conference expenses can be seen in this light; the FAO secretariat expected that FAO's influence would be insured by its financial contribution as well as the fact that most of the secretariat work would be done by personnel on loan from the FAO and documentation would be printed at FAO headquarters.[25] Thus, as at Stockholm, a pre-existing UN specialized agency recognized that global UN conferences could result in the establishment of new competitor machinery, something that was not seen to be in FAO's interest.

Unlike Stockholm and other UN global conferences, the World Food conferees only had two documents before them to consider. This was in large part a consequence of the limited time available to do the preparatory work for the conference. The limited preparatory time also meant that translations of documents were not as good as they might have been and some NGOs lacked the necessary time to raise funds to participate at the conference. Thomas G. Weiss and Robert S. Jordan opine that there may have been less need for NGO participation at this particular conference because the issues at hand were not as contested.[26] An important exception to the generalization on the limits to NGO input was the

International Peace Research Association's Food Policy Study Group that, along with some other NGOs, organized a meeting in Rome, prior to the conference. In fact, that meeting appears to have succeeded in influencing the world conference to refocus on issues of gender, and in fact the intergovernmental conferees passed an extensive and comprehensive resolution on women and food, one which indicated how women could contribute to the improvement of food supplies if they had better access to land, education, technology and funding.[27]

Twenty-six intergovernmental organizations joined the 133 countries,[28] six national liberation movements (all without a vote) and the ILO, FAO, UNESCO, WHO, the International Bank for Reconstruction and Development (IBRD), IMF, the World Meteorological Organization (WMO), GATT, IAEA, the United Nations (International) Children's (Emergency) Fund (UNICEF), UNDP, UNFPA, the World Food Program (WFP), UN High Commissioner for Refugees (UNHCR) and United Nations Institute for Training and Research (UNITAR) at the proceedings. Conferees elected Giuseppe Medici of Italy as the conference President. Unlike other UN conferences, the background documents in Rome included little new research; much of it was data previously collected by the FAO. Also unusual (and opposed by some conferees) was the fact that the conference secretariat drafted up substantive resolutions that became key to the conference deliberations and outcomes. What also distinguished the Rome conference from those in Bucharest and Stockholm was that there was a consensus about what the problem was. This, of course, did not mean that there was total unanimity on issues. For example, many governments expressed reservations or abstained from resolutions calling for reduced military expenditures so as to provide more resources for development, while others expressed reservations about the establishment of a global information and early warning system on food and agriculture, as this was seen as eroding national sovereignty.

All these unusual factors resulted in a fairly focused conference, where the conferees were able to spend their time debating specific action proposals. It also meant that the conference was less expensive than it might have been and public relations relating to the conference was more concentrated "and perhaps more effective as well." The NGOs also published an influential newspaper. Indeed, *Pan* may have been the most influential and useful intervention by NGOs at the conference. It raised critical issues and, as at other conferences, allowed participants at the various forums to know what was going on elsewhere.[29] Also, as in the past, the work of the conference was conducted in three main committees. The first dealt with issues of food production and consumption; the second with food security issues and conference follow-up mechanisms; and the third with international food trade and commodity stabilization issues.

Given the perceived inadequacies of the FAO and WFP to deal with the world's food problems, it is not surprising that institutional issues were central to conference deliberations. Developed countries began the conference opposed to new institutions, whereas economically less developed countries wanted them. Their proposals included a world fertilizer fund (sponsored by Sri Lanka and endorsed by the Economic and Social Commission of Asia and the Pacific), a worldwide food information system, a world food security council, an international fund for agricultural development, and a global food bank. Developed countries took the position that scarce resources should be spent on programs, not on new bureaucracies. They also asked for concrete evidence that the existing institutions were inadequate to deal with the global food situation. The representative from Sierra Leone responded with a case study to document how slow the World Bank's financial support was and Indian delegates noted that no existing intergovernmental organization was truly interested in the fertilizer problem until 1974. Positions on new institutions changed, perhaps because of suggestions that a couple of oil-exporting countries might be willing to shoulder some of the new institutions' financial burden.[30] The end result, which grew out of a proposal by Sierra Leone on behalf of the African group, was to set up a new UN specialized agency, the International Fund for Agricultural Development (IFAD), which the authors of the most detailed study of the conference contend

> must be regarded as a key achievement of the Conference. The implementation of many of the new program priorities—such as an increase in the production of fertilizers or the elimination of the tsetse fly in Africa—recommended by the Conference to increase national capacities to produce food necessitates a substantial augmentation in resources devoted to agricultural development. The institutional framework for the cooperation of countries with potential resources—particularly the responses of oil-producing countries that sponsored this resolution—was what many delegates and international officials believe to have been the essential raison d'être of the Conference.[31]

IFAD, which was established as a specialized agency in 1977, is unique in a number of ways. First, its target groups are the poorest of the world's people: small farmers, the rural landless, nomadic pastoralists, artisanal fishermen, indigenous people and rural poor women. Second, its funding sources were voluntary, and, third, its Executive Board comprised three groups of states (also seen to be the sources of funds): (1) advanced industrialized states; (2) oil-exporting countries; and (3) economically less developed countries. It is the only specialized agency where the oil-exporting countries' voting power and financial contributions are such a substantial proportion of the institution.

The conferees also called for the establishment of a World Food Council (WFC), to function as the primary coordinating mechanism for food policy in the UN system (reporting to the General Assembly through ECOSOC), a recommendation endorsed by the UN General Assembly within a month of the conference's conclusion.[32]

On the other hand, conferees' new commitments of grain were disappointing, as was the fact that the USA was not forthcoming in terms of immediate food aid. Other countries, however, were more forthcoming. "Some progress was made on increasing food security" as conferees agreed to further negotiations about systems of information and stocks that could improve the chances that adequate food would be available in the future.[33] They also called for special aid to countries most seriously affected by the energy crisis and for the establishment of an International Fertilizer Supply Scheme to benefit economically less developed countries. Further, conferees called upon governments to increase their agricultural research, extension and training programs and to enhance food productivity and to promote land, soil and water conservation. Finally, on November 16, 1974, conferees adopted a Universal Declaration on the Eradication of Hunger and Malnutrition, first proposed by Peru, that recognized the need for more food production and better distribution, the need to reduce the waste of food and of post-harvest loss of food to pests and poor handling and storage, and the need to reform domestic policies and obstacles to higher food production.

As at Stockholm, the conferees chose to invoke the language of human rights, declaring that "Every man, woman and child has the inalienable right to be free from hunger and malnutrition in order to develop fully and maintain their physical and mental faculties." The Declaration continued, making some interesting and contentious observations:

> Society today already possesses sufficient resources, organizational ability and technology and hence the competence to achieve this objective. Accordingly, the eradication of hunger is a common

objective of all the countries of the international community, especially of the developed countries and others in a position to help.[34]

This was declared as being consistent with the NIEO of May 1, 1974. Not surprisingly, then, the Food Conference was much more notable for its institutional outcomes, especially the establishment of a new UN specialized agency, than for its formal declarations, although, or perhaps because, some of them were clearly quite contentious. The notion of food as a human right, of course, is yet another example of the articulation of soft law. While the full realization of that right has still not been achieved, the World Food Conference's role in its evolution is as unmistakable as is the conference's contribution to meeting the goals of eliminating starvation and decreasing malnutrition throughout the globe. In both instances, of course, the conference was simply a part of an ongoing process, of which the institutions it called for are also ingredients.

World Conference on Women

As previously noted, the UN conferences of 1974 were a logical consequence of the increased proportion of UN members that were economically less developed and the UN's adoption of "developmentalism" as its guiding ideology. In preparing for those conferences, it had become abundantly clear to those involved that "unless the situation of women was addressed and their status and conditions improved, there would be no hope for alleviating food and population problems. Thus, the hard reality of the world's situation brought women into the spotlight." In this regard the 1974 conferences can be seen as achieving what the ECOSOC Commission on the Status of Women had been unable to do on its own. Indeed, Commission members had been frustrated that the first International Development Strategy, adopted for the Second International Development Decade (1970–1980), had paid scant attention to women. Their only real success had been the unanimous passage by the General Assembly, on December 15, 1970, of a comprehensive resolution [A/RTES/2715 (XXV)] outlining "a programme of concerted international action for the advancement of women."

The context in which the first World Conference on Women was proposed also included growth of the feminist movement, especially in industrialized countries. In its first phase, it was primarily what came to be characterized as liberal feminism, that is, a call for treating women like other human beings. The UN itself was not immune to the feminist movement; indeed, pressure was exerted on UN Secretary-General Kurt Waldheim, when he was appointed UN Secretary-General in 1971, to increase the proportion of women in the UN secretariat and in senior positions.[35] Notably, in 1972, the new Secretary-General appointed Helvi Sipilä of Finland as the first female UN Assistant Secretary-General. In December of that same year, the UN General Assembly declared [Resolution 3010 (XXVIII)] 1975 International Women's Year (IWY) with the objective of focusing attention on the status of women both within the UN system and within UN member states.[36]

> An oral tradition in the UN family says that the seeds for the IWY came from Finland. A non-governmental organization, the Women's International Democratic Federation [WIDF], first proposed the declaration of a women's year, and WIDF's president then was a prominent Finnish parliamentarian, Hertta Kuusinen. Representing her organization at the 1972 session of the UN Commission on the Status of Women, Ms Kuusinen, together with a number of other NGO observers, drafted a proposal which she convinced the Romanian representative on the Commission to present. The Finnish government representative at that time, Helvi Sipilä, seconded the proposal and, on Leap Year Day in 1972, the Commission decided to recommend to the General Assembly the declaration of 1975 as International Women's Year.[37]

The General Assembly was not enthusiastic when the recommendation went to its Third Committee in November 1972. The lack of enthusiasm was due to a concern about the proliferation of "theme" years and "partly due to doubts as to the wisdom of singling women's issues out for special attention."[38] The recommendation, however, was passed unanimously by the Assembly on December 18, 1972.[39] ECOSOC's follow-up resolutions of May 16, 1974 [1849 and 1851 (LVI)], which by now included the call for a global conference as the highpoint on the UN's year, were adopted "tardily" leaving little time for preparatory work before the conference was to begin.

As with other UN global conferences in the 1970s, it was customary for a comprehensive plan of action to be prepared. Preparation normally occurred in several stages so that drafts could be sent to participating states for comments, which would then be incorporated in subsequent drafts. In the case of the first Women's conference, however, there was no time for the draft plan of action to be handled this way.

The "first such document in the world to concentrate specifically on problems and concerns of women, covering all possible aspects of their lives from food, health, and education to family planning and political participation" had to be worked on by the conference secretariat and representatives of only twenty-three countries.[40] Of course, the authors of the document were able to draw on earlier UN resolutions, but still the limited number of countries represented in this stage of the process did not bode well.[41]

Still, the first ever global conference specifically organized to address women's issues and world problems from women's perspectives scheduled for Mexico City began on time (June 19, lasting until July 2, 1975). It also proved to be the first major UN conference where a vast majority of the delegates were women (73 percent of 1,200). As significant, 113 of the total of 133 delegations were headed by women. In addition, over 6,000 women participated in the NGO Forum in Mexico City, more non-official participants than at any previous UN world conference.[42] Of course, significantly different views and priorities among the women attending were evident throughout the Forum; for example, women from countries of the Eastern bloc were most interested in issues of peace, while women from the West emphasized equality and those from economically less developed countries placed a priority on development.

The conference was organized under the three themes of Equality (i.e. full gender equality and the elimination of gender discrimination), Development (i.e. the integration and full participation of women in development), and Peace (increased participation of women in the strengthening of world peace), which also became the overall theme for the UN Decade for Women and all subsequent UN women's conferences. One of the leitmotifs of the Mexico City conference was that the three elements of the conference theme were "interrelated and mutually reinforcing." The theme, however, also came to be connected to some of the main global political debates of the day. And indeed politicization came to plague this conference as well, especially in terms of the discussion of the Arab–Israeli conflict. The most contentious aspect of the Declaration of Mexico on the Equality of Women and Their Contribution to Development and Peace foreshadowed the infamous "Zionism is Racism" resolution passed on November 10, 1975, by the UN General Assembly (Resolution 3379; this was not revoked until December 16, 1991), namely that

> international co-operation and peace require the achievement of national liberation and independence, the elimination of colonialism

and neo-colonialism, foreign occupation, Zionism, apartheid and racial discrimination in all its forms, as well as the recognition of the dignity of peoples and their right to self-determination.

Less controversially, the Declaration called on women to play a vital role in all spheres of life including seeking to attain world peace.

Since only a small number of the participating countries had had time in advance to express their views and aspirations for the World Plan of Action for the Implementation of the Objectives of the International Women's Year, it is probably not surprising that it was not adopted unanimously. In fact, almost 900 amendments and additions were proposed to the Plan, whose original draft contained a mere 205 paragraphs. In a two-week conference, it proved impossible to handle that many proposed changes or to resolve key differences. Thus, the major part of the Plan, intended as a program of action for the advancement of women to be adopted during the forthcoming decade, was adopted as it had been originally drafted (i.e. rather than trying to achieve the unachievable, a wholly new compromised, consensual document).[43] The Plan called for a binding treaty to eliminate sexual discrimination, which—along with other items coming out of the conference—has been described as a "soft law" precursor to the Convention on the Elimination of All Forms of Discrimination Against Women (CEDAW).[44] It set targets and proposed actions for both national governments and intergovernmental organizations. The ones proposed for 1975–1980 were more specific and concrete (e.g. on securing equal access for women to resources such as educational and employment opportunities, political participation, health services, housing, nutrition, family planning and relating to the measurement of unpaid labor and including it in national statistics). Attached to the Plan of Action were separate regional Plans of Action for Africa and Asia; they had been prepared and adopted beforehand at the regional preparatory conferences. The Plan's "comprehensiveness and its lack of underlying causal explanation of women's status led some feminist critics to refer to the plan as a 'shopping list' of issues relating to women."[45]

In December 1975, the General Assembly endorsed the Declaration of Mexico and the World Plan of Action and proclaimed the years 1976–1985 as the United Nations Decade for Women. It also agreed to hold a mid-decade conference in Copenhagen to review and appraise achievements from the decade's first five years and to establish specific objectives for the remainder of the Decade.[46]

In institutional terms, the Mexico City conference led to the establishment, in 1976, of the International Research and Training Institute for the Advancement of Women (INSTRAW) and the United Nations Development Fund for Women (UNIFEM). INSTRAW promotes gender equality and women's advancement worldwide through research, training and the collection and dissemination of information, whereas UNIFEM's mandate is to support innovative and experimental activities benefiting women in line with national and regional priorities, and to serve as a catalyst, with the goal of ensuring the appropriate involvement of women in mainstream development activities. While both of these organizational initiatives were important and noteworthy, they both report to ECOSOC (i.e. they do not have the legitimacy, status or financial stability of a UN specialized agency).

Thus, while the Mexico City conference was important in drawing attention to the roles that women play in the world, including in the development process, and to many of the inequalities that afflicted them, it was much less successful in terms of outcomes, because of the lack of time for adequate conference preparation, politicization during the conference, and the lack of unanimity on the implementation plan. All these three phenomena, of course, are both interrelated and hardly unique to this particular UN global conference.

United Nations Conference on Human Settlements (Habitat I)

The context that gave rise to the UN Conference on Human Settlements was stated succinctly by then World Bank President, Robert S. McNamara, whose tenure was marked by concerns about overpopulation and the problems of economically less developed countries, particularly those in Africa.

> [Cities] are growing at an unprecedented rate in history. Twenty-five years ago there were 16 cities in developing countries with populations of one million or more. Today there are over 60. Twenty-five years from now there will be more than 200 ... At current trends, over the next 25 years the urban areas will have to absorb another 1.1 billion people, almost all of them poor, in addition their present population of 700 million.[47]

While the specific origins of the first separate conference on the topic of human settlements can be traced to the 1972 UN Conference on the Human Environment (UNCHE), there are important antecedents to that including the World Bank's 1970 *Annual Report* which contended that housing and human settlements should be a priority and to the prominent place given to housing and human settlements in the International Development Strategy for the Second UN Development Decade. But the UNCHE role in setting the stage of what came to known as Habitat I cannot be overestimated.

"The Planning and Management of Human Settlements for Environment Quality" was among the six main themes selected in Stockholm by its PrepCom for that conference. The PrepCom also specified the subject areas to be considered under each theme. For the theme concerning human settlements, fifteen subject areas were chosen, each of which became the subject of a background report:

- Comprehensive Development Planning
- Management of Settlements Development
- Population Growth and Distribution
- Rural Development
- Housing and Rental Facilities
- Transitional and Marginal Areas
- Recreation and Leisure
- Interaction between Building and the Environment of Human Settlements
- The Problems of Central City Areas
- The Environment of the Central Areas of Cities: A Case Study of Warsaw
- Industry
- Transportation and Communication
- Water Supply, Sewage and Waste Disposal
- Human Health and Welfare Factors
- Social, Cultural and Aesthetic Factors.[48]

The UNCHE secretariat, mainly its Centre for Housing, Building and Planning, a unit of the Department of Economic and Social Affairs, drew on these background reports in developing its related official documents, including the UNCHE's Declaration. Although much of the so-called Declaration on the Human Environment has relevance to the issue of human settlements, Principle 15 addressed the issue most directly:

> Planning must be applied to human settlements and urbanization with a view to avoiding adverse effects on the environment and obtaining maximum social, economic and environmental benefits

for all. In this respect projects which are designed for colonialist and racist domination must be abandoned.

Of the many UNCHE recommendations concerning human settlements, a few merit our attention as they tie together the UNCHE and Habitat I. Recommendation 2, for example, called for a "conference/demonstration on experimental human settlements" under the auspices of the UN, noting that "nations should take into consideration Canada's offer to organize such a Conference/Demonstration and to act as host to it," and Recommendation 17 called upon the UN Secretary-General to work toward the establishment of an international fund or a financial institution to work on human settlement programs. Interestingly, Recommendation 11 called on the Secretary-General, in the lead-up to the World Population Conference, to give attention to issues related to population and the environment and the environment and human settlements, whereas the third recommendation made the case for certain aspects of human settlements having international implications (e.g. the "export" of pollution from urban and industrial areas).

Moreover, in the aftermath of the UNCHE, on December 12, 1972, the UN General Assembly passed a number of relevant follow-up resolutions. Resolution 2997, for example, called on development agencies, such as UNDP and especially the World Bank, to give high priority to requests for assistance in housing and human settlements. On the same day, it passed Resolution 2999 calling on the Secretary-General, with collaboration from the World Bank, to study ways to set up an international fund or international financial institutions to support improved human settlements, and Resolution 3001 which accepted the Canadian offer to host a Conference-Exposition in 1975. Shortly thereafter, University of British Columbia Professor Emeritus Peter Oberlander wrote the proposal for what was to become Habitat I. Oberlander linked UNCHE and Habitat by asserting that rapid urbanization was the cause behind the physical destruction of the environment.

The conference convened in Vancouver from May 31 to June 11, 1976. Its express purposes were to serve as a practical means for the exchange of information about solutions to problems of human settlements and to set out guidelines for national and international action to improve the living places of people throughout the world. The conference was attended by 132 governments (but not the People's Republic of China), four national liberation movements, 160 NGOs and a number of intergovernmental bodies.

As had become traditional, NGOs convened an additional conference, the NGO Forum (Habitat or Jericho Forum). It was advertised as a coordinated conference, one aimed at complementing the inter-governmental agenda with issues and perspectives not part of the official discussions. It began on May 27, three days before the inter-governmental meeting. This was intended to give time for those attending to prepare their recommendations "as the basis for a working interface with the official delegations."[49] But at least one conference observer portrayed communication between the huge NGO Forum—more than 5,000 participants from over ninety countries—and the official conference as almost non-existent. This was explained, in part, by their geographical separation, but blame was also placed on the *Daily Jericho*, which was described as largely long-winded, ill-informed and lagged in news by a day (and thus not the sort of newspaper that had accompanied, enlivened and enlightened debate at the other UN global conferences). Moreover, discussions between the two "coordinated" forums seemed unusually out of synch. Jon Tinker underscores this point by noting how little "third world" opposition there was at the intergovernmental conference to developed country nuclear power proposals to solve poor countries' energy problems, in spite of the NGO Forum's call for a moratorium on nuclear energy. Tinker contrasted this inability to get the officials in Vancouver to take seriously the NGOs' calls for a moratorium on nuclear energy with the much greater success achieved by NGOs at the UNCHE when they called for a whaling moratorium, their touchstone issue.[50] Other issues discussed at the Forum included self-help and low-cost housing, land policy, appropriate technology and rural development.

As was also traditional, the official conference was preceded by three sessions of the Preparatory Committee, regional preparatory conferences and a series of expert meetings. Also the conference President—Barney Danson—was selected from the host country. One of the innovations, however, was that in addition to the traditional reports and background papers, an audio-visual program was devised to stimulate the exchange of information about human settlement problems. A total of 236 films and slide presentation were submitted by 123 governments. The presentations were shown during the conference and plans were made to make them available for subsequent showings worldwide.[51]

In addition to plenary meetings there were three main committees, which did most of the substantive work. Committee I dealt with the draft declaration of principles and with programs of international cooperation. Recommendations regarding national action were divided between Committee II, which examined settlement policies and strategies, settlement planning, and institutions and management, and Committee III, which dealt with shelter, infrastructure and services, land and public participation.

On June 11, 1976, the conference adopted a Declaration of Principles known as the Vancouver Declaration of Human Settlements, 1976. The Declaration, which was proposed by the "Group of 77" was adopted by a roll-call vote of 89–15–10. Most of the "no" votes (like the USA) and the abstainers (like Japan) opposed the Declaration's "implicit endorsement" of the UN General Assembly's "Zionism as Racism" resolution.[52] Others objected to the Declaration's references to the NIEO and to what they considered unwarranted political interjections, such as a reference in the preamble to "involuntary migration, politically, racially, and economically motivated, relocation and expulsion of people from their national homeland."

Conferees agreed to a set of sixty-four recommendations for action by governments intended to assure the basic requirements of human habitation: shelter, clean water, sanitation and a decent physical environment, and the opportunity for cultural development of the individual. Six resolutions, addressing the question of international cooperation in regard to human settlements, were also passed. The first of these called for the creation of an intergovernmental body of human settlements and the sixth, which received "no" votes from Israel, Paraguay and the USA and forty-two abstentions, recommended that the General Assembly request the UN Secretary-General to prepare and submit a report in 1977 on the living conditions of the Palestinian people in the occupied territories.

One unusual omission was the fact that the conferees did not take a decision on the section of the text before them dealing with the location and organizational link of the proposed human settlements unit—whether it should be integrated into the Secretariat or UNEP or somewhere else.[53] This particular omission is one of the conference's events and non-events that led Robert Allen to describe Habitat I as the "most inconclusive and divided UN Conference so far." Allen opines that the low-key, wait-and-see, diffuse views and demeanor of many of the delegates that contributed to the conference's politicization and inconclusive ending resulted from the delegates coming to Vancouver without answers. Paradoxically, he suggests that these selfsame characteristics resulted in a set of delegates unusually open-minded and eager and willing to learn from others, something he believes may be the best thing about the Vancouver conference.[54]

Another surprising omission, particularly given the origins of the conference, was the lack of much attention in Vancouver paid to issues related to the physical environment. A comparison of the UNCHE documents and the silence at the Habitat conference on physical environmental issues underscores the artificiality of the divisions among key conferences in the 1970s. Of course, this division was most obvious in the artificial separation of the Population and Food conferences, as if those issues were not intimately connected.

Other factors contributing to the unimpressive results at Vancouver included the belief among many from economically less developed countries that their housing problems were idiosyncratic and this required national or at most sub-regional or regional strategies, not global remedies—in spite of the fact that the focus of the conference was on the processes resulting in unplanned megalopolises throughout the "third world." How journalists around the world framed their articles about the conference, if they covered it at all, also limited the Vancouver conference's global impact. Because many of the topics were technical, many journalists either skipped the conference or focused their reporting on issues such as the debates related to the Palestinian people.[55] Such coverage was unlikely to contribute to the building of a groundswell of global support for providing new financial assistance to cope with the world's human settlements challenges, much less in the countries that might have the funds to provide such support (i.e. including those which had voted against or abstained from the Declaration). Although the Habitat I conference may have been a more extreme example of this, the way in which the (especially private) media focuses on drama, conflict and politicization is a constant theme in UN conference coverage, one bedeviling conference supporters and those seeking financial support for implementing conference recommendations.

United Nations Water Conference

The rationale for the convening of the United Nations Water Conference, held at Mar del Plata, Argentina from March 14 to March 25, 1977, was well described in "Resources and Needs: Assessment of the World Water Situation," the first of a series of background papers prepared for the conference. It noted that at least one-fifth of the world's city dwellers and three-quarters of its rural population lacked reasonably reliable supplies of drinking water. Not unrelated, there was a wide range in water consumption, from less than a gallon per person a day in economically less developed areas to 200 gallons per person per day for those with higher incomes. Further, it contended that irrigation demands in many areas would increase because of the need to increase food production, owing to the increase in population and to industrialization. In a similar vein, the FAO predicted the need by the year 2000 for a virtual doubling of the amount of water available for irrigation compared to what was available at the time of the conference.[56] Thus the conference background report warned that people and governments had to lose their complacent attitude toward water, that somehow it was an inexhaustible "gift of nature." If not, the time might come when it would become necessary to relocate populations closer to sources of available water.[57] Thus, conferees were told of an impending crisis, with the hope that such dire data and predictions would spur them to action.

ECOSOC's Committee on Natural Resources served as the conference preparatory committee. The conference agenda, as approved by the PrepCom, had two main substantive items: (1) the world water situation, prospects, problems and solutions; and (2) recommendations for action. Preparatory activities included the authoring of thematic papers by governments; the development of strategy papers and background documents by experts, regional commissions, specialized agencies and other UN bodies; and the convening of a two-day "encounter for journalists" to inform them of the basic problems related to water resources and to assist the media in effectively covering the conference. This appears to have been an interesting innovation, and perhaps an example of UN institutional learning, given earlier experiences with minimal media attention and on the media framing the conferences in ways that the conferees and organizers did not prefer.

Representatives from 116 governments participated at the conference. Notable among the absentees was China, a country already with well-established water recycling practices in industry as well as irrigation and thus one whose experience might have benefited others in attendance.[58] Partly offsetting the loss of their physical presence was their agreement to allow a UN study group to visit China later in 1977 to examine its achievements in irrigation and small-scale water works. On the other hand, the absence of China (and South Africa) decreased the potential politicization of the conference, that is, there would not be any "wrangling" between the Soviets and Chinese. Although their "wrangling" had become something of a "regular feature of United Nations meetings," the decision regarding the Water Conference continued an evolving Chinese practice of picking and choosing which conferences to attend. Also, what had become something of a regular feature of UN meetings was a resolution on the occupied territories; at this conference the resolution dealt with water policies, a denunciation of policies or actions by colonizing or dominating powers, "particularly in Palestine, Zimbabwe, Namibia and Anzania." This resolution required a vote (52–17–22), unlike the overall Action Plan and all of the other resolutions, save the one calling for a speedy conclusion to US negotiations with Panama over the Canal Zone and urging the restoration of total sovereignty to Panama. Apparently the absence of China from the conference did not mean it would totally lack politicization; it just refocused the contentious political dialogue.

Other countries skipped the conference either because they were not interested in the topic or didn't believe they had a water problem (see Appendix I for a list of how many countries attended the various conferences).[59] However, as always, specialized agencies and other UN bodies participated; and other intergovernmental organizations attended as observers, significantly including eight international river commissions. Sixty-three NGOs also participated as observers. US NGOs, in particular, saw themselves as already playing an important role in trying to provide water to those in need. They estimated that at least seventy US-based NGOs, mostly church-related, were operating in forty-two countries and the two largest, CARE and Catholic Relief Services, each channeled between $500,000 and $1 million annually to water development projects. They presented their real strength as being able to reach the people who needed help in getting clean water, and to get civil society involved in the process, that is, the classic roles of NGOs as contrasted to government and intergovernmental aid agencies. On the other hand, the NGOs' weakness was that their projects did not always fit into government water programs; NGOs often became discouraged when they had to work through bureaucratic channels. All recognized that achieving the conference's goals required overcoming these organizational cultural obstacles.[60]

The conference elected Urbano Jáuregui (of Argentina) as the conference President. Yahia Abdel Mageed (of the Sudan) served as the conference Secretary-General. The key result of the conference was the Mar del Plata Action Plan, a series of over 100 recommendations, nineteen additional specific regional recommendations and twelve resolutions, to be used as the basis for future work.[61] The Plan was something of a roadmap for the future; in this connection conferees proposed an International Drinking Water Supply and Sanitation Decade, 1980–1990, to be devoted to implementing the Plan. Underlying the Plan was the conviction that solutions to water resource development and management required higher priority at all levels of governance. Common themes included the need for strengthening local services, training personnel for water-related activities, improving planning methods, and coordinating national efforts under an overall development plan. It was this last point (i.e. integrating water planning and management into overall development plans) that was particularly notable. In this connection, conferees drew attention to the recommendations from the Vancouver conference that related to water and to the forthcoming conference on desertification, again underscoring the artificiality of the issue–area division of the UN global conferences of the 1970s.

On the other hand, somewhat surprising or at least disappointing given the recently concluded World's Women's Conference, was the lack of specific reference to the important role that women played in relationship to water. Less surprising was the invocation of the language of human rights in the document, something of a post-Stockholm tradition and clearly one of the means by which norms evolve: "[a]ll people have a right to have access to drinking water."

United Nations Conference on Desertification (UNCOD)

As with other UN global conferences, the origins of the 1977 United Nations Conference on Desertification (UNCOD) can be found in both natural and human events, material and ideational factors. Desertification or the encroachment of desert lands, is not a new phenomenon. Indeed, it is widely considered to have played a "salient role" in hastening the decline of civilizations since ancient times, including the Sumerian and Babylonian empires. Nonetheless, worldwide recognition of it and its far-reaching ecological impact is relatively recent.[62] In the 1950s and 1960s, a large number of international organizations, including UN specialized agencies — UNESCO, FAO, WMO — and NGOs, such as the International Council of Scientific Unions (ICSU, but now called the International Council for Science), and the IUCN conducted research and collected information on the economic constraints in arid zones. For example, UNESCO established an arid zone program as early as 1952.

But it was only when the Great Sahelian Drought (1968–1973) became an international issue-area some years later that the governments of most of the countries affected by various degrees of land degradation viewed desertification as a process that merited international attention.[63] The problems caused by the Sahelian drought were compounded by the fact that the 1972 drought in the Soviet Union had led the Soviets to make unusually large grain purchases from the USA, leaving little available for food relief elsewhere. In spite of this and in spite of pressures from African countries attending the Stockholm conference, desertification attracted little attention there. Although the word "desertification" was used at the Stockholm conference, it did not feature as a separate topic. There were, however, a number of resolutions from that conference that have relevance to desertification. For example, Recommendation 20 dwelt at length on the importance of improved knowledge and the transfer of experience on soil capabilities, degradation, conservation and restoration.[64]

Moreover, the energy crisis of 1973 had had an adverse impact on the ability of the Sahelian states to receive food relief.[65] Accordingly, in 1973 the UN set up the UN Sudano-Sahelian Office (UNSO), which was given the mandate of coordinating recovery and rehabilitation efforts in drought-affected regions of Africa, that is, it focused on drought relief and not on the underlying social and environmental problems linked to drought.

But, as in the past, natural disasters and concern by the affected parties alone did not suffice to convene a UN global conference. As Elisabeth Correll notes:

> While the Sahelian drought served as a catalyst to elevate desertification to the status of a "global" problem, there were nevertheless differing views on the desirability of holding an international conference on the subject. Developing countries maintained that desertification could not be solved nationally or regionally but must be approached through a global strategy. They also argued that such a strategy was appropriate since the most affected states lacked the financial and technical resources needed to effectively combat desertification. Industrialized countries, on the other hand, did not agree that an international conference was needed or would be effective—even if some did agree on the need for a world strategy for desertification. They argued that creating a new institution would not solve the problem and that the UN system already had adequate capacity to consider all aspects of desertification.[66]

Meanwhile Michael Glantz identifies the West German Neufeldt with the position that a new institution would not suffice unless there was the political will on the national and regional level to take effective action and a French representative as arguing that the UN system already had the capability to deal with all aspects of the problem.[67]

In spite of the fact that those with the money opposed it, Correll argues that the Sahelian drought had "galvanized world opinion in favor of the need to 'fight' desertification and a 'global desertification movement' demanded a fully fledged UN conference to bring political weight to addressing the problem." She admits that some of the rhetoric used to promote the conference was a bit extreme, however. For example, she quotes a UN document published prior to the conference stating that "if desert spreading is not stopped, two African countries will completely disappear within the next decade."[68] The movement also had the added "advantage" of a series of almost contemporaneous droughts that were being experienced in several other parts of the world.

> Up to that moment, droughts had been regarded as a "normal" aspect of climatic variability and even climatic fluctuations ... But now it was noticed that the droughts were also associated with a more permanent ecological damage or land degradation which was termed "desertification," and which was of a more global concern.[69]

The linking of droughts and desertification was a key conceptual and definitional linkage that was a long time in coming; until that happened, desertification had been understood by many as manmade, unlike droughts, and thus not considered a global issue.

The confluence of these natural and human pressures resulted in a series of General Assembly and ECOSOC resolutions, culminating in the December 17, 1974, General Assembly resolution [3357 (XXIX)] calling for a UN Conference on Desertification. It was introduced by the delegation from Upper Volta (now known as Burkina Faso); their country had been especially badly affected by the drought. The resolution placed responsibility for preparing the conference with UNEP. UNEP's Executive Director—Dr. Mostafa Tolba (from Egypt)—was charged with gathering all relevant data; he was subsequently named as the conference Secretary-General. Scientists working in anticipation of the conference, while not able to reach consensus on the definition of desertification, "agreed that desertification was caused by humans in their efforts to seek a living from their environment." They also agreed to commission nine country case studies, funded by UNEP, to analyze the feasibility of transnational attempts to fight desertification and to prepare world and regional desertification maps.

The conference, which met in Nairobi from August 29 to September 9, 1977, had three central goals: (1) to increase global awareness about desertification; (2) to collect all available scientific and technical information about the problem and possible solutions; and (3) to initiate a program to combat desertification. Ninety-five states, five UN agencies, and eight other intergovernmental organizations participated in the conference; an additional sixty-five NGOs attended as observers. Conference preparations went at least part-way in achieving the first two goals.

The Plan of Action to Combat Desertification (PACD), adopted on September 9, 1977, accomplished the third objective and has been described as the "Conference's most important outcome." It sought to prevent and arrest the advance of desertification, to reclaim desertified land for productive use, and to sustain the productivity of areas vulnerable to desertification in order to improve the quality of the lives of the areas' inhabitants. The PACD's recommendations were divided into three main areas. The first focused on national and regional actions, including desertification evaluation and land management, corrective anti-desertification measures, underlying socio-economic aspects, and on the strengthening of national science and technological capacities. The second focus was on international action and in particular the role of the UN in tackling desertification. It took into account the need for cooperation among contiguous states to deal with the problem. The third focus was on measures to be taken to implement the Plan. Implementation was left to governments, with an overall coordinating role assigned to UNEP.

The Conference on Desertification, as was true of others in the decade, suffered from politicization. For example, one of the resolutions passed at the conference condemned the use of chemical and biological weapons, the poisoning of water, and other techniques of war that destroyed the environment. Conferees also condemned South Africa's policy of bandtustanization for putting excessive pressure on agricultural land; they also condemned South Africa's continued occupation of Namibia and, in another resolution, denounced the Israeli case study for calling the Negev "a desert reclaimed."

As a result of the conference and pursuant to its goal of implementing the Plan by the year 2000, two groups were established: the Interagency Working Group on Desertification, which was to be responsible for giving guidance to UNEP on overall implementation of the Plan; and the Consultative Group for Desertification Control (DESCON), which was to assist in mobilizing resources for combating desertification. The seven-year period of 1978–1984 was chosen for implementation of required immediate action, at the end of which a first general assessment of progress could be made. UNEP's Governing Council was requested to report to the General Assembly through ECOSOC on follow-up action in 1978 and thereafter every two years.

Implementation, however, was beset with problems and became bogged down right from the outset:

> Serious inconsistencies made the Plan to a large extent irrelevant. Thus, while calling for a bottom-up approach and the recognition of the importance of local knowledge in tackling desertification, it also promoted large-scale technical solutions that were not commensurate with a bottom-up approach. Further, affected countries did not take implementation seriously. Overall, the Plan of Action generated further international awareness [one of the goals of any UN global conference] concerning the seriousness of the land degradation issue but failed to stem the spread of desertification. This was due in large part to the unavailability of sufficient funding to carry out required measures and by the lack of effective participation by affected people and communities.[70]

UNEP's own review of the situation in 1991 came to the conclusion that "little evidence of progress had emerged from the reports received."[71] Frank Cardy, who directs UNEP's Desertification Control Centre, was quoted as saying that

> the trouble with PACD was that it was an agreement which said that UNEP should coordinate everything and hoped that somebody would implement something … But by and large, there wasn't a real commitment of governments to really implement the plans of action and put programs in place.[72]

Indeed, when the General Assembly voted on the PACD, many countries essential to funding a special account as a means for financing the Plan of Action—such as France, West Germany, Japan, the United Kingdom, the United States, Sweden, Norway, Denmark, Australia, and Belgium—expressed objections. Some contended that the General Assembly was making demands on them that were not made at the conference itself.[73]

The failure of the PACD to promote effective action against land degradation led some states to demand immediate and renewed action in this field, including the development of a legally-binding Convention, something that did not happen until 1994. While that is certainly a long time in the making, UNCOD succeeded in focusing global attention on the problem of desertification and reinforced the notion that it was indeed a global problem demanding international action.

World Conference Against Racism

As noted above, one of the major foci of the Tehran conference was apartheid in South Africa, a clear reflection in the increased membership in the UN of former colonial states, especially African ones. This also provided part of the context for the first World Conference Against Racism. The context included the aforementioned 1975 UN General Assembly resolution equating Zionism with racism.

The specific charge to the conference was codified in Paragraph 13(a) of UN General Assembly Resolution 3507 (XXVIII) of November 2, 1973, which called for the Decade of Action to Combat Racism and Racial Discrimination beginning on December 10, 1973:

> As a major feature of the Decade, a world conference on combating racial discrimination should be convened by the General Assembly as soon as possible, but preferably not later than 1978. The Conference should have as its main theme the adoption of effective ways and means and concrete measures for securing the full and universal implementation of United Nations decisions and resolutions on racism, racial discrimination, *apartheid*, decolonization and self-determination, as well as the accession to and ratification of the international instruments relating to human rights and the elimination of racism and racial discrimination.

Subsequently, ECOSOC [in Resolution 2057 (LXIII)] requested that the UN Secretary-General appoint C.V. Narasimhan, the UN Under-Secretary-General for Inter-Agency Affairs and Coordination, as the conference Secretary-General, and to convene the conference in Geneva from August 14 to August 25, 1978. Mooki V. Molapo of Lesotho was elected conference President.

Some 125 governments were represented at the conference. Among those absent was the United States; it boycotted the conference because of the 1975 UN resolution equating Zionism with racism. Israel did not participate either. In this regard, the conference Declaration stated:

> The Conference recalls with deep regret the cruel tragedy which befell the Palestinian people ... expresses grave concern over this continuing situation and deplores Israel's refusal to comply with

the relevant resolutions of the United Nations and it calls for the cessation of all practices of racial discrimination to which Palestinians, as well as other inhabitants of the Arab territories occupied by Israel are being subjected.

But the conferees paid "far more attention" to the problem of apartheid in South Africa. First, the Declaration recognized apartheid as a crime against humanity and a threat to international peace and security, the language necessary to invoke Chapter VII of the UN Charter.[74] Second, it "acknowledged" a government "obligation" to prevent multinational corporations from assisting or supporting the "racist regimes" in South Africa and Rhodesia. Third, it stated that all those profiting from or assisting apartheid regimes were "accomplices in the perpetuation of this crime against humanity." The Declaration also declared that "Any doctrine of racial superiority is scientifically false, morally condemnable, socially unjust and dangerous, and has no justification whatsoever." This was understood to be an allusion (and response) to Nazism and the rise of neo-Nazi and fascist organizations. Furthermore, the Declaration noted the importance of education (singling out UNESCO's work) in fighting racism, and endorsed in Paragraph 21 "the right of indigenous peoples to maintain their traditional structure of economy and culture, including their own language" and recognized their special relationship to their land. In Paragraph 22 it noted that women are often doubly discriminated against.

The Program of Action called on governments "to ensure that legislative, judicial, administrative and other measures are adopted to prohibit in their respective countries any manifestations of racism and racial discrimination, regardless of whether or not discriminatory practices prevail." But much of the Program focused on racist regimes. For example, the Program called on governments to terminate their relations with apartheid regimes. It also requested that the UN Security Council, operating under Chapter VII, impose mandatory and comprehensive sanctions against the apartheid regimes. Moreover, it called for the cessation of all collaboration with South Africa in its nuclear program and in its manufacture of arms and military supplies. Conferees called for the prohibition of all loans and investment in South Africa, the termination of all credits by the IMF and other international financial institutions, the termination of all trade promotion with South Africa, and an embargo on the supply of petroleum, petroleum products and other strategic commodities to South Africa. Moreover, conferees requested for a special study on the status of women and children under apartheid and called on the General Assembly to study the possibility of the establishment of an international fund, on a voluntary basis, to help support national liberation movements, recognized by the OAU in their struggle against racial discrimination and apartheid. (The General Assembly had specifically asked the Secretary-General to invite those movements to the conference; they attended in the capacity of observers.)

Consistent with earlier UN conferences, inclusion of items such as this in the Declaration and Plan of Action did not prevent their passage, but did prevent their approval by consensus. A number of governments, including Bolivia, Finland, Sweden, Switzerland and San Marino, entered explicit reservations or disassociated themselves from particular paragraphs in the two documents. Eastern European representatives spoke out against apartheid, but were silent about Zionism. Arab representatives spoke out against both. Austria, while remaining at the conference, made it clear that it found the discussion of Zionism "extraneous" to the deliberations. In explaining their vote in favor of the Declaration and Program including the most controversial paragraphs, the Chinese delegates stated that the Declaration and Program of Action reflected, in the main, the statements and demands of numerous "third world" countries and "other justice-upholding countries."[75] The Chinese, at the time, were working hard to play a leadership role for the "third world."

More unusual was the fact that a total of fourteen delegations, including West Germany, on behalf of the then nine member countries of the European Economic Community (EEC), Australia, Canada, New Zealand, Norway and Iceland ceased participation in the conference altogether. Per Fischer of West Germany told his fellow conferees that the anti-Israeli statements "deviated from the purpose" of the anti-racism campaign.

As a sign that the East–West conflict was still alive and well in the summer of 1978, Soviet President Leonid I. Brezhnev, in a message to the conference, attacked unspecified NATO countries for their "interventionist actions" in Africa. In addition to urging the "independent development" of newly decolonized states, Brezhnev assured the conferees that there was no discrimination in the USSR based on race or national origin.[76] Interestingly, the Somali representative at the conference denounced "a superpower" (meaning the Soviet Union) for "instigating Cuba to interference in Africa's affairs." He noted that that "the Cuban mercenary troops are equipped with modern weapons provided by a superpower."[77] Prior to the conference, the Somali UN office in Geneva had issued a press release stating that they believed that Cuba was not

> qualified to be the genuine spokesman for those who are firmly committed to the struggle against racism and racial discrimination so long as she is engaged in proxy wars in Africa on behalf of the Soviet Union in the execution of a systematic plan to suppress the legitimate aspirations of African peoples for justice, freedom and human dignity.

Chih-Yuan, the head of the Chinese delegation, both to curry favor in the "South" and to continue their anti-Soviet diatribe, condemned both superpowers (the USA and the USSR), but especially the Soviets and "their mercenary troops" (meaning the Cubans, although the Cuban representative argued that his country's troops were not mercenaries, but rather shedding their blood in the spirit of "internationalism") for their aggression and expansion in South Africa and on the Horn of Africa. After Chih-Yuan's speech, the Soviet representative made a counter-attack, which was, in turn, refuted.[78]

A detailed study of the UN race conferences by the legal advisor to the US Delegation at the most recent such conference concludes the following about the 1978 conference: "Although the U.N. set lofty goals for its first Decade for Action to Combat Racism and Racial Discrimination, the Decade's flagship event [the conference] ended in discord."[79] Not surprisingly, the conference President's summary judgment was not as harsh. While deeply regretting that delegates were unable to reach a consensus, he asserted that the conference had "gone a long way in the struggle against racism."[80] Unfortunately, history did not prove him a good prophet. And as vividly as any UN global conference held to date, the anti-racism conference demonstrated the high costs of politicization.

United Nations Conference on Science and Technology for Development

The last UN global conference of the decade of the 1970s was the UN Conference on Science and Technology for Development. Haas's judgment about the conference (as well as the earlier Conference on Desertification) is probably not too harsh. He writes of it (them) failing "to spark international concern or to catalyze robust international commitments and action."[81] This is true even though in the lead-up to the conference, US President Jimmy Carter had proposed the creation of new instrument—an Institute for Technological Cooperation—within which was to be a reorganized and upgraded foreign aid administration.

The decision to hold the conference was reached on December 21, 1976; the UN Committee on Science and Technology for Development was to serve as the PrepCom. Accordingly it developed a draft program for the conference, which was convened in Vienna, August 20–31, 1979. The conference's purpose was straightforward: identifying and effectuating strategies to build up the science-based, problem-solving capacity of poorer countries in the world.

The UN Secretary-General opened the conference noting that much human ingenuity was going into refining military technology and "wasteful consumerism." Thus, it was a major task of the conference to ensure that scientific and technological potential were directed to more constructive ends. It was also noted that 70 percent of the world's research and development took place in industrialized countries; thus, developing countries were excessively dependent upon imported technologies. In setting forth the requirements for specific action in the field of science and technology, the conference's Vienna Program of Action on Science and Technology for Development sounded the same themes. It called for: (1) creation and/or strengthening of the policy-making capacity of economically less developed countries; (2) promotion of efforts to strengthen those countries' self-reliance; (3) strengthening such countries' capacity through, *inter alia*, external support and assistance; (4) restructuring international cooperation to improve the distribution of world production and resources; (5) allocating adequate financial resources; and (6) adoption of special measures in favor of the economically least developed, land-locked and island developing countries and those most seriously affected by economic crises. To help effectuate these actions, conferees called on the General Assembly to establish a high-level Intergovernmental Committee on Science and Technology for Development, which it did on December 19, 1979 (Resolution 34/218). Conferees also passed a resolution inviting governments to facilitate women's participation in the decision-making process related to science and technology and their equal access with men to training and careers in the field. Significantly, agreement was not reached on key draft resolutions on the transfer of technology, supplementary financing for national capacities, increasing support to developing countries for the production and marketing of capital goods, or on the role of multinational corporations.

The General Assembly (also on December 19, 1979) voted to create a United Nations Interim Fund for Science and Technology for Development, to be funded by *voluntary* contributions of at least

$250 million targeted for the two-year period 1980–1981, and to be administered by UNDP. This was to be replaced when a more permanent financing system came into place. While the $250 million was found, it consisted "mostly of reallocations of existing aid commitments" and was "trivial in relation to the size of the problem."[82] Moreover, the USA and other key states balked at the idea of setting up a Centre for Science and Development headed by an Under-Secretary-General (rather than an Assistant Secretary-General).[83]

Thus, the decade ended on a much less promising note than it had begun: many countries resisted the notion of an ever-larger international bureaucracy, and the rich refused to increase what they were paying for the achievement of the conference's goals. Moreover, the costs of the UN global conferences had continued to escalate:

> The bill for the Science and Technology Conference [was] close to $50 million—not just the United Nations Secretariat and conference costs ($8 million alone), but the travel, food and lodging for 5,000 people for two weeks in Vienna and for 1,300 delegates and United Nations officials in five preparatory meetings, preparation of 110 national papers, the holding of 160 special seminars, and meetings all over the world, and so on.[84]

None of this boded well for the future of UN global conferences. If there were a silver lining in the last two conferences of the decade, it was that the anti-racism conference demonstrated the willingness, at least in theory, of the UN to address one of the most politically difficult of questions confronting member states, and the Secretary-General's opening remarks at the Conference on Science and Technology for Development demonstrated his willingness to avoid mincing words and to seek to identify the root causes of global problems, something avoided at earlier conferences and something that conference critics suggest almost never happens.

And while the conferences of the 1970s in general fell way short of their conveners' hopes and expectations, their value should not be dismissed too quickly. The challenges of overpopulation and desertification, the lack of clean water, adequate housing, and investment in science and technology, especially in economically less developed countries, had never received as much global attention. Everyone realized at the decade's end that none of these issues had been adequately addressed. But all were now on the global agenda and indeed all would be the subject of subsequent conferences.

While the problem of food scarcity was certainly not solved by the World Food Conference, important new intergovernmental institutions were established, which had the capacity to make important strides in that direction. On the other hand, the Women's Conference ended without agreeing to set up a new intergovernmental UN specialized agency. Still the demands for rights of women were on the UN and global agenda in a way that they had never been before. While effective transnational gendered networks crossing the North–South divide were only in their infancy, the importance of those initial conversations in Mexico City cannot be overstated. And, of course, promises were made to quickly return to the issue of global gender equality.

4 Conferences during a period of crisis and distraction, 1980–1989

- **World Conference on the United Nations Decade for Women**
- **United Nations Conference on New and Renewable Sources of Energy**
- **United Nations Conference on Least Developed Countries**
- **World Assembly on Ageing**
- **Second World Conference to Combat Racism and Racial Discrimination**
- **International Conference on Population**
- **World Conference to Review and Appraise the Achievements of the United Nations Decade for Women: Equality, Development and Peace**

In international relations circles, the 1980s are known for the "crisis of multilateralism" or, better put, one of the crises of multilateralism.[1] According to Robert W. Cox, the crisis that emerged in the 1980s is usually attributed to

> a tendency on the part of the United States and some other powerful countries to reject the United Nations as a vehicle for international action and a movement by these countries toward unilateralism [acting alone, outside of multilateral institutions] in world economic and political matters.

Cox goes on to explain this shift by the aforementioned economic crises of the mid-1970s, including the increase in OPEC oil prices and related NIEO demands by the "third world" for more economic and political influence on the world scene, the decrease in financial aid by the "rich countries" of the North and their increased tendency "to insist upon free-market, deregulating, and privatizing economic policies both at home and abroad." Part of this shift, however, was also a consequence of changes of leadership in the USA, Britain and major European countries where leaders committed to market solutions (i.e.

limited government or international organization roles in the economy) to domestic and international problems gained political office. Cox, however, further suggests that there was also increased "suspicion that the United Nations system had become an unfriendly political forum and a potential obstacle to economic liberalism [i.e. so-called market solutions to problems]."[2] The former could be tied to the infamous "Zionism as racism" resolution in the UN General Assembly and the latter to some of the elements of the NIEO agenda which explicitly called for greater interference with the free market, such as the support for OPEC-like commodity organizations (i.e. organizations whose goal was to increase prices by regulating how much of a particular commodity was on the market at a set price, including through production limits). Complementing these political-economic explanations for the "crisis" are a series of geo-strategic explanations including the re-emergence of the Cold War, first focused on tensions in the Middle East and Africa, and culminating in the Soviet invasion of Afghanistan on December 24, 1979, and later in the decade, the significant improvement in Soviet–American relations which, as Mohammed Ayoob notes, lessened the importance of the "third world" in the eyes of the globe's superpowers. No longer was competition for "third world" countries a motivation for providing them with economic assistance.[3] But while disenchantment with the UN was most pronounced among developed countries, even economically less developed countries

> always known as staunch supporters, had also adopted an ambivalent attitude towards the United Nations but for different reasons. The United Nations had been credited with bringing about the decolonisation process and providing a global forum to address the demands of developing countries. At the same time, criticism was voiced about the inability of the Security Council to abolish apartheid by imposing comprehensive sanctions, to bring independence to Namibia, and to ensure peace in the Middle East. The failure of the "global negotiations" [relating to the NIEO agenda] remained a disappointment for the developing countries. Third World nations deplored the "ignorance of the minority," while industrialized countries rejected the "tyranny of the majority" [i.e. an allusion to the fact that economically less developed countries now dominated the General Assembly].[4]

Thus, as argued throughout this volume, the systemic context (or evolving world order of the time) conditioned the role of UN global conferences. In this instance, the world order provided the conditions for a decade of lessened support for world conferences, whose major beneficiaries were intended to include economically less developed countries.

But as the preceding chapter underscores, some of the seeds for the crisis in multilateralism and turn from UN global conferences were either planted or germinated with the conferences of the 1970s themselves, with Stockholm possibly being the exception that proved the rule. Thus, it should probably come as no surprise that the 1980s witnessed a significant decrease in the number and size of UN global conferences, while at the same time those that were held were often highly politicized and highly contentious, and that the responses to the financial demands from the South were negligible.

World Conference on the United Nations Decade for Women

The 1980s began with the Second World Conference on Women, something previously agreed to at the highly politicized Mexico City conference. In part, it was scheduled to review the progress to date on Mexico City's Declaration and Program of Action. But it was also aimed at refining programs, as needed, and proposing a Program of Action for the Second Half of the United Nations Decade for Women (i.e. 1981–1985). It was, however, impossible for the Second World Conference on Women, convened in Copenhagen, July 14–30, 1980, to be free from the highly charged atmosphere in which it was convened. Judith Zinsser's succinct summary suggests as much:

> According to U.S. press coverage of the 1980 Mid-Decade Conference in Copenhagen, and the accounts of the Western women participants, politics, politicians, and political ideology dominated the governmental meetings. Representatives from the group of 77, supported by the delegations from the Eastern bloc, used every opportunity to insert a condemnation of "Zionism" into the Programme of Action and [the forty-eight] separate resolutions presented at the Conference.[5]

Along with the 145 government representatives, five UN specialized agencies, ten intergovernmental organizations and a number of NGOs and other UN organs, the Palestine Liberation Organization (PLO), the South West People's Organization, the African National Congress and the Pan African Congress of Anzania sent observers. The conference agenda covered four substantive areas, again underscoring the conference's charged atmosphere: the effects of apartheid on women in southern Africa and measures to assist them; a mid-point review and evaluation of progress in and obstacles to attaining the objectives of 1975–1985 Decade for Women; elaboration on the Program of Action for the second half of the UN Decade for Women; and the effects of Israeli occupation on Palestinian women inside and outside the occupied territories.[6]

The Program of Action's aim was to promote attainment of equality, development and peace (again seen as three interrelated and inseparable goals), with special emphasis on employment, health and education. It contained "practical measures" for advancing the status of women and overcoming obstacles and constraints on women's quest for full and equal participation in development. For example, stress was placed on literacy efforts and equal access to educational opportunities as well as on removing sex bias from learning materials.

Zinsser noted that the USA voted against the Program of Action as a whole, once the inflammatory word "Zionism" had been inserted into the fifth paragraph. The USA, Canada, Australia and Israel (all of which voted against the Program; another twenty-two governments abstained; many more voted against the fifth paragraph) saw it as favoring the PLO and also blaming the West for "third world" underdevelopment. It should also be added that the USA voted against Paragraph 2 which stated that the Mexico City Declaration was still relevant and which referred to the social and economic recommendations of the May 1979 Conference of Non-Aligned and Developing Countries on the role of women in development. The USA noted that the Mexico City Declaration was not approved unanimously and that it had not been invited to the Conference of Non-Aligned and Developing Countries.[7]

North–South debates also included debates over the meaning of feminism, the merits of the NIEO and the evils of hegemony, racism, colonialism and apartheid.[8] The USA and Canada complained that by emphasizing political disputes, the Program went beyond the scope of issues of real concern to women. Many Western European governments also expressed reservations about the conference's political atmosphere. The Holy See objected to the inclusion of language in the Plan of Action about family planning. On the other hand, others such as the representatives from Albania and Mozambique took the position that it was impossible to deal with the problems of women in isolation from the political context, "or to talk about education, health, and employment without referring to the fundamental causes of oppression."

In spite of all this, Zinsser concludes, on balance, the "Copenhagen Programme did advance women's interests."[9] She notes that women's activities in the economy and the family were applauded; that there was support for women receiving education of all sorts; and that there was even "a veiled gender critique of the international order in clear statements about the adverse effects for women, as distinct from men, of contemporary economic structures and cultural attitudes."[10] She also notes that, as with the documents from the Mexico City Conference, the Copenhagen Program of Action had development as its major objective, focusing on health, employment and education "but now women are central, not peripheral to its realization" and it was more specific than its predecessor had been in identifying impediments to progress.

Many sections of the 1980 Program of Action call for the gathering, analysis and dissemination of statistics to reflect "unpaid work in the household and in agricultural tasks," to document the extent of women's absence from paid employment "because of maternity," and for new "census and survey forms" that will provide data for evaluating the progress made by women toward development. The Program also envisions governments setting "qualitative and quantitative targets," commissioning "periodic reviews," setting "timetables" for increasing the number of women active in politics, and "statistical indicators" to measure and monitor women's "progress toward equality."[11]

Conferees adopted forty-five resolutions on a wide range of issues. These included (number 32, adopted by a vote of 100–0–17) a denunciation of the "criminal acts" of the South African regime against Angola; number 33 (no vote) recommending the General Assembly consider the convening of another world conference on women in 1985; and a series that dealt with the employment of women in the UN system. Another set of resolutions dealt with the integration of women in the development process; two dealt with the situation of women in rural areas; another encouraged governments to ratify the Convention for the Suppression of the Trafficking in Persons and of the Exploitation of Others; four others dealt with women refugees and internally displaced women; and yet others made specific recommendations concerning violations of the human rights of women for political reasons. The latter proved controversial and many delegates abstained from voting for them as did many from resolutions dealing with colonialism, neo-colonialism, racism, and apartheid and with women detained for political reasons by the El Salvadorian government.

On a somewhat more positive note, the Copenhagen conference had a ceremonial signing of the Convention on the Elimination of All

Forms of Discrimination Against Women (CEDAW), which had been adopted by the General Assembly the preceding year. It is often referred to as the international bill of rights for women and "from women's point of view, the single most important legal instrument adopted by the UN."[12] It includes all the provisions aimed at the elimination of discrimination against women from earlier conventions as well as new provisions, including the right to a family as a basic human right. An optional protocol to CEDAW, endorsed by the General Assembly in October 1999, and entering into effect in December 2000, provided CEDAW with the mandate to hear petitions and complaints of individual citizens, groups of individuals and concerned NGOs about treaty violations.[13] In this regard, the Copenhagen conference can be seen as part of the process of encouraging countries to ratify a treaty and contribute to the evolution of global norms. Moreover, as will be seen again, such symbolic events can add, perhaps unjustifiably, to a conference's reputation.

United Nations Conference on New and Renewable Sources of Energy

While the UN General Assembly resolutions (33/148 and 34/190) calling for the convening of the UN Conference on New and Renewable Sources of Energy trace its origins to the Sixth Special Session of the UN General Assembly's Declaration and Program of Action for the NIEO, one really needs to think of its origins as including the hikes in oil prices in the early 1970s, if not before. The UN actually first addressed the issue of energy, including the search for sufficient, affordable and inexhaustible energy, in 1949. It was then discussed under the rubric of "conservation and utilization of resources."[14] The UN's first international conference to address this issue was convened in Rome, August 21–31, 1961. That conference, the United Nations Conference on New Sources of Energy, was, not surprisingly, in an era when functionalism was the UN's dominant organizational ideology, an experts' conference.[15] There the focus was on solar, geothermal and wind power. That conference is given considerable credit for helping publicize the benefits and possibilities of using geothermal energy as a reliable source of electricity.

As the UN itself evidenced by the labeling of a subset of countries MSA (most severely affected), those that were most hurt by the hike in oil prices in the early 1970s were the oil-importing countries in the South. They were unable to offset those price hikes by increasing their own exports (i.e. countries where increases in price meant decreases in sales). So even though the issue of new and renewal sources of energy is obviously relevant to all countries, the General Assembly made it clear that the 1981 conference should focus "especially" on the needs of economically less developed countries, "in particular in the context of efforts aimed at accelerating" their development.[16]

The scope of the conference was confined to

> [such] new and renewable sources of energy as solar, geothermal and wind power, tidal power, wave power and thermal gradient of the sea, biomass conversion, fuel-wood, charcoal, peat, energy from draught animals, oil shale, tar shale, and hydropower.[17]

Given this focus, a lot of attention was expected to be devoted to the availability and accessibility of relevant technologies. Perhaps it is best to think of the conference, which met in Nairobi on August 10–12, 1981, and had as its Secretary-General the Uruguayan Enrique V. Iglesias, as looking for alternatives to expensive oil imports and in light of the impending exhaustion of wood as an energy source, long the sole energy resource for heating, cooking and cottage industries for the rural poor.

Coming into the conference, the World Bank had estimated that economically less developed countries needed to spend $12–$16 billion a year on new, renewable energy sources over the next decade if they were to "rejuvenate" an energy base capable of supporting their populations. In light of this crisis and their own estimates, the World Bank had proposed to set up a new body to lend $30 billion more than its current levels to poor countries for alternative energy projects over the period 1981–1986. The idea for such a body can be traced to a proposal at the end of the 1970s by Sheikh Ahmed Zaki Yamani of Saudi Arabia. At the time, the idea was embraced by Edward Fried, the Carter administration's US Executive Director at the World Bank. With that endorsement, a "Bank" proposal came forward, in the form of setting up an energy affiliate that would provide a way of enlarging and concentrating the Bank's work in the whole energy field. The proposal moved ahead until the Carter administration's successor administration, that of President Ronald Reagan, withdrew US support. From the Reagan administration's perspective, the World Bank could foster policies that encouraged private sector investment, but it should not make loans to governments or state-owned oil and gas companies:

> A U.S. note to World Bank directors explaining the new adminis- tration's opposition to the energy affiliate said that the United

States would not approve development bank action that borrowed from private capital markets to make long-term loans to governments of developing countries for energy development.[18]

Thus, on the eve of the conference, notwithstanding support from members of the EEC, the Bank's proposal was suspended.[19] The Reagan administration preferred to rely on private enterprise to develop and market new sources of energy and to give energy aid directly to receiving countries,[20] without the involvement of economically less developed countries that would come with the establishment of a World Bank energy affiliate.[21]

Accordingly, all Yves Rovani, the head of the World Bank's energy department committed the Bank to during the conference was $3 billion in 1981 for energy projects in developing countries and a promise to give high priority to energy projects in future years. He made no mention of the controversy over the establishment of a Bank energy affiliate to lend money for energy projects in economically less developed countries.[22]

As if this were not ominous enough, even though the conference focused on a rather technical topic and one that was of particular interest to economically less developed countries, especially those in Africa, it suffered from politicization. Twice Arab and some African delegates walked out of the conference when an Israeli delegate rose to speak. Arab delegates and the observer from the PLO objected to Israel's plans to build a canal from the Mediterranean to the Dead Sea. The Israelis contended that dams on such a canal could generate 600 megawatts of vitally needed power. Mohammed Jabir Hassan, an official in the Iraqi Oil Ministry, told the conferees that the Israeli plan represented "aggression and [a] violation of people's legitimate rights."[23] Conferees also condemned Israel's attack in June against Iraq's nuclear facility, warned of the danger of joint military activities between Israel and South Africa, condemned the exploitation of Namibian energy resources by South Africa and multinational corporations, and demanded the withdrawal of South African troops from Angola.[24]

What the conferees could agree to was the Nairobi Program of Action for the Development and Utilization of New and Renewable Resources. The Program of Action aimed to help the world move away from its dependence on depletable supplies of petroleum and natural gas and called for an intergovernmental body in the UN specifically concerned with new and renewable sources of energy and charged, *inter alia*, with monitoring and implementing the Nairobi Program. But it left it to the General Assembly (at its 37th session) to make final arrangements as to what shape that intergovernmental body would take. This, of course, was a far cry from what was agreed to at earlier conferences like Stockholm or Rome, but in keeping with the times (i.e. those of ever-expanding commitments to an ideology of neo-liberal economics). In this context, it is noteworthy that implementation of the Program required both public and private financing. The Program also urged

> international and regional development financial organizations and institutions, in particular the World Bank, to provide additional and adequate resources specifically for large-scale supporting actions, pre-investment and investment activities in the field of new and renewable sources of energy.

Further, it urged "all interested parties to accelerate consideration of other possible avenues that would increase energy financing, including the mechanisms being examined in the World Bank, such as an energy affiliate." Apparently this last provision was too much for the Reagan administration even though it paralleled the language from the final communiqué from G-7's Ottawa Summit (issued July 21, 1981)[25] and even though James Stromayer, the US representative at the conference, said that he was "very, very thrilled at the outcome" of the conference. He went on to say, however, that "The notion that this conference should endow renewable energy with a large amount of money is not a legitimate question." Accordingly, the USA entered a reservation after the Plan of Action had been adopted by consensus. The reservation stated the strong opposition of the USA to a new energy affiliate. Eastern European delegates agreed with the Americans that there should be no additional financial implications for the UN.

Not surprisingly, delegates from non-oil-exporting developing countries were very disappointed with the conference outcome, suggesting that without guaranteed money or a permanent coordinating body, the Program of Action was a hollow statement. One delegate was quoted as referring to it as "the Nairobi plan of inaction."[26] Marvin Soroos simply concludes that the conference

> fell short of the goals of its organizers, in large part because of the reluctance of the United States to support international programs for assisting less [developed] countries develop their fossil fuel resources or make use of renewable resources of energy.[27]

As a follow-up to the conference, the General Assembly agreed on December 21, 1982, to establish a (permanent) Committee on the

Development and Utilization of New and Renewable Resources of Energy, open to all states. It was to report to the General Assembly through ECOSOC and was to meet once every two years. The Committee's functions included recommending policy guidelines, formulating plans to implement the Nairobi Program and mobilizing resources. In what was hardly a good omen for the future, there was considerable opposition to the General Assembly resolution. Eastern European countries opposed it because they considered "its administrative and financial implications unjustified;" the USA opposed it because they wanted the committee's mandate to be more explicit and Turkey opposed it because they thought a more central administrative unit would eventually be needed.[28]

As the events of this conference vividly demonstrate, the global hegemon has considerable influence even at conferences with consensual decision-making procedures and practices. And while shifts in global material and ideational power significantly affect the outcome and potential success of UN conferences, so do (the not unrelated) shifts in the internal politics of major powers.

United Nations Conference on Least Developed Countries

The background to the first UN Conference on Least Developed Countries is to be found in late 1960s. It is then that the UN began paying attention to a group of countries characterized by severe poverty and economic misfortune, deemed the most vulnerable of the international community. The International Development Strategy for the second UN Development Decade for the 1970s [adopted by the UN General Assembly on October 24, 1970, Resolution 2626 (XXV)] incorporated (in Section five) special measures in favor of the least developed countries. Although stated in quite general terms, there was a call for "exceptionally soft loans," attention to their "scarcity of indigenous technical and managerial cadres," building an economic and social infrastructure, assisting them in formulating and implementing national development plans, and a variety of special trade considerations. In 1971, both ECOSOC and the UN General Assembly took decisions on the identification of the least developed among the economically less developed countries. It was deemed vital to reach agreement at an early date on a list of the least developed countries so that special measures could be initiated that favored them, at least by the beginning of the Second UN Development Decade. Before both these major organs of the UN were a number of committee reports, including those of the Committee for Development

Planning and UNCTAD's Trade and Development Board, that had considered questions concerning the least developed countries. But setting criteria for qualifying as a least developed country proved difficult. While a list of least developed countries was eventually agreed to, it was also agreed that it could and indeed would be revisited (as it has been repeatedly over the years).[29]

The least developed countries had also been singled out in the Program of Action on the Establishment of a New International Economic Order adopted on May 1, 1974, without a vote at the Sixth Special Session of the UN General Assembly [Resolution 3202 (S-VI)]. In that document, Section X discussed a special program of emergency measures to mitigate the difficulties of the developing countries most seriously affected by the economic crisis, "bearing in mind the particular problem of the least developed and land-locked countries." It also called for a larger annual transfer of resources from richer countries to economically less developed ones, a better balance between the prices of imported and exported goods, enactment of a code of conduct to regulate the practice of multinational corporations, alleviation of "third world" debt problems, a reform of the international monetary system to provide greater power to economically less developed countries, and encouragement of trading opportunities for economically less developed countries, including preferential treatment and greater access for developing countries' manufactured goods in developed markets. While little of this agenda was adopted, including at the abortive 1975–1977 CIEC (Conference on International Cooperation) negotiations—the first to be designated a North–South dialogue—there was a general acceptance that the *least* developed countries required some special (and immediate) attention.[30]

Accordingly, on June 3, 1979, UNCTAD V, convened in Manila, agreed to launch a two-phase Comprehensive New Programme of Action for the Least Developed Countries, comprising an Intermediate Action Program (1979–1981) and a Substantial New Programme of Action for the 1980s, aimed at transforming these countries' economies toward self-sustained development. In the same UNCTAD resolution [122 (V)], UNCTAD invited the General Assembly to convene a conference on the least developed countries to finalize, adopt and support the Substantial New Programme of Action. Accordingly, on December 19 of the same year, the General Assembly did just that (in Resolution 34/203), setting 1981 as the date for the conference. It also asked the UN Secretary-General to name the UNCTAD Secretary-General, Gamini Corea of Sri Lanka, as the conference Secretary-General. (Jean-Pierre Cot, French Minister for Cooperation and Development, served as conference President). UNCTAD conferees designated UNCTAD's Intergovernmental Group on the Least Developed Countries as the Conference Preparatory Committee, opening that Committee to all members of UNCTAD.

Aware that development assistance was declining rather than increasing, the General Assembly passed a second resolution (35/205) on December 16, 1980. In addition to accepting the French invitation to host the conference—it was originally scheduled for Geneva, but moved to Paris "at the insistence of President Valéry Giscard d'Estaing, who was eager to improve France's position in the third world"[31]—and setting the dates for it (September 1–14, 1981, preceded by a two-day conference among senior officials on August 27–28), the Assembly urged

> all developed countries, developing countries in a position to do so, multilateral institutions and other sources to take urgent steps to implement without further delay, and in any case before the end of 1981, the commitments undertaken in the Immediate Action Program.

The reasoning behind the Assembly's action became even clearer and more public when at the ECOSOC meeting in July 1981, members, after receiving information from the UN Secretary-General, expressed their "deep concern" that the Immediate Action Program had not been fully implemented more than two years after its adoption and nearly at the end of the Program period.

At the conference itself, the Substantial New Program of Action for the 1980s for the Least Developed Countries was adopted by acclamation. The Program consisted of a preamble and three chapters. The chapters dealt with national and international support measures and arrangements for implementation, follow-up and monitoring. "The Group of 77 felt the Conference had been a positive, though not decisive, sign for resumption of the North–South dialogue."[32] On the other hand, the Tanzanian delegate, speaking for the African Group, said he would have wanted a stronger and more unequivocal commitment on the flow of resources in real terms and within a specific time frame. The spokesman for the EEC noted that as their donor members sought to meet the overall UNCTAD I goal of 0.7 percent/GNP as official development aid, that they would aim to allocate 0.15 percent/GNP toward the least developed countries. Some EEC members had already reached that goal and French President François Mitterrand promised that France would increase aid to the least developed countries and also cancel their debts to France. He also urged other wealthy countries to do the same. While other developed countries, like Japan, promised to try and increase their contributions, the US delegate made clear that its position of not accepting specific ODA targets had not changed. In addition, it opposed the notions of the IMF's creation of Special Drawing Rights (SDRs) linked to aid, and the concept of international taxation as a means to redistribute wealth to the world's poorest.

On December 17, 1981, the General Assembly endorsed the conference's Program of Action and called upon member states and international organizations to implement it immediately as part of action on the establishment of an NIEO. Of course, the likelihood of it being implemented depended, in part at least, on the G-77's ability to hold together a large coalition of countries, whose individual national interests might overlap, but certainly did not coincide.

Even if had been implemented, the commitments were so much greater in terms of rhetoric than anything else, something they had in common, of course, with the NIEO itself. This is the sort of outcome that gives pause to UN conference supporters and ammunition to their opponents. But what this volume tries to suggest is that both are probably missing one of the key impacts of conferences such as this one: they have the potential to change the mindsets of key policy-makers; those preparing for, attending and following up on the conferences. Here this "conference concentrated the attention of the international community on the plight of some 270 million of the globe's most desperately poor people."[33] Cot puts it this way:

> The results obtained after fifteen days of particularly intense discussions might have appeared modest with respect to the needs of the least-developed countries, but its outcome was far from negligible. The Paris Conference led to a recognition of the problems that are confronted by these countries. The message of the conference was listened to, and it was understood.[34]

World Assembly on Ageing

The question of aging first came before the UN in 1948, when Argentina presented a draft declaration on old-age rights to the General Assembly. Pursuant to this, the UN Secretary-General issued a report entitled "Welfare of the Aged: Old Age Rights," published in 1950. But it was not obvious then what a substantial proportion of the population the aging population would become both in developed and in economically less developed countries. Thus, it was not until 1969 that the UN turned its attention again to this topic. Then it was at the initiative of a Maltese delegate who placed the issue on the General Assembly agenda. On December 14, 1973, the General Assembly passed a resolution (3137/28) noting the need for well-designed policies and programs for the elderly and the aged.

As Dr. A.h.B. de Bono, the Maltese chairman of the Main Committee of the UN General Assembly, wrote, "it was very much the United States that provided the impetus for the World Assembly to take place." It was actually the US Congress that pressed the executive branch which, in turn, pressed the UN throughout the 1970s to take some initiatives on this area. According to de Bono, it was the first time that the US Congress had urged a worldwide assembly on a particular topic.[35] Members of Congress explained US interest as at least partly a consequence of the magnitude of the aging population in the United States itself. The idea that the UN should consider convening a conference was first proposed in the US Congress on September 13, 1977, by Senator Frank Church, Chairman of the Senate Committee on Aging. On October 5, a US Senate resolution called on the US President to work with other countries in getting the UN to take up this idea. A similar resolution was passed in the House, by the House Select Committee on Aging, headed by Representative Claude Pepper. On December 7, 1977, the US designated funds for the Assembly. Ultimately, the US Congress appropriated $650,000 of the $1 million for the Assembly Trust Fund. And on December 16, 1977, (Resolution 32/132), the UN General Assembly passed a resolution calling for an International Year and a World Assembly on Ageing (initially called a World Assembly on the Elderly). The UN resolution calling for the conference came a year later on December 24, 1978. Moreover, in May 1981, William M. Kerrigan was named the conference Secretary-General, the first US national ever to be named as head of a UN conference, suggesting that members of Congress were not wrong in pressing for the USA to assume an effective leadership role throughout the process.[36] Obviously this is a vivid contrast to the US position—seemingly consistent in the"dragging of its collective feet"— on most of the other UN global conferences of the 1980s.

Consistent with other UN conferences, however, the World Assembly on Ageing was preceded by regional meetings—three in this instance (Asia and the Pacific, Africa, and Latin America). There was also an NGO Forum. Held in Vienna from March 29 to April 2, 1982, it was attended by 336 delegates from 43 countries representing 159 NGOs that had consultative status with ECOSOC. The Forum developed a set of recommendations for governments to act on in providing for the needs of the aging. It is also worth noting that ECOSOC, on May 4, urged that the Assembly to devote attention to the special problems of elderly women.

Some 124 governments were represented at the World Assembly on Ageing, which met in Vienna from July 26 to August 6, 1982. Its objectives included promoting awareness of major demographic shifts in progress and identifying the impacts of those shifts on socio-economic development, especially in economically less developed countries. On August 6, by consensus, conferees adopted the Vienna International Plan of Action on Aging, 1982. Although there had earlier been discussion of a separate declaration on the rights of the aging, it was agreed that they could be included in the Plan's preamble: "The Plan's general policy recommendations were aimed at a shift from policies and practices limited to providing protection and care to a vulnerable and declining minority to policies based on a positive, active and developmentally oriented view of aging." To implement the Plan,

> full use was urged of opportunities existing for technical cooperation between developed and developing countries in three areas: data collection and analysis by means of censuses and surveys or statistics systems; training and education; and research on the developmental and humanitarian aspects as identified by the Plan.

There were also recommendations for increased bilateral and multilateral (including UN) aid and for bringing the issue of aging to the attention of those preparing for the 1984 International Conference on Population. The Plan was adopted by the General Assembly on December 3, 1982 (Resolution 37/51) by a vote of 149–0. The resolution also called on the UN Secretary-General to ensure sufficient funds were expended to implement the Plan, called for a strengthening of the international network of information, and called on UNFPA to strengthen its assistance in the field of aging. In spite of the fact that President Reagan was only one of three heads of state who sent messages to the Assembly, the USA still tried, unsuccessfully in the end, to amend the text to ensure that the Plan would be carried out within existing UN resources or with voluntary contributions that would be available from the Trust Fund.[37]

Given this last-ditch effort by US conferees, it is probably not surprising that members of Congress concluded that consciousness-raising might have been the most important product of the Assembly and that the money available in the UN Trust Fund for

Ageing was quite meager. In fact, in the first round of grants, $344,000 was allocated, mostly in grants of $5,000–7,000 each. There were requests for $4,000,000. Other follow-up activities, however, were arranged. For example, the UN established an international interdisciplinary network of institutes related to aging and the WHO worked with relevant NGOs. In terms of the USA itself, Congress passed a resolution on November 17, 1983 asking the President to follow up on the Assembly with new programs within the USA.[38] Throughout the process, it appears that it was the US Congress, rather than the US executive branch or economically less developed countries, that was pushing this effort. Indeed, at the conference, Richard S. Schweiker, the US Secretary of Health and Human Services, told conferees that "Americans want less government interference in their lives," a position consistent with the neo-liberal perspective of the US administration at the time.[39]

Thus, while the World Assembly on Ageing appears to be an anomaly in many ways—the US taking the initiative during an era of unilateralist foreign policy when the UN was far from the top of its agenda—a closer look at the conference explains how this occurred. It was one of those rare Congressional initiatives in foreign policy, one where the administration's grudging participation limited whatever major impact the conference ever could have hoped for in terms of coping with the graying of the globe's population. Of course, conferees' calls for adding the issue to the agenda of the upcoming population conference not only signaled their frustration at how little the conference on aging had accomplished, but it also underscored the then practice of the UN conferences to separate out logically connected issues, often for political reasons. Having said all this, it is still somewhat remarkable how far ahead of the curve the UN was in convening a conference on this topic in 1982, decades before the issue was really being wrestled with by the USA and Europe, much less in economically less developed countries.

Second World Conference to Combat Racism and Racial Discrimination

It would be hard to imagine a more vivid contrast in terms of US participation in world conferences that that of the World Assembly on Ageing and the Second World Conference to Combat Racism and Racial Discrimination. Continuing its protest of the UN General Assembly resolution equating Zionism with racism, the United States, along with Israel, boycotted the Second World Conference to Combat

Racism and Racial Discrimination. In spite of their boycott, 124 governments were represented, along with representatives of national liberation movements recognized by the OAU; the UN Council for Namibia, and various intergovernmental organizations, NGOs with consultative status with ECOSOC and a variety of "interested" committees, including the Committee on the Exercise of the Inalienable Rights of the Palestinian People and the Special Committee to Investigate Israeli Practices Affecting the Human Rights of the Population of the Occupied Territories.

While the first World Conference to Combat Racism and Racial Discrimination was held at the midway point during the first Decade to Combat Racism and Racial Discrimination, the second conference was held in Geneva at the end of the decade, i.e. August 1–12, 1983. The original plan had been to hold the conference in Manila, in spite of Filipino financial problems. Indeed, at one point the UN had suggested it would deviate from past practice [and a policy it had codified in General Assembly Resolution 2609 (XXIV) of December 16, 1969] and use UN regular budgetary funds to pay half the additional cost of holding the conference in the Philippines.

In accordance with the authorizing ECOSOC (1982/32, dated May 5, 1982) and General Assembly resolutions (A/RES/37/41, dated December 3, 1982), the purpose of the conference was to review and assess the activities undertaken during the first decade and formulate specific measures to ensure the implementation of UN documents aimed at eliminating racism, racial discrimination and apartheid. ECOSOC acted as the PrepCom for the conference; it, in turn, established a Preparatory Subcommittee comprised of twenty-three states. The UN Secretary-General appointed James O.C. Jonah as conference Secretary-General. The conference elected Héctor Charry-Samper (of Colombia) as its President.

In explaining the need for a second conference so soon after the first, Jonah conceded that the achievements of the (first) Decade to Combat Racism and Racial Discrimination had been "quite minimal, because the decade itself was plagued by serious political difficulties." He explained this in part at least by the fact that the "Europeans, the United States and, I think, New Zealand and Australia have practically withdrawn from the Decade." Basically all that had been accomplished were

> a lot of seminars, which have focused primarily on, first, the recourse procedures available to victims of racial discrimination, and then, encouragement of Governments to adopt legislation

domestically to help these victims. But by and large, not much progress has been made.[40]

Jonah's hopes for the conference were connected to his belief and expectation that issues relating to Zionism would not be discussed there. It was on the basis of that belief and expectation that the Europeans agreed to attend. But Jonah realized that the USA would not attend until the 1975 General Assembly resolution equating Zionism with racism had been rescinded.[41] Thus, from the outset, the possibilities for the conference were bounded. But still the conference, like those preceding it, issued a fairly comprehensive Declaration and Program of Action.

The conference Declaration stated that "Racism and racial discrimination are continuing scourges which must be eradicated throughout the world." It also declared apartheid totally abhorrent to the conscience and dignity of mankind, a crime against humanity, and a threat to international peace and security.[42] The conferees also noted "with concern the insidious propaganda by Israel against the United Nations and against Governments that are firmly opposed to *apartheid*." The word "insidious" is pretty strong in terms of diplomatic parlance. The Declaration went to on to recall "with deep regret the practices of racial discrimination against the Palestinians as well as other inhabitants of the Arab occupied territories."[43]

Conferees called for steps to be taken against all ideologies and practices, such as Nazism, fascism, and neo-fascism based on racial or ethnic exclusiveness or intolerance, terror, or systematic denials of human rights and fundamental freedoms. They also noted the "double discrimination" often experienced by women. The Declaration further spoke of the urgent need to protect the rights of refugees, immigrants and migrant workers and spoke in favor of the establishment of the UN Working Group on Indigenous Peoples.

Among the resolutions passed at the conference was one demanding the "immediate and unconditional release of Nelson Mandela and all South African and Namibian political prisoners." Significantly, the paragraph expressing solidarity with Nelson Mandela and the National Liberation elements of South Africa and Namibia were voted on separately (78–0 with 10 abstentions) so that the rest of the resolution (Resolution 2) could be passed without a vote.[44]

The conferees' recommendation to the General Assembly that a Second Decade to Combat Racism be launched was quickly acted upon. In its November 22, 1983, resolution endorsing the Second Decade for Action to Combat Racism and Racial Discrimination

(1983–1992), the General Assembly referred to the second conference's report and expressed concern that the objectives of the first decade had not been attained. Indeed, the report noted that millions of people continued to be victims of varied forms of racism and racial discrimination. The second decade's Program of Action included a plan for initiating a world public information campaign for human rights and the drafting of "model national legislation" to guide governments in the enactment of legislation against racial discrimination. It charged the UN Commission on Human Rights with drafting up the "model" legislation.

Whereas the measures proposed to combat apartheid in South Africa, namely economic sanctions and a total curtailment of all sports, cultural and scientific contacts, were unanimously endorsed, most Western delegations in attendance abstained or voted against the measures condemning Israeli cooperation with South Africa and Israeli racial discrimination against inhabitants of the Arab occupied territories.

Clearly, the conference fell well short of its proposers' hopes and Jonah's own expectations. The boycott by the USA, in particular, was a bad omen from the outset. One lesson was not lost on the conferees, however. It would not make much sense to convene another global conference on this topic until the "Zionism as racism" resolution had been dumped in the dustbin of world history. Only then would it make sense to convene a third global conference on the "continuing scourges" of racism and racial discrimination.

International Conference on Population

The International Conference on Population was held in Mexico City from August 6–14, 1984. Like the Bucharest conference that preceded it, the idea came from the Population Commission. Accordingly, in 1979, ECOSOC asked the Population Commission, in consultation with other UN bodies, to consider the possibility of holding such a conference. Its aim would be to appraise the implementation of the World Population Plan of Action adopted at the 1974 Bucharest World Population Conference. In November 1981, ECOSOC reviewed the Population Commission's proposal. Compared with Bucharest, this time there was a great deal of support among economically less developed countries for such a conference. Indeed, India, the Philippines, and Mexico strongly supported the proposal. On the other hand, many developed countries were not so keen and the Soviet Union and some Eastern European countries preferred that the Bucharest consensus not be disturbed in any way. Countries' reservations explain why the conference agenda was focused on the Bucharest Plan of Action and on furthering its implementation. Not surprisingly, given the lack of enthusiasm of some rich countries and given the economic situation at the time,

> the question of how much such a conference would cost was raised repeatedly by a number of delegations in informal discussions, and they wanted to make sure that if a conference were to be held, costs would be held down to a minimum.[45]

ECOSOC finally agreed on November 25, 1981, to convene the conference (ECOSOC Resolution 1981/87).

The Mexico City conference was attended by 146 governments, as well as representatives of the UN Secretariat; ECOSOC regional commissions and other UN bodies; five specialized agencies; thirteen other intergovernmental organizations; 154 NGOs; and three national liberation organizations, the African National Congress of South Africa, the PLO and the Pan-African Congress of Anzania. The United Nations Council for Namibia represented Namibia. Manuel Bartlett Diaz (of Mexico) was elected conference President and Rafael M. Salas served as the conference Secretary-General. Salas's appointment by the UN Secretary-General "recognized the emergence of UNFPA as the major actor in the area of population within the UN system." There was also the hope that he "would be in a position to raise most of the money needed for the Conference."[46]

The conferees agreed that although progress had been made in the decade since the last conference and although the World Population Plan of Action was basically sound, problems persisted and the Plan needed to be revisited and revised. Demographic differences between developed and economically less developed countries remained striking (e.g. the average life expectancy in developed countries was 73 years but only 57 in economically less developed countries). Millions still lacked access to safe and effective family planning methods. Accordingly, the eighty-eight recommendations that comprised the Recommendations for Further Implementation of the World Population Plan of Action (E/CONF.76/L.3, dated August 13, 1984), that was the main product of the Mexico City conference and was officially described as a "refinement" of the Bucharest Plan, dealt with socio-economic development, the environment and population, the role and status of women,[47] population goals and policies, morbidity and mortality, population distribution, migration, and the promotion of knowledge and policy.

What the conferees recognized was that considerable demonstrable progress had been made in the decade between the conferences, not least of all because many more governments had adopted population policies, linked demographic issues to developmental efforts, and, significantly, had shown a willingness to assume more of the cost of their family planning programs (i.e. drawing funds from their national budgets). In terms of statistics, the global population rate had declined from 2.03 to 1.57 percent per year.[48] "That these developments were attributable to Bucharest alone is unlikely—and impossible to prove—yet it would be foolish to deny that the conference played no role, at least as a catalyst." Perhaps as significant as any other positive change was the fact that ten years after Bucharest, it was the economically less developed countries (and UNFPA) that provided most of the impetus for the Mexico City conference, whereas they had left Bucharest insisting that development, not population control, was their overriding objective and that they would not cede national sovereignty to a coordinated global plan designed by rich industrialized countries.[49] Sonia Corrêa puts it this way:

> Although an explosive North–South conflict permeated the population debates at the 1974 Bucharest Conference, the Southern critique of demographic imperatives did not restrain Southern countries from rapidly expanding their internationally funded family planning programmes. Surprising as it may seem, developing countries have not been entirely loyal to the Bucharest agenda. By the end of the 1970s, India and China—countries that led the Southern position in 1974—had already reframed their former policies to adopt clear fertility control measures. When the Second International Conference on Population was held in Mexico in 1984, most Southern governments had incorporated family planning programmes in their policies. In some cases states had, in fact, defined draconian fertility reduction targets.[50]

Paul Demeny implies that the change may have been due to the realization that the "deleterious consequences of rapid population growth for development deserved greater recognition" and thus "programs aimed at moderating such growth deserved higher priority" at least than they had received in Bucharest.[51]

On the other hand, the USA, "the one unfailing advocate at Bucharest of the overriding importance of family planning programs as a solution for problems caused by rapid population, appeared in Mexico City ready to champion a new approach to population policy."

At Mexico City, the USA, now guided by the Reagan administration and with the active support of the Vatican, lobbied heavily against initiatives to define abortion as a legally enforceable universal human right and indeed made clear, even before the conference, that it was no longer going to provide funds to any organization that underwrote abortions.[52] The US delegation to the conference was led by James L. Buckley, a former Republican US Senator from New York, and an outspoken opponent of abortion. The US representative

> threw a largish bombshell into the proceedings on the first day by arguing for "market-based solutions" to population and by threatening to withdraw US funding for international population programmes run by the UN and the IPPF (International Planned Parenthood Federation) unless it could be demonstrated that these bodies were not, directly or indirectly, supporting coercive abortion in China.[53]

In the end, the USA claimed victory on this point, as conferees agreed to a recommendation that abortion "in no way should be promoted" as a family planning method. This proposal, which was opposed by the Chinese and Soviet bloc, was, however, less than the total ban that the Vatican had sought.[54]

The US administration took the position that the best way to reduce population growth was to accelerate economic growth; family planning programs were deemed not to be up to the task. It almost seemed as if the USA had taken up the "third world's" mantra from Bucharest, namely that "development is the best contraceptive," suggesting that "too many governments [had] pursued population control measures without [the] sound economic policies that create the rise in living standards historically associated with decline[s] in fertility rates." The USA contended that this approach had not worked

> primarily because it has focused on a symptom and neglected the underlying ailments … [P]opulation control programs alone cannot substitute for the economic reforms that put a society on the road toward growth and, as an aftereffect, toward slower population increases as well.[55]

While the US delegates had abandoned their traditional belief that family planning was important, they went on and suggested that, based on past experience, there was a clear recipe to achieve rapid economic growth that could *assist* in controlling population growth.

That was reliance on markets and entrepreneurial initiative.[56] This particular suggestion did not go down well with the other delegates, except the Japanese, and was largely absent from the conference's final documents, which were adopted by consensus, with only the Vatican dissenting.[57] Not surprisingly the Soviets and Chinese were opposed to the US position, noting that they had both made significant advances in population control *without* the benefit of free market economies.[58]

What the conference did not resolve and perhaps could not resolve were two fundamental problems central to dealing with the population challenge. First, many of the economically less developed countries lacked the administrative capacity and financial wherewithal to implement the commitments that they made in Mexico City, especially if one considers all of the other competing demands on them, including those coming out of other UN global conferences. Second, all governments have a major challenge in dealing with implementing social policies, like fertility, that deal with the most private of individual decisions. At best, perhaps, a conference like that at Mexico City, could suggest processes for wrestling with the tensions between the individual and collective in decisions like these.[59]

Consistent with other conferences of the 1980s, the Population conference suffered from debates on other politically contentious topics not clearly germane to the conference's main focus. For example, over the objections of the USA, conferees passed a recommendation condemning the establishment of settlements in the occupied territories, although it did not mention Israel by name.[60] In a similar vein, the Soviets proposed a resolution stressing the importance of disarmament and an end to the arms race as a means for providing more resources for economic and social development.[61]

The politicization of yet one more UN conference led some at the meeting to raise

> new concern about the inability of world forums, even those engaged in politically neutral subjects, to keep from being snarled in highly charged international conflicts … In the nine days of meetings at the Mexican Foreign Relations Ministry, many delegates asserted, the longest debates and the greatest attention were inspired by matters that had the least direct relation to planning of the world's future population growth.[62]

In a somewhat more positive vein, unlike many of the other conferences which were largely derailed by politicization early on in the conference, in Mexico City the political controversies did not appear in full force until near the end of the meeting and thus had a less damaging effect on the conference.

World Conference to Review and Appraise the Achievements of the United Nations Decade for Women: Equality, Development and Peace

In July 1985, the end of the United Nations Decade for Women (1975–1985) was marked by the third UN-sponsored World Women's Conference. It met in Nairobi, from July 15–26. While 157 governments sent delegations, Margaret Kenyatta (daughter of Jomo Kenyatta, Kenya's first president) was elected President of the conference by acclamation and Leticia Ramos Shahani of the Philippines was appointed conference Secretary-General (she was the UN's Assistant Secretary-General for Social Development and Humanitarian Affairs, one of the highest-ranking women in the UN secretariat). Women were there in greater numbers than ever before at a UN global conference—83 percent of the delegates were women.[63] Still the context in which the conference was convened was inauspicious:

> Renewed cold war rhetoric had attended the increased competition between the United States and the Soviet Union. Women's concerns were generally out of favor in the 1980s with conservative governments in the United States, the United Kingdom, and the Federal Republic of Germany. The rich states of the industrial North and the economically poor states were deadlocked over solutions to growth and Third World debt; financial crises preoccupied multilateral institutions and their member governments.[64]

And, of course, there was the history of highly politicized women's conferences, with condemnations of Zionism, neocolonialism and apartheid in Mexico City and denunciations of Israel and the Palestinian issue in Copenhagen. Even more immediately, going into the Nairobi meetings, of the 372 paragraphs in the draft document, 58 had not been agreed upon. Moreover, US President Reagan sternly warned the US delegation to the conference that they should be sure that the conference sticks to its focus on women, not on "propaganda."[65]

In addition to reviewing the activities of the previous ten years in implementing the World Plan of Action and the Programme of Action for the Second Half of the Women's Decade, conferees adopted the Nairobi Forward-Looking Strategies for the Advancement of Women

(NFLS), a set of measures aimed at overcoming the obstacles of the decade's goals and furthering the objectives of equality, development and peace during the remainder of the twentieth century. Agreement on the document, by consensus, was one of the conferees' key goals, especially the US delegation, which had voted against the final document coming out of the Copenhagen conference. In fact, the USA had tried, at the outset of the conference, to require that all documents from the conference be approved unanimously. In effect, that would have given any one member a veto.[66]

The Strategies document began with an historical background and stated that the measures being proposed were for immediate action, with monitoring and evaluation every five years. Each country was given the option to set it own priorities, based on its own development policies and resource capacities. Likewise, the mode of implementation would vary with countries' political processes and administrative capacities. The NFLS then went on to describe the obstacles previously encountered in meeting the objectives of equality, development, and peace, and plausible means for overcoming those obstacles. In the area of the equality, these focused on constitutional and legal steps, equality in social participation and equality in political participation and decision-making. In the area of development, recommendations were made as to employment, health, education, food, water and agriculture, industry, trade and commercial services, science and technology, communications, housing, human settlements, community development and transport, energy, environment and social services. The recommendations on development were influenced by two reports in particular, *Development, Crises and Alternative Visions*, produced by Development Alternatives with Women for a New Era (DAWN), an NGO based in India that was formed in 1984 and which believed that everyone needed to rethink past practices for integrating women in the development process, and the *UN World Survey on the Role of Women in Development*, which was "more diplomatic and subtle." Both, however, agreed that economic development as it was now taking place was not serving the needs of women and did not correspond to women's values and aspirations. When the General Assembly finally (in 1985) endorsed the NFLS, it also decided that world surveys on the role of women in development should be prepared every five years as part of the conference follow-up.[67]

The section on strategies for peace singled out women and children under apartheid, Palestinian women and children, and women in areas affected by armed conflicts, foreign investment, and threats to peace. Subsequent sections of the NFLS dealt with the situation of women in areas affected by drought, urban poor women, elderly women, young women, abused women, destitute women deprived of traditional means of livelihood, women as sole supporters of families, physically and mentally disabled women, women in detention and subject to penal laws, refugee and displaced women and children, and minority and indigenous women. Although most of the document stressed national strategies, the concluding section focused on international and regional measures including in the areas of monitoring implementation, training, and policy analysis and information dissemination.

The bulk of the resolutions passed at the conference focused on the role of women in development. Others, however, focused on women's contribution to peace, women in areas of conflict (e.g. Afghanistan, the Iran–Iraq conflict, Chadian women, Palestinian women, women in Namibia, those living where apartheid was practiced,[68] Syrian women in the Golan Heights), health issues, and the social advancement of women. There was also a call for strengthening the ECOSOC Commission on the Status of Women, the United Nations Development Fund for Women, INSTRAW, the International Centre for Public Enterprises and Developing Countries, and for increasing the participation of women in the UN system.

The proposal for a draft declaration was not passed due to "lack of time." In addition to declaring that the objectives of the UN Decade for Women remained valid and calling on governments to seek to meet them with a view to eradicating all forms of discrimination against women, the unapproved draft declaration included a variety of highly contentious elements. For example, it would have declared that only the total eradication of apartheid could lead to a just and lasting solution to the problems in South Africa, and it would have strongly condemned Israel for oppression and repression of the Palestinians and called upon the international community to insure their inalienable rights. The United States had, early on, made it clear that it would walk out of the conference if the phrase "Zionism as racism" were retained in any of the documents. The phrase "all other forms of racism and racial discrimination" was used instead. While East–West splits were less pervasive than issues related to South Africa and the Middle East—dozens of delegates chanting "Zionist terrorists go home" walked out of the conference as the head of Israeli delegation, Sarah Doron, began to speak—they were not entirely absent, in spite of pleas by the US delegates to stick to the topic.[69] There was, for example, criticism of US policies in Nicaragua and of its proposed Strategic Defense Initiative (SDI).[70]

While the official, intergovernmental conference was deadlocked on familiar, politically contentious issues, the NGO Forum in Nairobi, which opened on July 10 (i.e. before the intergovernmental conference), "witnessed an enormous increase in representation from around the world" and "provided the occasion for the formation of three regional networks focused on women and rights."[71] "The networking and strategies initiated in Mexico City and further developed in Copenhagen matured at Forum '85."[72] Particularly path-breaking were the contacts made by women from all over Africa.[73] Indeed, it has been argued that the "end of the Decade of Women marked the beginning of an international women's movement the world [had] yet to recognize." More specifically women from across the globe, estimated at upwards of 15,000, meeting in Nairobi Forum '85 reached consensus on a number of points related to the conference theme and the NFLS (Box 4.1).

Not surprisingly, however, there were differences between the positions held by many of the American women attending Forum '85 and the official US delegation (e.g. regarding the size of the military budget, the impact of multinational corporations on women's employment, the equal rights amendment). And there was limited interaction between the two groups:

> Many Americans who attended Forum '85 [left] disappointed that they were not given the chance to exchange views with Maureen Reagan [the President's daughter and the head of the US delegation] … or Mr [Alan L.] Keyes [the key US negotiator at the conference], the only two members of the delegation who appeared to be willing to answer questions on substantive foreign-policy issues.[74]

At the conclusion of the conference, the head of the US delegation described the conference as "an orgy of hypocrisy" and suggested that the USA should rethink its degree of participation in UN global conferences: "There is something wrong with a system that is more interested in the system than in what it accomplishes."[75] Alan Keyes added that there was some feeling within the US delegation that the USA should be selective about attending, funding and participating at conferences, ensuring that they are not used "for the political purposes of a few countries."[76]

On December 13, 1985, the General Assembly adopted the conference report without a vote, but it took no action on any of the appended resolutions, much less the draft declaration. Many of the

Box 4.1 Points of agreement at the Nairobi conference

- Women's universal oppression and inequality are grounded in the patriarchal systems that ensure the continuation of female subservience and secondary status everywhere.
- Women do two-thirds of the world's work, yet two-thirds of the world's women live in poverty. Their work is usually unpaid, underpaid and invisible. Their fiscal dependency is perpetuated despite the fact that they do almost all of the world's domestic work, plus working outside the home and growing half of the world's food.
- Women are peace-makers, yet they have no voice in arbitration. War takes a heavy toll on them and their families as they struggle to hold them intact, in the face of physical and mental cruelty that leaves more women and children tortured, maimed, and killed than men in combat.
- There is universal sexual exploitation of girls and women, too often resulting in sexual domination and abuse throughout their lives.
- Women provide more health care (both physical and emotional) than all of the world's health services combined. They are the chief proponents of the prevention of illness and the promotion of health. Yet, they have fewer health care services, are likely to experience chronic exhaustion due to overwork, and to be deprived emotionally and physically by "their" men, their families, their communities, and their governments.
- Women are the chief educators of the family, yet outnumber men among the world's illiterates at a ratio of three to two. Even when educated, they generally are not allowed to lead.[1]

Note

1 Janice Wood Wetzel, *The World of Women: In Pursuit of Human Rights* (London: Macmillan, 1993), pp. 5–6.

delegates, however, have used the NFLS in their reports to their national legislatures and governments. This was true, for example, in New Zealand, Mexico, Yugoslavia and the USA.[77] In assessing the Nairobi Conference, one analyst put it this way:

> Some question the premises of success of the Nairobi Conference or the Decade for Women when women in many areas were worse off at the end of the 1980s than at the beginning. We suggest that the new standards of women's equality, recognition of social and cultural stereotypes about women as sources of discrimination, the acknowledgement of women's roles in peace and development, women's global movements for social reform, and adjustments in North–South issues in the global women's movement need to be understood as the very dynamic long-term consequences of the Nairobi Women's Conference, 1985.[78]

Interestingly, in November of 1985, Maureen Reagan went to the UN and urged that it take a leadership role by increasing the roles of women at the UN itself. This was in the context of the UN discussions of how to implement the NFLS. "While women at the United Nations were pleased to hear Miss Reagan's remarks about the world body, they were disappointed that she said nothing about how the United States would put the recommendations of the Nairobi document into effect." Actually she repeated her position that as a decentralized government the USA could not enforce the conference's recommendations: "Ideas may be picked up by the city of Denver or the state of Illinois," she added.[79] Such statements merely underscored the importance of the networking that had "matured" in Nairobi.

As called for by the General Assembly, in 1990, the UN Commission on the Status for Women issued an evaluation of the progress made toward implementing the NFLS. The findings were mixed: "A greater proportion of women are literate, and more of them are visible at high political levels. At the same time, many women are poorer than ever before, and women's human rights are being violated on an unprecedented scale." In sum, there was progress in the education and health areas, but the overall commitments of Nairobi had not been fulfilled. Thus, ECOSOC recommended the UN convene in 1995 a Fourth Conference on Women and that the Commission on the Status of Women serve as its preparatory body. The General Assembly accepted this recommendation in December 1990. It was charged with examining the major obstacles to women's progress in twelve interconnected areas: poverty, decision making, education, human rights, health, media, violence, environment, armed conflict, girl-child, economic equality, and national machinery for the advancement of women.[80]

While the Nairobi conference is probably rightfully best known for its impact on contributing to the "maturation" of global feminist networks, it is also noteworthy that the conference's documents were able to be used by members of those networks in countries throughout the world as they sought to accelerate the pace of women's achievement of equality. These positive outcomes, of course, occurred in spite of the conference's politicization, the ambivalence, at best, of the US conference delegation, and the focus of the media.

The 1980s were something of an *intermezzo* in terms of the UN global conferences, an interlude between the rush of the mid-1970s and that of the 1990s. In large part, this was a consequence of the end of one world order—the Cold War confrontation between the USA and the Soviet Union—and the beginning of new one, with an emerging hegemonic United States. Or as noted at the outset of the chapter, a transition from one crisis of multilateralism—a turn from the UN by the USA—to another crisis, the challenges of multilateral institutions to remain relevant and legitimate in a hegemonic world. In this sense, it seems clear that UN global conferences reflect fairly the world orders of which they are part and which they try to influence, perhaps more so than the UN itself. Thus, as the Cold War and bipolarity ended, not simply did the Cold War politicization lose its place at the table of UN global conferences, but the role of the USA loomed ever larger. This, of course, is made evident by contrasting the women's conferences discussed in this chapter. But while the importance of that geo-strategic shift cannot be overemphasized, it should not overshadow several other notable trends that were evidenced by the conferences of the 1980s, including the maturation of global transnational social networks; the recognition of the increasing interconnectedness between issues on the global agenda; the relationships between world conferences, norm creation and treaty law; the rising global attractiveness to neo-liberal economic solutions; and the economic and political consequences for economically less developed countries of fissures in their coalition.

5 United Nations global conferences in the post-Cold War era (1990–1999)

- **(Second) United Nations Conference on the Least Developed Countries**
- **World Summit for Children**
- **United Nations Conference on Human Environment and Development (UNCED)**
- **World Conference on Human Rights**
- **International Conference on Population and Development (ICPD)**
- **World Summit for Social Development (WSSD)**
- **Fourth World Conference on Women**
- **United Nations Conference on Human Settlements (Habitat II)**

Given the negative reaction, especially by the USA, to the politicization of the UN conferences in the 1970s and early 1980s, it is hardly surprising that they virtually ceased being convened in the late 1980s. In fact, the US Congress attached a key amendment related to the UN conferences to the 1986–1987 fiscal year budget (P.L. 99–93, dated 1985). The so-called Kassebaum Amendment is best known for the fact that it set a limit to US assessments of 20 percent of the regular UN budget unless the UN reformed itself in such a way as to give influence (weighted voting) to countries in accordance with their budgetary contributions. But it also contained a provision that set a limit of 25 percent of contributions to UN global conferences "whose sole or partial purpose is to implement the provisions" of the UN General Assembly resolution equating Zionism with racism (i.e. the element of politicization of UN global conferences that most irked the USA and a position consistent with the views President Reagan had articulated just prior to the Nairobi conference).[1] These actions, of course, reflected the evolving world order of a single dominant power. They also reflected what came to be called American unilateralism or selective or *à la carte* multilateralism and the related US approach to its treaty obligations. In this instance, the decision by the US

Congress to treat the UN's rules on funding obligation as negotiable rather than a law binding the world's strongest power is noteworthy, as was the USA's refusal to ratify the 1989 Convention on the Rights of the Child, the most ratified international human rights instrument in history.

Of course, there were other obvious and important structural explanations for the decline in UN conferences in the mid-late 1980s. The late 1980s was a period in world history when attention was focused on events in the Soviet Union and subsequently in Central Europe. The Soviet Union imploded as a superpower and with it the global attractiveness of communism or, more accurately state socialism, as an ideological competitor to capitalism evaporated. This, of course, facilitated the global spread of classical liberalism (i.e. both liberal economics and democracy) and many, especially in the USA, saw many of the conference recommendations as calling for interference with the global "free market" as well as providing assistance to non-democratic governments. The collapse of the Soviet Union and its former empire, the removal of Soviet troops from Eastern and Central Europe, and the at least temporary removal of the old guard from positions of leadership contributed to the unleashing of long-standing ethnic conflicts and the migration of peoples across national boundaries, the rise of civil unrest, civil wars and even genocide in Central and Eastern Europe. And as the 1980s faded into the 1990s, civil unrest and civil wars proliferated, especially in Africa. All these events, of course, diverted attention from global conferences, whose traditional focus was on non-military security issues.

For a short period, especially 1987–1990, unprecedented great power consensus existed in the UN, but this was largely limited to the security arena, even though the Soviet leader Mikhail Gorbachev had called for a new UN Special Fund for Humanitarian Cooperation and there were those who expressed the hope that the anticipated post-Cold War "peace dividend" would be expended in support of the needs of the economically less developed countries. Instead, much of the reform was focused on the Security Council, including a renaissance of UN peacekeeping. Even after that short-lived consensus broke down, peacekeeping missions and an unprecedented number of so-called Chapter VII activities (i.e. the UN use of economic sanctions and military troops to respond to threats to international peace and security) were authorized. While this is not the place to discuss these activities in detail,[2] the evolving hegemonic world order and the increased attention paid to military security issues, with the concomitant Security Council's overshadowing of activities by the General Assembly, set the context for the global conferences of the last decade of the twentieth century.

But while the conferences may have been on hold for several years, the problems that had given rise to them in the first place were not. Indeed, that may explain why many of the conferences of the 1990s returned to topics of earlier conferences, including the first one. Close on its heels, however, was something very novel: the World Summit for Children, an idea "first publicly floated—very carefully—in December 1988 in the *State of the World's Children* report as a suggestion of which UNICEF strongly approved, not as a definite proposition."[3]

(Second) United Nations Conference on the Least Developed Countries

The decision to convene the second United Nations Conference on the Least Developed Countries was reached by the General Assembly on December 11, 1987 (Resolution 42/177). The context and justification were clearly stated by UN Secretary-General Javier Pérez de Cuéllar in his opening statement at the conference. He spoke of the "dismal record of the 1980s, which had produced increased indebtedness, a decline in public and private finance, a drop in the price of raw materials, increased inflationary pressures and natural calamities." He contended that these problems were not simply attributable to the less developed countries' structural weakness, but were also due to the fact that the responsibilities undertaken at the 1981 conference had not been fully implemented.[4] Thus, not surprisingly, even prior to the conference, the foreign ministers of Bangladesh, Somalia and Togo, representing the least developed countries, had met with the heads of governments of seven major rich countries, urging them to persuade the rest of the industrialized countries to grant them further concessions at the upcoming global conference.[5]

The conference's mandate was to review progress made by governments in the 1980s; to review progress on the international level, especially in terms of official development assistance; and to develop new policies and measures to accelerate development in the 1990s for the least developed countries. UNCTAD was given the chief responsibility in preparing for the conference and the UNCTAD Secretary-General, Kenneth Dadzie, was named the conference Secretary-General. The French offer to host the conference was accepted.

The major documents coming out of the conference, which met from September 3–14, 1990, were the Paris Declaration and the Programme of Action of the Second United Nations Conference on the Least Developed Countries.

The Paris Declaration (A/CONF.147/18) stated that successful revitalization of the effort of the least developed countries to develop depended on national policies, a favorable international economic climate, and a strengthened partnership based on mutual commitments. The Declaration identified five priority areas: (1) to conduct macroeconomic policy that takes into account market signals and debt issues and aims at accelerating long-term growth and development, showing concern for the most vulnerable groups in society; (2) to develop human resources (with an emphasis on education and training, health and sanitation, and overpopulation); (3) to reverse the trend toward environmental degradation; (4) to promote an integrated rural development policy; and (5) to develop a diversified productive sector based on private initiative, efficient public enterprise, regional cooperation, increased access to the international market and international action in the field of commodities.

Many of these priorities underscore the expanding global pervasiveness of neo-liberal economic convictions, something certainly pleasing to the ears of policy-makers in Washington. Success in achieving the priorities identified by conferees also depended upon a significant increase in official development assistance, something presumably less pleasing to the ears of policy-makers in the then deficit-riddled United States.

The Program of Action identified two main areas: mobilizing and developing human capacities in the least developed countries, and development, particularly expansion and modernization, of the economic base. It also identified a set of basic "principles," including:

1   "Success depends on a shared responsibility and a strengthened partnership for the growth and development of LDCs."
2   "The least developed countries have the primary responsibility for the formulation and effective implementation of appropriate policies and priorities for their growth and development."
3   "The strengthened partnership for development necessitates external support from LDCs' development partners."
4   "Commitments undertaken should be measurable and sufficiently transparent to enable monitoring and assessment of the Programme of Action for the 1990s."[6]

UNCTAD was given the ongoing responsibility to monitor the Program's implementation. But the Program also suggested that the General Assembly might consider a possible additional conference at the end of the 1990s. The lesson had been learned: "The recognition of effective follow-up and monitoring as key to the successful implementation of the Programme of Action was one of its significant features." Conferees also recognized that implementation strategies had to be flexible enough to accommodate changes in the international economic environment.[7]

Implementation, however, did not get off to a good start. In spite of pleas for a specific target for funds to the least developed countries— their preferred figure was twenty-one hundredths of a country's GDP, whereas the USA was then at four one hundredths and Japan seven— none was agreed to, principally because of US opposition. Instead what was agreed to was a menu of options, including one where a country was asked to pledge to increase its aid, but without specifying any amount. That is the option that was preferred by the world's two largest aid donors, the USA and Japan.[8] Thus, even though the conference's main documents had adopted economic policies that accorded with the neo-liberal economic preferences of the major industrialized countries of the world, most notably the United States, concrete and significant financial commitments from them were not forthcoming. This was not simply an inauspicious outcome for the Least Developed Countries conference but an omen of things to come in the decade of the 1990s.

World Summit for Children

Given the context, it is not surprising that the origins of the World Summit for Children differed from the other conferences and summits discussed in this book. Its format—a global summit—and the procedures leading up to its convening were more unconventional than its goal: to obtain agreement on health, education and development goals for children.

Described as a "typical Grant pipe-dream" (i.e. an innovative but against-the-odds idea of James P. Grant, the Executive Director of UNICEF, see Box 5.1), the idea was first floated very cautiously as a UNICEF suggestion in its widely publicized annual *State of the World's Children* report.

> Grant hoped the idea would be picked by those who could run with it, but the question was not left to chance. Informal overtures had already been made to Swedish Prime Minister Ingvar Carlsson and to President Robert Mugabe in Zimbabwe. Personal statements of approval for the Summit idea from Carlsson and Mugabe were issued on the day the report was launched.[9]

Beginning early in 1989, Grant sought support for his idea with leaders, initially in West Africa. While "most leaders in developing

Box 5.1 James P. Grant

Grant, an American citizen who was born in China on May 12, 1912, began serving in 1946 as a representative of the United Nations Relief and Rehabilitation Agency (UNRRA) relief program in the communist-held areas in China. In the 1950s and 1960s he worked for the US International Cooperation Administration, and the US Agency for International Development (USAID). In 1969, he became President of the Overseas Private Development Council (ODC), a private think-tank based in Washington, DC. UN Secretary-General Kurt Waldheim, after years of hesitation, finally appointed Grant, on the recommendation of the UNICEF Board, as Executive Director of UNICEF in 1979. He was appointed in preference to the Swedish candidate, whose candidacy was advocated by the Nordic countries, who were major UNICEF contributors. Grant resigned from his post on January 23, 1995, five days before he died.[1]

Note

1   Yves Beigbeder, *New Challenges for UNICEF: Children, Women and Human Rights* (New York: Palgrave, 2001), pp. 29–30.

countries welcomed the Summit idea," it quickly became clear that there would be resistance from richer countries. Not surprisingly, they feared a "cheque-book conference" (i.e. "an occasion leading to extra demands to their aid budgets"). Others "had become very resistant to Unicef's involvement in public relations extravaganzas of which they regarded this as another example."[10] Still others were not prepared for the idea of a summit, i.e. a conference to which all of the world's leaders would be invited. Prior to this, summits were much more intimate gatherings. But UNICEF took the position that "only something as dramatic and unprecedented as a summit meeting of world leaders to discuss the subject of children could significantly upgrade the priority which the world will give to children."[11]

Given the focus on the resistance, gaining the support of Joe Clarke, the Canadian Foreign Minister, was a major turning point in Grant's and UNICEF's quest to convene such a meeting. Clarke offered "both political and financial support for the Summit so long as the event was substantive, inexpensive and took place in New York." With Canada on board, an "initiators group," comprised of Mali, Egypt, Pakistan, Mexico, Sweden and Canada, began meeting. In November 1989, UN Secretary-General Javier Pérez de Cuéllar gave permission for the summit to be held at the UN headquarters. Even with the Secretary-General's support, however, the summit almost failed to come about, not least of all because Grant had left the UNICEF Executive Board out of the planning process. As a consequence, it was not until early 1990 that planning began in earnest. The planning committee was composed of representatives of the WHO, UNESCO, UNFPA, the World Bank, the ILO, and the UN itself as well as twenty-five UN members.

By spring of 1990, a draft Declaration and Plan of Action (based on the "Strategies for Children in the 1990s" agreed to by the Executive Board in April 1989) was in circulation. It listed quantifiable goals the world should aim to reach by the end of the twentieth century, including significant reductions in infant and child mortality (reduction by one-third or to a level of 70 per 1,000 live births, whichever is greater); malnutrition (reduction of severe and moderate malnutrition among children under 5 by one-half of 1990 levels) and illiteracy, improvements in diarrheal disease control and immunization levels, and reductions in acute infections; universal access to safe drinking water and improved access to family planning services; and protection for children in difficult circumstances, particularly in situations of armed conflicts.

The Summit met, September 29–30, 1990. Up to that point, it was the largest gathering of world leaders—seventy-one attended—ever to have been convened. Brian Mulroney, the Canadian Prime Minister, and Mussa Traoré, the President of Mali, served as joint chairmen. While the high point of the summit was the joint signing of the World Declaration on the Survival, Protection and Development of Children and the Plan of Action for implementing the Declaration over the next decade, it is ironically often thought of in connection with the Convention on the Rights of the Child. That is ironic although, as readers of this volume will know, not unique, because the convention had been adopted by the UN General Assembly a year earlier and all that the summit conferees did was urge that those governments that had not yet ratified it do so. But it was also ironic because initially Grant was skeptical about such a convention, not least of all because he (rightfully as it turned out) did not believe that the US government would be anxious to grant legal rights to children, independent of those of their parents and other adults and because UNICEF was not assigned to be the convention monitor. It is also ironic because a convention initiated chiefly by NGOs has come to be seen as UNICEF's unofficial constitution.[12] The point, however, is not that people are totally confused when they connect the convention with the summit, for its convening clearly affected the pace and probably the number of convention ratifications. Indeed, it came into force in September 1990, again underscoring one of the by-products of UN world conferences. And by 2005, 192 countries had ratified it, making it the most ratified of UN conventions. The United States and Somalia are non-ratifiers, although both have signed it. The USA signed in 1995, but the Senate has not yet given its advice and consent, a necessary prerequisite to Presidential ratification.

The funding strategy for achieving the summit's goals had precedents in early conferences, namely another attempt to use the so-called 20/20 initiative whereby the economically less developed countries would devote at least 20 percent of their budgets to basic needs and the richer countries would earmark 20 percent of their development assistance for the same purpose. The summit launched the so-called Children's Vaccine Initiative, involving UNICEF, UNDP, the Rockefeller Foundation, the World Bank and WHO.

The summit was also noteworthy in terms of its attention to follow-up actions and monitoring. The Plan of Action set out a range of measures for follow-up actions and monitoring at both the national and international levels. These included the formulation of national and subnational plans of action; the re-examination of existing and national and international programs, policies and budgets to see if they could give higher priority to children's issues; and the encouragement of communities, social and religious institutions, businesses and the mass media to support the Plan's goals. It also called for the regular and timely collection *and publication* of data relating to the well-being of children and progress toward achieving the summit's goals. Accordingly, the UN Secretary-General submitted reports to the 45th, 51st and 53rd sessions of the General Assembly on progress in implementing the Declaration and Plan of Action, while UNICEF submitted annual reports on progress to its Executive Board. Key issues were also signaled in UNICEF's major publications, *The State of the World's Children* and *The Progress of Nations*. Some 155 countries submitted national programs of action and over 100 countries conducted monitoring surveys. Moreover, in 1996 there was a mid-decade review and in 2000 there was a wide-ranging end-decade review that culminated in national progress reports from more than 130 countries and an end-decade review by the UN Secretary-General, *We the*

Children: Meeting the Promises of the World Summit for Children, prepared for a Special Session of the General Assembly on Children, convened in June 2001. While this is not the place to repeat all the data in that report, the "bottom line" was that "real progress" had been achieved. For example, sixty-three countries had achieved the summit goal of reducing by one-third the death rate of children under 5, while over 100 countries had cut such deaths by one-fifth.

> Consequently, there are now 3 million fewer under-five deaths each year than at the beginning of the 1990s; one third of these young lives are saved just by achieving the Summit goal of reducing child deaths from diarrhoeal disease by 50 per cent.[13]

Much of the funding for achieving these ends came from foundation sources rather than governments, as had been hoped for. And while it's impossible to credit all of the achievements to the summit, it is hard to totally dismiss the impacts of getting the world's leaders to focus on children as the summit (and the Special Session) did.

United Nations Conference on Human Environment and Development (UNCED)

Peter Haas voiced a widely shared opinion about the United Nations Conference on Human Environment and Development (UNCED), also known as the Earth Summit, when he wrote of it as being the "high water mark" in terms of UN environmental conference outputs. It is because of that opinion that the discussion of this conference merits a somewhat more sustained discussion than many of the others.

UNCED conferees in Rio adopted the Framework Convention on Climate Change; the Convention on Biological Diversity (CBD); the Statement of Principles to Guide the Management, Conservation and Sustainable Development of All Types of Forests; the Rio Declaration on Environment and Development, with 287 principles of guiding action; and Agenda 21, "a sweeping action plan to promote sustainability, with 2,509 specific recommendations applying to states, international institutions, and members of civil society." In addition, conferees agreed to set up a new ECOSOC Commission, the Commission on Sustainable Development (CSD), to increase the likelihood of effective implementation of Agenda 21.[14] While Haas's statement is technically correct, it seems to suggest that the Framework Convention on Climate Change and the CBD were negotiated at Rio; actually they were signed there, but negotiated before then, "although they will always be associated with the Earth Summit." On the other hand, the date of the "Earth Summit offered a useful deadline by which the negotiations could be completed—and the political impetus provided by UNCED helped both treaties enter into force with unusual rapidity."[15]

This, of course, is a recurrent theme noted throughout this volume, that is, the mere convening of a conference to address a set of problems sets in motion a variety of actions that can address the problem even before the conference's opening gavel is banged. This can take the form of data gathering, the reorganization of national bureaucracies, the gearing-up of the NGOs, the passing of national legislation or work by intergovernmental organizations so as to be able to brag or not be embarrassed at the conference.

Strictly speaking, then, the main outputs of UNCED were the statement of forest principles, Agenda 21 and the Rio Declaration. All of these were designed to build on the Stockholm conference: "the Rio Declaration recast the Stockholm Declaration in the new language of sustainable development, while Agenda 21 was intended to be the UN's blueprint for implementing sustainable development." And the CSD was "created to maintain peer pressure on states to fulfill their Rio commitments."[16] Rio also built on Stockholm in the sense that UNCED dealt with so-called second-generation environmental problems—acid rain, depletion of the stratospheric ozone layer, climate change, deforestation and desertification, preservation of biodiversity, international traffic in toxic and dangerous products and waste, and the destruction of the environment in times of armed conflict; Stockholm had focused on "first-generation" environmental problems, those relating to water, air and land degradation caused mostly by industrial activities and those activities exacerbated by poverty and underdevelopment.[17]

Thus, the origins of UNCED can be traced back to Stockholm. But more specifically and directly the origins are to be found in the General Assembly's (1982) ten-year review of the Stockholm conference. Then it was noted that any progress that had been made in achieving Stockholm's goals had been modest. And, not surprisingly, most of the progress that had been made was in areas of interest to wealthy industrialized countries (e.g. marine and river pollution and air pollution). Moreover, UNEP's activities in promoting implementation of the Stockholm Action Plan and other agreements had been based on a tri-level program strategy, all of which had had very modest impacts on the environment. First, there was its annual *State of the Environment* report. Second, there were efforts at stimulating activities in priority areas; this usually took the form of consciousness-raising conferences and facilitating the creation of multilateral environmental agreements. Finally, there was support for technical and scientific monitoring and research activities. While the global environment had become measurably worse in the decades since Stockholm despite all the efforts deployed,[18] that, in and of itself, does not prove that UNEP's actions were meaningless, simply that it was not up to the task of the environmental challenges of globalization and its attendant economic growth.

In order to try and meet these challenges and indeed to regain lost momentum, the General Assembly had agreed in 1983 (Resolution 38/161) to establish a special independent commission, the World Commission on Environment and Development (WCED), under the leadership of then Norwegian Prime Minister (subsequently WHO Director-General) Gro Harlem Brundtland. By the time the results of the WCED, better known as the Brundtland Commission, were published in 1987, the political climate for reinvigorating the environmental movement had improved: economic prospects of the industrialized world were more positive and threats to the global ecosystem were being more widely publicized. Most notably, the Commission developed, or more correctly publicized, the conceptual relationship between the environment and development. As previously noted, the Founex meetings in 1971 had concluded that there was no inherent contradiction between attention to environmental issues and a commitment to economic development. It was the Brundtland Commission, however, under the rubric of "sustainable development" (i.e. growth that satisfies the needs of today without jeopardizing the needs of the future) that was able to make both the North and South commit to further conversations about environmental improvement and economic development. What the allusion to the Founex meeting and the Brundtland Commission proves is that some of the many UN commissions of eminent people drawn together to deal with perplexing issues have had significant impacts on some UN global conferences.[19]

The idea of a new global conference on the subject was first raised in the General Assembly in 1986 and tentatively agreed to in 1987 (Resolution 43/196). On December 22, 1989, the General Assembly (in Resolution 44/228) formally agreed to convene UNCED in 1992. The aim was to recommend strategies to halt and hopefully reverse environmental degradation in the context of increased efforts to promote sustainable and environmentally sound development throughout the globe.[20] Brazil, whose environmental attitudes and policies had undergone major changes since Stockholm, offered to be the June 3–14,

Box 5.2 Maurice Strong

Maurice Strong has often been referred to as the international civil servant who contributed more to bringing global attention to environmental problems than any other. A Canadian, born in 1929 in Manitoba, Strong made his money in the Alberta oil boom. However, his lifelong ambition and métier were public service. In addition to serving as the Secretary-General of the Stockholm and Rio conferences, Strong served as Director-General of the Canadian External Aid Office, the first Executive Director of UNEP and Under Secretary-General and Senior Advisor to UN Secretary-General Kofi Annan, where he has been assisting with UN reform. But nothing in Strong's long and impressive public service record compares in his or anyone's estimation to his work in the environmental field. Indeed, in his best-selling autobiography, he refers to the Rio conference as "the summit to save the world."[1] While optimistic, Strong is hardly naïve. Five years after Rio he boldly asserted that: "The world community has still not made the fundamental transition to a development pathway that will provide the human community with a sustainable and secure future. Environmental deterioration continues, and the forces which drive it persist."[2]

Notes

1   Maurice Strong, *Where on Earth Are We Going?* (Toronto: Vintage Canada, 2001), p. 215.
2   Ibid., p. 284.

1992, conference host. On the other hand, the USA, which had played a leading role twenty years earlier, played a much more restricted role in 1992. Still, this post-Cold War conference took place in a spirit of high expectations. These expectations were multiplied when Maurice Strong (see Box 5.2) agreed to again serve as conference Secretary-General. (Brazilian President Fernando Collor was elected conference President.) Strong reportedly accepted the challenge of Rio because he thought that in the post-Cold War era he could get action on many of the topics that could not be resolved at Stockholm.[21]

The 1992 conference was significantly bigger than the one in Stockholm:

> Physically, Rio eclipsed Stockholm in terms of the number of participants involved. [More than 1,100 NGOs were accredited to UNCED as contrasted to 134; it staged a Global Forum in tandem with the intergovernmental one and attracted 30,000 participants, including 3,738 NGOs from 153 countries.] It also generated much more media attention and attracted many world leaders [a total of 176 national delegations and two-thirds of the world's heads of state attended, whereas only two went to Stockholm].[22]

Among the most innovative activities undertaken by the NGOs was a treaty-writing exercise. It began, in part, because of NGOs' frustration at the slow progress made at the initial PrepComs, but it was also seen as a way to exercise direct citizen diplomacy. The connections between the Forum and UNCED, however, were much less direct than rhetoric at the time suggested and indeed Forum participants didn't get a chance to present their treaties at the Earth Summit.[23]

As was traditional, a series of PrepComs were held prior to the scheduled opening of UNCED. As the first of these, in New York, Strong put forward an ambitious agenda for UNCED, calling for an "Earth Charter" that would spell out clear, internationally acceptable principles on the environment, and a detailed Plan of Action. PrepCom members also urged negotiators of the climate change and biodiversity conventions to complete their work so that both conventions could be opened for signature at the conference. Later PrepCom meetings— which were held in Nairobi, Geneva, and again in New York, "an example of the kind of compromises that had to be struck in order to achieve consensus"[24]—were much more divisive. European and North American governments, in particular, sought binding global commitments to protect the environment from dangerous development policies (such as destruction of the rain forest, indiscriminate use of fossil fuel technologies or pollution of water by toxic effluents). On the other hand, many governments in the South continued to see the Northern goals as threats to their national sovereignty and as efforts to limit their pursuit of the development paths previously followed by the industrialized North. Thus, they sought commitments from the richer governments to give additional aid for any new costs arising from externally imposed environmental requirements. And they were relatively successful at the PrepComs (and in the final documents) in limiting governments' obligations to statements of aspiration (e.g. Agenda 21 does not even require governments to report on their strategies or their implementation of the Agenda).

The Rio Declaration on Environment and Development contains twenty-six broad principles that outline the general obligations and rights of states regarding the environment and development processes. It reflected the many compromises that emerged at the conference. In the opening Principle, the Declaration proclaims that "human beings are at the center of concerns for sustainable development." This discouraged some environmental activists because it seemed to demote the preservation of "nature" and the "environment" as primary interests of the world community. It also seemed to provide a strong rationale for the defense of development policies in the economically less developed countries, even if those policies hurt the environment. This concern was reinforced in Principle 2, which recognized the sovereign right of states to exploit their natural resources. Moreover, despite US resistance, Principle 3 stated, for the first time in an international document, that there was a right to development.[25] In addition, Principle 15 recognized the "Polluter Pays Principle," which required states to pay not only for pollution prevention on their own territory but also for damage costs from pollution. This principle, while pleasing to environmentalists, was unlikely to go down well with politicians in Washington. The Declaration also reaffirmed the Stockholm (and Trail Smelter) principle that governments are responsible for environmental injuries beyond their boundaries, but it went beyond earlier norms by calling upon governments to conduct environmental impact assessments before undertaking possibly hazardous development activities. Governments were also expected to notify other governments when environmental emergencies arose. The details for implementing the Declaration's broad outlines were left to Agenda 21 and its more than 1,000 specific recommendations.

Conferees also agreed to a "Non-legally Binding Authoritative Statement of Principles for a Global Consensus on the Management, Conservation and Sustainable Development of All Types of Forests." This document, whose title reveals all, fell well short of the World Convention on Forests that developed states (the G-7 and especially the USA) and some NGOs had sought. Indeed, some NGOs came to refer to it as a "Chain-Saw-Charter." The opposition to the kind of convention sought by developed states was led by Brazil and Indonesia, key states in any such binding treaty, but also "fast-developing countries" like Malaysia, which questioned the need for such a treaty. The Indian magazine *Down to Earth* noted that in Rio the economically less developed countries had gained considerable time in their struggle against a binding forest convention. The Malaysian ambassador Ting Wen Lian was quoted as saying: "We have not even given them a window. We have just given them a chink."[26] The non-binding statement declared that states had the sovereign right to utilize, manage and develop their forests, including the right to convert them to other uses, in accordance with their own development plans and level of socio-economic development. Governments were "urged," however, to manage their forest resources and lands so as to meet the social, economic, cultural, ecological, and spiritual needs of current and future generations. As of 2005 there is no binding convention; in its stead ECOSOC has established the United Nations Forum on Forests (UNFF), which meets annually for two weeks at a time.[27] Indeed, while there was considerable support for such a Convention immediately after Rio, it has since dropped off. By 1996, the USA, one of the strongest supporters earlier, had changed its position "completely, as industry opposition grew because of the inclusion of boreal and temperate forests in the agenda of the various panels and forums addressing deforestation."[28] Some environmental organizations, too, were opposed to a global forest agreement and wished, instead, to see forest conservation addressed through the Convention on Biological Diversity. The final straw was when discussions surrounding the Kyoto Protocol began to focus on forests for their potential for sequestering carbon and thus allowing countries to avoid the need to reduce greenhouse gas emissions in other sectors, such as transportation and industry.[29]

Agenda 21 set international and national objectives and provided programmatic suggestions on how to fulfill those objectives. It identi-fied multiple areas for action, including world trade, poverty eradication, population, cities, atmospheric pollution, deforestation, drought, desertification (largely sought by African governments, who complained bitterly about the low profile given to desertification on UNCED's agenda),[30] marine resources and management, waste management, agriculture, biodiversity, and the transfer of technology. It also included a chapter, "Global Action for Women towards Sustainable and Equitable Development," that acknowledged the importance of the active involvement of women in economic and political decision-making, especially in the environment and develop-ment fields.[31] It looked to NGOs and other members of civil society as well as governments and intergovernmental organizations to imple-ment its recommendations. Moreover, to ensure continuing attention to the issues raised at UNCED, Agenda 21 urged the General

Assembly to create a new ECOSOC functional commission, which became the CSD. The economically less developed countries hoped that the CSD would provide it a forum for pressing the rich for additional financial aid. They also saw it, if strong enough, as a way to counterbalance the power of the multilateral financial institutions to impose environmental and other conditions for getting financial aid. The North saw it as a means through with they could stipulate that any financial aid contribution toward implementing decisions from the conference would be given on the condition that the protection and preservation of the environment be given priority. It should also be noted that some governments—especially those in the North—argued that it was not rational to set up a new institution, while the UN was going through a reform process. The North and South also disagreed on a reporting line, with most countries from the South preferring that it report to the General Assembly. The North, and a few countries from the South, opted for ECOSOC. Although the North wanted the Commission to be kept small, it was agreed that it would have fifty-three members. The number was chosen, according to rumor at least, to keep it below the size of ECOSOC (which had fifty-four members), as was the practice for functional commissions, but as large as possible. UNCED also recommended that specialized agencies, NGOs and intergovernmental organizations be allowed to participate in the Commission. In December 1992 the General Assembly formally established the CSD (Resolution 47/191), charging it with reviewing progress on Agenda 21 and making recommendations for implementing it. But the European Union's (EU) request that it be allowed to participate fully in the CSD, as it had at UNCED, was not resolved until 1995. It is not allowed to vote.[32] The CSD is the only functioning ECOSOC Commission that has a government minister as its chair; that may be the reason why it has also given civil society the "greatest involvement in the work of any UN Commission." In fact, none of the CSD's sessions are now closed; even small working groups are open to civil society and in many of them representatives of civil society can speak. However, this is an *ad hoc* arrangement, contrary to formal ECOSOC rules, and is totally at the discretion of the chair of the CSD. But what it has meant is that the CSD has proven to be the most interesting UN "experiment with individual and joint advocacy, and with multi-stakeholder engagement."[33]

While the CSD was the institutional innovation coming out of UNCED, post-UNCED there was also a "greening" of other international institutions. UNEP came "to focus more precisely on the goals of sustainable development" and the UNDP began "to integrate the environmental component into its operational activities." And although the UNDP had proposed the concept of sustainable development prior to UNCED, it became more of a systematic concern after the Earth Summit.[34]

To implement all of Agenda 21's recommendations, the conference secretariat estimated that $125 billion in foreign assistance would be needed, nearly ten times the 1992 level of global aid. The economically less developed countries were less successful when it came to getting money than they were in getting documents to their liking and the CSD to take the form they wished. With the USA in the lead, the major powers refused to go much beyond what they had previously committed in terms of development aid.[35] The major constraint was lack of additional financial resources. This not simply raised questions about the seriousness of developed countries regarding UNCED's agenda, but also laid bare the lack of priorities in the huge Agenda 21 document.

In fact, a follow-up study suggests that Agenda 21 has not been viewed by governments as a document for structuring domestic policy agendas or framing issues for national debate (i.e. it is not viewed as a plan to implement or even a general set of principles for problematizing and working towards sustainable development), but the issues, ideas and policy recommendations in it have permeated some national debates.[36]

The only new source of multilateral aid agreed to at Rio was to be in the form of the Global Environmental Facility (GEF), originally established "by World Bank staff and a few officials in Western European government ministries as a 'green window' of the Bank, intended to finance projects supportive of the United Nations Convention on Biological Diversity [and on] Climate Change."[37] It was believed that some sort of fund was needed to persuade Southern governments to agree to the conservation and constraints on development that these documents implied. And the North chose the World Bank because they did not "want to become liable for all the potential costs arising from the treaties, nor to put more money into the United Nations system—with its relative accountability to Southern governments and 'inefficient' political debates and processes." In the lead-up to Rio, the GEF attracted opposition from Southern governments and NGOs' mistrust as

> [an] opaque entity, a *fait accompli*, based in a World Bank accountable to "donor" rather than "client" governments, let alone to environmental science or popular movements. In light of the World Bank's past investments and unfavorable experiences with the GEF so far, some said giving the Bank responsibility for global conservation was like putting a fox to guard chickens. They argued

instead for reparations from the damage done to Southern and the global environment by Northern expansionism, as well as help for the billions of people whose environmental priorities are more immediate, for example, clean water to drink and air to breathe.[38]

In response to the critics, the donor governments promised to review and restructure the GEF to operate more openly, accountably and participatorily. It was made "nominally" independent of the World Bank and charged with supporting

[the] national development priorities of recipient governments, while making global "partnerships"—not least with green NGOs and the private sector. A sufficient number of Southern governments and international environmental interests therefore accepted the promise of funds, innovation and access, for the GEF to be refinanced in 1994 and designated "interim financial mechanism" to implement the Conventions on Climate and Biodiversity.[39]

Criticism continued and still continues, claiming that it didn't provide as much funding as had been promised and suggesting that it was really a tool of Northern firms and consultants exploiting Southern resources and "bribing" Southern governments to give up some of their sovereignty.[40]

The consequence of all of this was to place tremendous burdens on the new institutions, especially the CSD. Sharing the burden, however, was the benchmarking system called for in the Agenda and which the UN Statistical Office had already begun to work on prior to Rio. Of course, Agenda 21 also gave NGOs direction in their own efforts in the follow-up to the conference.[41]

The signing of the climate change and biodiversity conventions helped to offset the passage of relatively weak documents and compromised institutional arrangements. But these events were bittersweet at best. Under a threat from US President George H.W. Bush that he would not attend the Rio Conference and that the USA would not sign a climate convention that contained specific greenhouse gas emission reduction targets, the convention was modified, "watered down" in the words of critics.[42] It can be argued, however, that the fierce debate surrounding the elimination of target dates or omissions levels "watered down" the convention so much that it became merely a framework convention and "gave rise to the 1997 Kyoto Protocol."[43] It should also be noted that while small island states and countries with long coasts like Bangladesh and Egypt wanted a strong climate change convention, even one that included the precautionary principles, oil-exporting countries were concerned that people might actually start doing something about climate change if a strong convention were signed and ratified.[44] The G-77 consensus was eroding.

Then, on the eve of the conference itself, President Bush announced that, contrary to the recommendations of his Director of the Environmental Protection Agency (EPA), he would not sign the Biodiversity convention, ostensibly because the financial implications of the convention had not been worked out sufficiently. Most believed, however, the real reason was because of US concern for the patenting of genetic materials and their reluctance to transfer the recombinant DNA technology to economically less developed countries.[45] Representatives of the US biotechnology industry had complained bitterly about the efforts of economically less developed countries to "undermine intellectual property rights with respect to plant and animal materials, and to apply instead self-serving notions of sovereign control over these living materials."[46] It has been argued that delegates from the South may have thought they conceded too much on the Climate Change Convention and thus were not going to "water down" the Biodiversity treaty to meet US requirements. Plus it can be argued that they had more at stake in this convention.[47]

During his brief appearance in Rio, where the USA was seen by many as isolated, President Bush proposed that countries meet on January 1, 1993, to report on specific plans to reduce emissions of pollutants related to global warming. He also stated that "America's record on environmental protection is second to none, so I did not come to apologize."[48] Hempel contends that:

> while Bush's positions on the climate and biodiversity treaties officially isolated the United States from its traditional allies and from the other nations of the globe, there is no doubt that his administration's views were privately shared by a number of other world leaders. Part of the evidence can be seen in the meager funding commitments that many of the wealthy nations made to implement the treaties and to enact the hundreds of other provisions agreed to as part of Agenda 21.[49]

In spite of all of this, the conference and the massive media attention it generated succeeded as a consciousness-raising exercise and, perhaps as importantly, provided the impetus for many national governments to establish domestic environmental programs and agencies. Those agencies, of course, were also mandated by UNCED to provide national progress reports. The UNCED secretariat saw the preparation of such reports as a way to increase public participation in environmental decision-making. Reporting allowed for new institutional channels with affected groups (NGOs, women's groups, industry, the Church, even the Army) to get involved. Some of the economically less developed countries initially feared that the reports would require that they share "proprietary information" and that they might lack the necessary administrative capabilities to gather the necessary information. They also feared that the information might be used as a kind of conditionality for future World Bank loans or IMF borrowings.[50]

Also as a consequence of the Rio conference, the General Assembly committed its members to negotiating a convention to combat desertification (eventually completed in 1994 as the UN Convention to Combat Desertification), and to future conferences on sustainable development of small island countries and the protection of migratory fish stocks. Moreover, the mere convening of the conference contributed to a significant increase in the knowledge about the environment, including as governments prepared for it[51]

However, in the end:

> Rio failed to secure a long-term agreement on the need for the more equitable world order that Brundtland and others had called for.[52] As was the case with Stockholm, Rio conspicuously failed to reconcile the conflicting demands of industrialized and industrializing countries. If anything, it helped to clarify the limits of environmental mega-diplomacy at a time when many assumed that the world's ills could be solved by holding a big environmental conference.[53]

As Michael Grubb and his associates concluded:

> Even those close to the process hoped for much more than actually emerged. They sought agreement on a sweeping Earth Charter; conventions to assist development whilst containing binding and quantified commitments on greenhouse gas emissions and the preservation of species and forests; and an Agenda 21 backed with targets of achievement and agreement on associated funding requirements, mechanisms and contributions for achieving those targets.[54]

They explain this by the continuation of two general tensions, one was North–South and the other, not unrelated, between perceived national interests on the one hand and international responsibilities on the other. Even if post-Rio sustainable development was "much more firmly rooted as an important concept, on each specific issue at least some governments will have strong reasons related to their perception of short-term political and national interests for resisting the desires of the broader international commitment."[55]

Hempel is more concrete in explaining why Rio didn't live up to the hopes and expectations that so many had for it. First, he points to the "greed and recalcitrant leadership style at the summit by the United States and some of its key allies." He also points to the unfortunate timing of the conference (i.e. a US Presidential election was in the offing; the US economy was in the doldrums and unemployment was high,[56] and the GATT negotiations were "in an unsettling state of suspended animation").[57] Furthermore, potentially generous donor countries were suffering from "donor fatigue," especially given the necessity for paying for the 1991 Gulf War and for the rebuilding of post-Cold War Eastern and Central Europe. He also suggests that scientific uncertainty "permeated key UNCED debates about climate protection" and there were North–South clashes over side issues, like fair trade and development assistance.[58] Moreover, the European Community,

> which had been squaring up to fill the leadership vacuum left by the US ... ran into complex internal difficulties over EC integration and consequent harmonization of environmental and development policies. Japan, perhaps the only country which seemed set to offer large increases in international assistance, was ... still finding its place in the world, nervous of straying too far from the US fold.[59]

Plus, the Japanese also had domestic difficulties.

Conca adds a number of additional "inherent problems" that ensured that Rio's follow-up would be limited: (1) many environmental problems operate within a single country's borders and there national sovereignty rules supreme; moreover, UNCED focused on interstate and transnational environmental issues (i.e. only a subset of the environmental problems plaguing the globe); (2) too much of the environmental process depends on states acting, whereas they often lack the capacity to do so, or at least they cannot do so effectively without other key stakeholders, few of whom are explicitly mentioned in the UNCED documents; and (3) although NGO networks proliferated in the post-UNCED era, many of them avoided working through the UNCED framework because it visualized "nonstate actors as a quasi-institutionalized presence at periodic global events or as one of the interested groups" credentialed to the CSD (i.e. farmers, children, corporations, and women).[60]

While the specific accomplishments at UNCED may often be over-stated and its implementation stymied, the rhetoric and documents rightly or wrongly connected with it marked an important development in the environmental movement and, again rightly or wrongly, convinced many—perhaps especially outside the USA—of the value of more global *ad hoc* conferences, including those connected to environment and development.

World Conference on Human Rights

In accordance with a decision taken by the General Assembly on December 18, 1990 (Resolution 45/155), the June 14–25, 1993 World Conference on Human Rights was convened in Vienna in the celebratory context of the end of East–West confrontation, the blossoming of civil society in Central Europe, and the knowledge that human rights had played an important role in the dissolution of the Soviet bloc, not least of all as a consequence of the Helsinki Accords and the related Conference on Security and Cooperation in Europe (CSCE) process.[61]

The aim of the conference was to evaluate progress made in the field of human rights since the adoption, in 1948, of the Universal Declaration of Human Rights; to consider the relationship between human rights and development and democratization; to examine ways to strengthen the protection afforded human rights; and to improve the UN's human rights program and machinery. The main topics identified for the conference were self-determination, universality or cultural particularity of human rights, whether donors should tie economic aid and loans to human rights conditions, and whether the UN should appoint a high commissioner for human rights.

In spite of the Vienna Conference's celebratory context, controversy pervaded it, from its PrepComs and NGO Forum to the host government's invitation to Nobel Peace Prize recipients, including the Dalai Lama, to address the conference's opening ceremony. In the last regard, UN Secretary-General Boutros Boutros-Ghali reportedly

> quickly deferred to what was readily perceived to be pressure from China, disinviting the Dalai Lama, and the late afternoon sessions of the NGO meetings broke into a furor of incriminations that the UN Conference on Human Rights could not stand by its own principles.

As a compromise, the Dalai Lama spoke outside the Amnesty International tent set up in a park adjacent to the Vienna Centre where the meetings were being held. Boutros-Ghali explained his decision as being necessary to insure that the Chinese attended the conference; if they did not attend, one-quarter of the world's population would be unrepresented. He also suggests that the Dalai Lama readily agreed to speak at the NGO Forum instead, and repeatedly emphasized that it was the Austrian government that had invited him to speak in the first place, not the UN, and who indeed had not even given advance notice to the UN.[62]

The NGO Forum, which had at least 2,000 representatives from 813 NGOs, formally met June 10–12, 1993, that is, prior to the official conference, but it continued to run sessions through until June 25. The official UN liaison to the NGO Forum, the Joint Planning Committee, issued instructions to the Forum organizers to insure that human rights violations of particular countries were not to be targeted. Given the size of the gathering and the fact that the UN had not held a global human rights conference since 1968, it was not surprising that the Forum was a bit undisciplined. One observer noted that "The NGO sessions were litanies of tearful pleas concerning impoverished peasants, terrorized tribes, and embattled ethnic communities, and each of the audience had his own cause." Somewhat ironically, former US President Jimmy Carter, known as the US President most committed to human rights as a high foreign policy priority, was shouted down at the NGO Forum. Apparently there was resentment that the USA appeared to be playing the role as the champion of universal human rights, which it actually was in Carter's time.[63] On the other hand, it has been argued that NGOs, especially women's groups, deserve much of the credit for whatever successes there were in Vienna.[64] One of the more innovative activities relating to the rights of women was the Global Tribunal on Violations of Women's Human Rights, which was held on June 15. The Tribunal was seen to have "made a very strong and symbolic statement about the failure of existing human rights law and mechanisms to protect and promote women's human rights."[65] NGOs took part in virtually all the activities at Vienna, with the significant exception of the drafting of the Vienna Declaration, in which they were permitted limited involvement.[66] "China reportedly also led the move to exclude NGOs from observing the government drafting sessions."[67]

The conference's regional PrepComs were not even able to agree on a conference agenda. Thus, it was decided that UN General Assembly Resolution 45/155 of December 18, 1990 that called for the convening of the conference would have to serve that purpose, even though it was a series of quite broad statements. The resolution, in fact, referred back to the UN Charter noting that "all Member States have pledged themselves to achieve the promotion of universal respect for and observance of human rights and fundamental freedoms in conformity with relevant articles of the Charter."

In many ways, the regional meeting for Asia (convened in Bangkok March 29–April 3, 1993, and serving as one of the PrepComs) turned out to be a kind of omen of what was to come at the world conference. The "Final Declaration of the Regional Meeting for Asia of the World Conference on Human Rights" can be seen as a kind of cultural declaration of independence from the efforts of the UN to establish a set of universal human rights. While "stressing the universality, objectivity and non-selectivity of all human rights and the need to avoid the application of double standards in the implementation of human rights and its politicization," the Asian Final Declaration also included these provisions:

- "Recognizing that while human rights are universal in nature, they must be considered in the context of a dynamic and evolving process of international norm-setting, bearing in mind the significance of national and regional particularities and various historical, cultural and religious backgrounds."
- "Recognizing further that States have the primary responsibility for the promotion and protection of human rights through appropriate infrastructure and mechanisms, and also recognize that remedies must be sound and provided primarily through such mechanisms and procedures."
- Discouraging any attempt to use human rights as a condition for extending development assistance.
- "Emphasize the principles of respect for national sovereignty and territorial integrity as well as non-interference in the internal affairs of States, and the non-use of human rights as an instrument of political pressure."[68]

In light of this and the fact that the African regional meeting (held in Tunis, November 2–6, 1992) also indicated that different societies had culturally distinct needs, it is probably not surprising that the final PrepCom (Geneva, April 19–May 7, 1993) was unable to follow the practice of most UN global conferences, namely to agree on a document that could serve as a draft for the Vienna Declaration and Programme of Action. Instead, the Conference Secretary-General, Ibrahima Fall (of Senegal, then the UN Assistant Secretary-General for Human Rights) and Jan Martenson (then Director of the Centre for Human Rights in Geneva) decided that the conference secretariat would draft a document based on the regional meetings. After protracted negotiations, the extensively bracketed draft was accepted with the various regional documents and position papers serving as appendices.

The Vienna Declaration's recommendations addressed racism, racial discrimination, xenophobia and other forms of intolerance; the rights of national or ethnic, religious and linguistic minorities; the status and human rights of women; children's rights; freedom from torture; rights of disabled persons; national and international action to promote democracy, development and human rights; and human rights education.

In a number of places, the final document tried to square the circle. For example, while the Declaration reaffirms that "[t]he universal nature of [human] rights and freedoms is beyond question," it adds that

> [w]hile the significance of national and regional particularities and various cultural and religious backgrounds must be borne in mind, it is the duty of states regardless of their political, economic and cultural systems, to promote and protect all human rights and fundamental freedoms.

And while conferees declined to endorse proposals to include in the Declaration that the promotion and protection of human rights should be conducted on the basis of respect for national sovereignty and non-interference in a country's internal affairs, they also declined to endorse proposals to state explicitly that the promotion and protection of human rights can never be considered as interference in domestic affairs. Instead, the Declaration declares that "the promotion and protection of all human rights is a legitimate concern of the international community."[69]

Where the three regional groups that held preparatory meetings (Asia, Latin America and Asia) agreed, there was a lot of support for inclusion of those agreements in the final document. For example, they all agreed that the Vienna Declaration should restate the "right to development" as agreed to in UN General Assembly Resolution 41/218 (dated December 4, 1986). Fearing that such an endorsement would lead to pressure on the US government to provide development assistance, the USA led an ultimately successful fight to insure that the final Declaration stresses the human person as the central subject of development (a position consistent with the General Assembly resolution).

While the Vienna conference's final document has been widely ridiculed for being inconsistent and compromised, the conference has been widely praised for boldly asserting that "the human rights of women and of the girl-child are an inalienable, integral and indivisible part of universal human rights." And while conferees encouraged universal ratification of the CEDAW, they simultaneously acknowledged the convention's weaknesses, notably the many reservations that signatory governments had to its various provisions. Thus, they urged that governments withdraw any reservations that were contrary to the convention's objective and purpose. Conferees also suggested that the Commission on the Status of Women and the Committee on the Elimination of Discrimination Against Women consider adding an optional protocol to the Convention to allow for the right of petition.[70] These critiques of CEDAW can be seen as evidence of how the women's movement was progressing and how norms and, in this instance, hard law can evolve with the aid of a progression of related world conferences.

Similarly, conferees were widely praised for finally agreeing on the need for a United Nations High Commissioner for Human Rights. The idea for a centralized Human Rights office, responsible for coordinating and promoting human rights activities, fact-finding and monitoring, and emergency responses was first discussed in 1950. At Vienna, the idea was pushed particularly hard by Amnesty International. While the Western states were united in the idea of creating an office and the post of a key human rights advocate, there were disagreements over specifics. Major opposition to the office and post came from the Asians. Their opposition followed logically from their belief in human rights implementation as resting with individual governments or regions. They found an ally in the UN Secretary-General, Boutros Boutros-Ghali, who was also against it. He argued that it would simply add one more UN bureaucracy in the already crowded human rights field:

> Moreover, the effort to "coordinate" would be regarded as an attempt to consolidate pressure against countries of the third world, and that would only strengthen their resistance to progress in human rights. The very title "high commissioner" was a vestige of British colonialism and should be abandoned.[71]

In the end, the conference recommended that the General Assembly establish such a post, which it did on December 20, 1993 (Resolution 48/141). (Five years later, many reported that they believed that the decision to create the post of High Commissioner "could justifiably be considered as one of the most important results of the Vienna Conference.")[72] The first appointee was Ambassador José Ayala Lasso of Ecuador, who had successfully lobbied for the General Assembly resolution establishing the post. Although he had no human rights background, his name was proposed by the USA and he was appointed by Boutros-Ghali. He spent much of his time in office fighting with the head of the UN Centre for Human Rights and was widely criticized, in part because he emphasized "quiet diplomacy," contending that his strategy would win permission for visits of special rapporteurs who would otherwise by denied entry. His definition of the role also seemed to fit with Boutros-Ghali's preference that the High Commissioner post be a weak and ineffective one. He was replaced on September 12, 1997, by former Irish President, Mary Robinson. Her appointment was widely praised by human rights NGOs. Later, her troubled leadership in the Durban World Conference Against Racism marked a period of bumpy relations especially with the USA, but also with UN Secretary-General Kofi Annan, who had appointed her, seeking more emphasis on human rights in the post-Rwanda, post-Bosnia era. He "sometimes found it difficult to work with a high commissioner so unschooled in the ways of bureaucracy and so often out in front of him."[73] Among Robinson's many acts of publicly giving voice to human rights concerns was her call for a bombing halt a week after the USA started to bomb Afghanistan in the post-9/11 attacks on the USA. Significantly, the UN resolution that dealt with the appointment of Robinson's successor (effective September 12, 2002), Sergio Vieira de Mello, noted that he would function under the authority and direction of the UN Secretary-General.[74] He remained a popular and effective High Commissioner, but was assigned by Secretary-General Annan as his special representative in Iraq, where he was killed in the bombing of the UN headquarters in August 2003. Effective July 1, 2004, his successor was named, Canada's Justice Louise Arbour, who had served as the prosecutor for the UN tribunals for the former Yugoslavia and for Rwanda (Box 5.3).

One area where the conference was not successful related to money. Conferees failed to make any specific recommendation in response to calls for a drastic increase in the UN's funding for human rights. For years, the UN's human rights budget had stagnated at approximately 1 percent of the overall UN budget, notwithstanding a dramatic expansion in the UN's human rights activities.[75] And even more recently, with the significant attention devoted by the international community to human rights issues, it still accounts for less than 2 percent of the UN's regular budget.

> This means that in the early twenty-first century the UN Human Rights Centre had about $25 million available for its global work in human rights ... The United States alone was spending about $500 million per year to promote democracy around the world.[76]

While the Vienna conference's documents have often been ridiculed, they provided some useful language that NGOs were able to

**Box 5.3 United Nations High Commissioners for
Human Rights**

José Ayala Lasso (Ecuador)   1994–1997
Mary Robinson (Ireland)   1997–2002
Sergio Vieira de Mello (Brazil)   2002–2003
Louise Arbour (Canada)   2004–

use in subsequent conferences. Similarly, while the High
Commissioner office has got off to a rough start, most agree that it is
beginning to have an impact on human rights practices around the
world. But what Vienna most clearly demonstrated was the impact
that well-organized NGOs could have on UN-sponsored global
conferences, most notably the women's groups, but also Amnesty
International.

International Conference on Population and Development (ICPD)

One frequent criticism of the Rio Conference was that it failed to
sufficiently address the relationships between demography, the environment and development. While Chapter 5 of Agenda 21 addresses
"Demographic Dynamics and Sustainability," it fails to draw the
connections between demography and the issues discussed in the
thirty-nine other chapters. The Vatican and Saudi Arabia have been
credited with limiting the inclusion of more precise, elaborate and
clear statements about demography in the Rio documents, including
the Declaration.[77] To deal with this major shortcoming, it was agreed
that contacts and negotiations should be undertaken after Rio with
the ultimate aim of preparing a convention on demography.[78] The
most visible post-Rio initiative undertaken by the UN in this regard
was the International Conference on Population and Development
(ICPD), agreed to by the UN General Assembly on December 22,
1992 (Resolution 47/176) and convened in Cairo, September 5–13,
1994. Convening the meeting in Cairo turned out to be a felicitous
choice: as a moderate Muslim state, it was able to reassure the
Vatican and prevent most other Muslim governments from
boycotting the conference for fears of the positions that the USA
might take.

The context for the Cairo conference is key to understanding what happened there:

> The collapse of the Soviet Union, prefigured by the fall of the Berlin Wall two years before the main preparations for the conference got underway, removed a source of tension and introduced a new dynamic into global politics that was ultimately reflected in the Cairo process. Gone was the ever-present fear among conference organizers that East–West conflicts might erupt to derail the proceedings, as indeed they had almost done at Bucharest and Mexico City; in its place was a new openness and willingness to cooperate among members of the former Soviet bloc, which simplified the work of the ICPD Secretariat. The political climate in which the conference and its preparatory process took place was also improved by the signing of a peace agreement between Israel and the Palestine Liberation Organization.[79]

But the end of the Cold War had also led some Americans to be less concerned about problems in economically less developed countries and less willing to provide generous development assistance to countries no longer deemed essential to global stability. Of the most likely candidates to fill the vacuum left by the US retreat, the Germans were suffering economic woes of reunification and the Japanese, as the world's most successful mercantile state, did not want to offend any potential customers. Moreover, Japan remained uncomfortable with its place in the world, given its behavior in WWII. Also relevant to the conference's geo-strategic context was the lessened visibility of the post-NIEO G-77, now a much less cohesive body than it had been in the past.[80]

Among the conference's objectives were to review the implementation of the World Population Plan of Action, adopted at the 1974 Bucharest World Population Conference, and to establish a program of action for the next twenty years under the theme of population, sustained economic growth and sustainable development. In many ways, the ICPD can be seen as the "mirror image" of the Bucharest conference twenty years earlier.

> In the lead-up to Bucharest, action programs in population had no universally acknowledged "home" within the United Nations, and the Secretary-General of the conference was appointed from outside the UN system. By 1990, UNFPA had emerged as a relatively strong organization within the UN, capable of attracting sufficient funds— based on voluntary contributions from governments—to recruit a

worldwide staff and to make its presence felt in population programs throughout the developing world. Its executive secretary, Nafis Sadik, was appointed Secretary-General of the conference [Egyptian President Muhammad Hosni Mubarak served as conference President] and was determined to make Cairo the most significant UN meeting in the decade that commemorated the fiftieth anniversary of the founding of the United Nations. Although the Bucharest draft Program of Action was comprehensively reworked by delegates to the conference, retaining its population orientation while deleting most references to family planning, at the ICPD, the draft program that was taken to Cairo had already rejected the demographic rationale for family planning and substituted the introduction of reproductive health services as a way to improve health. Whereas the preparatory process for Bucharest was largely closed to nonscientific influence, the Cairo process was influenced by the participation of a broad coalition of more than 1,500 NGOs whose interests spanned development, reproductive and adolescent health, women's rights and empowerment, violence against women, female genital mutilation, the rights of indigenous peoples, and family planning, but which paid little serious attention to the determinants or consequences of population growth.[81]

Unlike the development agenda at Bucharest, the reproductive health and rights agenda that constituted the thrust of the Cairo conference was originally elaborated in the USA, before the Women's Decade, but it later benefited from research undertaken as part of the decade.[82] "Reproductive rights and health emerged at Cairo as the new norm that should guide global population policy." Conferees

> declared that women should no longer be treated as a convenient means toward the end of population control ... In the Cairo Programme of Action there is an entire chapter dedicated to reproductive rights and health, but in previous UN conference documents on population there is not even a single *mention* of the phrase *reproductive rights*.[83]

This significant shift, in part at least, can be explained by the evolution of the transnational network of NGOs, especially women's groups, and the fact that "NGOs were accorded more extensive rights to participate in the meetings that mattered" than at other UN global conferences in the 1990s.[84] Paige Eager explains that the ICPD was eagerly anticipated by women's networks and NGOs. The Rio conference had been important in the implementation of a global strategy to advance a broad feminist agenda through UN conferences, most immediately ICPD, because it was at Rio that "many newcomers to the environmental movement" had been introduced to the negative feminist view of family planning.[85] By PrepCom III, NGOs, especially the Women's Caucus, had become active. The ICPD Secretary-General welcomed NGOs' participation in Cairo and indeed frequently credited their presence as essential to the development of a strong Program of Action.[86] Such groups were particularly hopeful of getting attention focused on reproductive rights and health included in the Cairo documents because of the election of President Clinton in the USA.[87] And, indeed, his Under-Secretary of Global Affairs, Timothy Wirth, was cited as saying that the USA was back in the forefront of global population efforts.

But the women's activists were opposed by the Vatican and "like-minded actors" (i.e. some countries where Muslims and Catholics constitute a numerical majority) who feared that the women's activists were seeking to secure an international right to abortion. Especially at PrepCom II (April 4–22, 1994), the Vatican and others registered their opposition to the use of terms such as "reproductive and sexual health," "reproductive rights," "unsafe abortion," "family planning," "safe motherhood," and "reproductive health services." They feared these were code words for the eventual acceptance of abortion. Thus they insisted that these words be bracketed in the documents (i.e. noting that because there wasn't agreement on these words they would have to be returned to later).

Not surprisingly, the final document tried to please all parties. Chapter VII, Paragraph 7.1, for example, spoke of the "sovereign right of each country consistent with national laws and development priorities, with full respect for various religious and ethical values and cultural backgrounds of people" while the document also spoke of the need to undo cultural norms and religious practices that perpetuate violations of women's reproductive rights.[88] Hilary Charlesworth portrays the introduction of these contradictory clauses as a "watering down" of the language from Vienna, something she credits to Islamic states.[89]

The conference's Program of Action included such principles as ensuring women's ability to control their fertility, that the family as the basic unit of life should be strengthened, and the need to attend to the treatment of children and of migrants. The Program of Action also stressed the need for all governments to incorporate population concerns into their relevant national development strategies, policies, plans and programs, but many at the NGO Forum thought there was too little emphasis on development and too much time spent debating the abortion issue.[90] The Program of Action also set out twenty-year goals in four related areas: (1) universal education; (2) reduction of infant and child mortality; (3) reduction of maternal mortality; and (4) access to reproductive and sexual health services, including family planning. It was agreed that the active discouragement of harmful practices, such as female genital mutilation, should also be understood as an integral component of primary health care.[91]

Of course, getting countries to agree to a final document is one thing, getting them to live up to their commitments is quite another. No voices were raised against the Program of Action as a whole and the fact that the Vatican limited its reservations to parts of the Program of Action was considered quite a triumph.[92]

Many reports, however, have indicated that donor commitments have consistently fallen short of what was anticipated at Cairo to be the cost of implementing both family planning and health programs. The Program of Action called for an increase in the amount of money spent yearly on family planning, reproductive health care, and other population programs in economically less developed countries to rise from about $5 billion to $17 billion by the year 2000, with two-thirds from developing countries and one-third from developed countries. It also sought to stabilize world population at or below 7.8 billion. One estimate suggests that less than a half of the expected annual developed country contribution of $5.7 billion for the year 2002, which was proposed at the ICPD, has been forthcoming.

> Moreover, although most observers are sympathetic to the need for broader programming in reproductive health, such programming is likely to come at the cost of family planning services, which are now required to compete with many other services for every dollar.[93]

Two and a half years after the conference, the US Under-Secretary of State Wirth reportedly referred to Cairo as "unquestionably the most successful of all post-Rio conferences," citing three reasons for its success: (1) it had a clear agenda; (2) it was a very well-run conference; and (3) the Program of Action was very specific. At about the same time, NGO leaders spoke of the conference's ability to empower women.[94] Somewhat more sanguine (and perhaps less biased) views were made a bit later. For example, at the outset of the five-year review and appraisal conference, UN Secretary-General Kofi Annan explained the lack of full implementation of the Cairo Program of Action this way:

> In Cairo, everyone agreed on the need to mobilize new financial resources—from within developing countries, but also from the international community. Since then, developing countries have proved their commitment. But they are cruelly limited in what they can achieve without outside help. Too often—let's admit it— they are also limited by the effects of conflicts, by arms spending, or by inadequate leadership. But too often, also, they have to give priority to debt servicing, or to draconian budgetary austerity imposed in the name of "structural adjustment."[95]

While the ICPD documents were important in the evolution of soft law, the conference also showed the integral connections between issues of population and development, and between the policies of donor countries and organizational success or failure. Post-Cairo it was hard for anyone to fail to see the connection between debt service ratios and the ability of economically less developed countries to implement effective population policies.

World Summit for Social Development (WSSD)

The context for the World Summit for Social Development (WSSD) also seemed promising. The end of the Cold War "presented a historic opportunity to achieve a common vision of social development and poverty reduction."[96] And perhaps no other UN global conference was focused as clearly as ever on the interconnectedness of issues. As UN Secretary-General Boutos Boutros-Ghali implies, this met, to an unprecedented degree, the long-standing goal of UN conferences in the sense of tying together issues that the UN's bureaucratic structure and governments' national bureaucracies are not organized to accommodate, yet which many believe are the only ways to cope with the problems of the contemporary era:

> The World Summit for Social Development in Copenhagen in March [6–12] 1995 stressed the interconnectedness of the entire continuum of conferences. It is obvious that economic problems have social consequences and the social deterioration in turn undermines economies. The ills that societies feel most acutely all have social origins and social consequences, and the Copenhagen summit focused on these: the urgent and universal need to eradicate poverty,

expand productive employment, reduce unemployment, and enhance social integration.

The decision to focus a summit entirely on the most deprived segment of global society was a dazzling statement. One hundred and eighty-seven countries were represented at Copenhagen, no fewer than 117 of them by their heads of state or government.[97]

The WSSD was also portrayed as representing "a landmark shift by Governments to support policies that promote a people-centered framework for social development and justice." Some saw this as a response to governments putting economic growth first.[98]

But the convening of the summit was not without controversy, right from the start when it was suggested by the Chilean Ambassador to the UN Juan Somavia. A number of governments, including the USA, were wary of a gathering that would raise unrealistic hopes and commit itself to unworkable goals.[99] As the editors of *The Economist* sarcastically noted at the conference's conclusion: "To the surprise of nobody, the world leaders who congregated in Copenhagen last week for the United Nations' social summit failed to achieve their modest aim of 'abolishing poverty.'"[100]

That is, some portrayed the virtue of the breadth of its mandate as the conference's biggest vice. But with the same sort of creativity and perseverance that had led to the implementation of his call for NGOs to address formally the UN Security Council for the first time and to his subsequent selection as Director-General of the ILO, Somavia succeeded in convening a conference designed as a kind of synthesis of all that preceded it.[101]

The key documents coming out of the World Summit were the Copenhagen Declaration on Social Development and the Programme of Action of the World Summit for Social Development. Both focused on the summit's three core issues: (1) eradication of poverty; (2) expansion of productive employment and reduction of unemployment; and (3) social integration.

The Declaration underscored the summit's uniqueness: "We are deeply convinced that economic development, social development and environmental protection are interdependent and mutually reinforcing components of sustainable development." Then, reflecting the optimism of the times, the Declaration spoke of the meeting as the "Summit of hope" and particularly the belief or at least hope that liberal democracy was sweeping the globe. In this context, the conferees declared their conviction "that democracy and transparent and accountable governance and administration in all sectors of society are indispensable foundations for the realization of social and people-centered sustainable development."

But the conferees also recognized that while "we are witnessing in countries throughout the world the expansion of prosperity for some, [it is] unfortunately accompanied by an expansion of unspeakable poverty for others." In part, this was portrayed as the dark side of globalization. Indeed, some of the statements in the Declaration were quite pointed, including those related to the environment: "The major cause of the continued deterioration of the global environment is the unsustainable pattern of consumption and production, particularly in industrialized countries, which is a matter of grave concern, aggravating poverty and imbalances."[102] In this connection, Boutros-Ghali thought

> [t]he most innovative idea of the summit was endorsement of the principle of spending 20 percent of overseas development assistance on basic social services, in return for which poor countries would agree to devote 20 percent of their budgets to such programs.[103]

But, to the disappointment of NGOs in particular, the proposal was made voluntary for interested governments. (The idea of such a 20/20 proposal, which had its origins in the UNDP in 1991 and was elaborated further in UNICEF in 1993, was discussed at the Cairo conference, but didn't make it into the final document.[104]) In a similar vein, the G-77 proposal for the establishment of an International Fund for Social Development (IFSD) did not even get that much support. It was deleted from the draft Program "on the understanding that the issue would be considered" by ECOSOC in 1995.[105] Still, the conference Declaration enumerated ten "commitments" (see Box 5.4).

The Copenhagen conference's Program of Action was organized to meet these ten commitments, for example, to achieve equality between women and men it called for the removal of restrictions on women's right to own land, inherit property or money, and the devising of "suitable means to recognize and make visible the full extent of the work of women and all their contributions to the national economy, including contributions in the unremunerated and domestic sectors." The Program of Action also included an extensive section on "implementation and follow-up" with this revealing introductory statement: "Nothing short of a renewed and massive political will at the national and international levels to invest in people and their well-being will achieve the objectives of social development." Considerable emphasis was placed on civil

> **Box 5.4 The ten commitments of the Copenhagen Conference Declaration**
>
> - To create an economic, political, social, cultural and legal environment that will enable people to achieve social development.
> - To eradicate absolute poverty by a target date *to be set by each country.*
> - To promote full employment.
> - To promote social integration based on the enhancement and protection of all human rights.
> - To promote full respect for human dignity and to achieve equality and equity between women and men.
> - To promote and attain the goals of universal and equitable access to quality education, the highest attainable standard of physical and mental health, and access to primary health care, making particular efforts to rectify inequalities relating to social conditions and without distinction as to race, national origin, gender, age or disability.
> - To accelerate economic, social, and human resource development in Africa and in the least developed countries more generally.
> - To ensure that structural adjustment programs include social development goals.
> - To increase significantly and/or utilize more efficiently the resources allocated to social development.
> - To improve and strengthen the framework for international, regional and sub-regional cooperation for social development, especially through the UN.

society's role. This is probably not surprising given the times (i.e. exuberance over the blossoming of civil society, especially in Central Europe) and that about 4,500 representatives from NGOs attended the parallel NGO Forum '95 (held March 3–12 at Holmen, a former naval base near Copenhagen) and 811 NGOs (representing 2,315 individuals) participated in the Social Summit itself.

In spite of this, at the conclusion of the summit, a "Copenhagen Alternative Declaration" was signed and released by over 600 NGOs in which they expressed disappointment with the summit. The Alternative Declaration, which was actually completed before the end of the summit and circulated to delegates and by the conference news-papers,[106] called for more forthright action on such issues as "third world" debt cancellation (only Denmark and Austria announced plans to cancel debts owed them by the forty-seven least developed coun-tries; those debts amounted to $266 million of the approximately $1.3 trillion owed by "third world" countries),[107] democratization of the World Bank and the IMF, regulation of multinational corporations and financial transactions, and community participation in decision-making. Much of the disappointment resulted from the ability of rich countries to insure that the final summit documents did not formally *bind* them to much of anything.[108] Thus, the follow-up to this summit is particularly important.

Among the "immediate" consequences of the summit was a reorien-tation of UNDP programming activities to target poverty as its overriding concern. Moreover, in 1996, the General Assembly proclaimed the International Year for the Eradication of Poverty and a decade on the same theme beginning in 1997.[109] The significance of these steps, of course, depended upon systemic events over which the UN has little control, including the degree of prosperity and the polit-ical predilections of leaders in key donor states and geo-strategic developments, including the degree of civil and interstate conflict.

Perhaps the summit charge was too broad, even if the interconnec-tions are indisputable. And perhaps it was naïve to believe that getting heads of government and heads of state to attend a summit would significantly increase the chances of garnering the resources needed to meet the challenges of the day. And while the immediate, demonstrable "bottom line" clearly is that the WSSD feel way short of the summit conveners' expectations, like conferences before it, the goals and very conception of the social summit seem to have had a long-term, albeit impossible to precisely measure, impact. Its goals have become embedded in almost every UN agency's program, including those of the World Bank Group and the IMF. Clearly one of the latent, but nonetheless essential, impacts of UN conferences is their role in norm creation and ideational change, part and parcel of the evolving world order of which the conferences are a part and which they also, often in very subtle ways, help to shape.

Fourth World Conference on Women

In 1990, when UN members first started discussing holding another conference on women, it was agreed that it should be in Asia, although the venue was not part of the General Assembly resolution (A/REES/45/129, dated December 14, 1990) that formally recommended such a conference. In 1991 China offered to serve as the host, committing themselves to the requisite major financial and human resources (estimated at $250 million); the only other offer was from the Australian government and after they withdrew in 1992, the Chinese offer was accepted.[110] China's goals in offering to host the conference were basically two-fold: to overcome the damage done to its international reputation as a consequence of its actions in 1989 in Tiananmen Square, and to demonstrate its political, administrative and logistical skills. The challenge for the Chinese regime was that it wanted to host the conference, but at the same time it wanted to maintain internal control:

> The incompatibility of these goals became apparent when the media, groups critical of either the conference itself or China's policies, and China's own actions [including trying to exclude some NGOs, denying visas and tightening security despite prior agreements with the UN that all groups, except those presenting a security risk, would be admitted to China, and arresting dissidents, detaining human rights activists and executing several criminals right before the meetings][111] all combined to produce a highly charged international atmosphere that diverted people's attention from the actual stated purpose of the conference.[112]

It is worth noting that one detailed study of the US press coverage of the conference emphasized that the press reports reflected the "dominant capitalist ideology within the USA," which played itself out in terms of the "deceitfulness of the regime" as well as the Chinese government's problem and failures, in this instance, logistical problems: "the underlying structure of the mainstream American media content" which tends to marginalize and trivialize feminist issues was also seen to contribute to the focus on issues of logistics and politicization rather than to the core of the events being discussed at the conference.[113] But it is also important to note that when the Chinese made their bid, NGOs were not the force at UN global conferences that they had become by the time the conference was convened.

In the end, however, the official conference was attended by 189 governments, more than any other UN conference. It had 17,000 participants, with 6,000 government delegates and more than 4,000 accredited NGO representatives. In addition, there were 4,000 journalists and many officials from all the organs in the UN system. The NGO Forum also broke all records, even though the Chinese thought they could discourage NGOs from attending by accommodating them in Huairou, 40 miles from the official conference site. An estimated 30,000 participants from around the world were joined by 5,000 Chinese, making a total of 40,000 people, if one includes performers, Chinese police and security officers:[114]

> Billed as a conference on equality, peace, and development, the Beijing meeting, at its core, was about eliminating coercion, discrimination, and violence in the public and private lives of women. Governments urged that: economic and employment policies recognize women's unpaid contributions to the economy; eliminate differentials in pay between men and women for equal work; and women be guaranteed equal access to public office, education, basic health care, and all other aspects of private life. In addition, they called for elimination of violence in the home and in public, where rape is not only a crime against the individual, but is still used as a weapon of war.[115] Finally, the governments represented in Beijing reaffirmed what they had agreed in Vienna in 1993, that international human rights laws and standards must not be diluted by religious practices, or tradition when applied to women.[116]

The outcome of the 1994 Cairo Conference had provoked some conservative delegations (e.g. the Vatican, conservative Islamic countries and several countries in Latin America) to threaten to use the Beijing Conference to turn back agreements on women's rights that had been written into that earlier conference's final documents. Despite this challenge the Beijing Platform for Action for Equality, Development and Peace included verbatim language from Cairo as well as language that actually extended, concretized and operationalized the Cairo Platform. In fact, the key Beijing documents consolidate all of the decisions made by preceding world conferences on women *and* the relevant statements from the conferences of the 1990s dealing with the environment, human rights, population and social development. But it also added specifics, such as men's equal responsibility as sexual partners and partners sharing family responsibilities, and concerns with discrimination against and the exploitation, abuse and other problems of the girl-child.

The Beijing Platform of Action specified twelve specific areas of concern for which it set strategic objectives and proposals for action: poverty, education and training, health, violence against women, armed conflicts (even though there was pressure to steer clear of this topic),[117] economy, power and decision-making, institutional mechanisms, human rights, the media, the environment, and the girl- child. The Platform's mission statement begins by asserting that it is an agenda for women's empowerment (i.e. the goal is not simply achieving equality and eradicating discrimination). The Platform's main themes are: (1) the primacy of women's rights, even where culture and tradition may seem to sanction restrictions on those rights; (2) reproductive and sexual rights; (3) abortion rights; (4) adolescent rights relative to the duties, rights and responsibilities of parents; and (5) women's control over their sexuality. The Platform also called on governments to commit themselves to effective mainstreaming of a gender perspective throughout their operations, policies, planning and decision-making.[118] Moreover, governments accepted the obligation to carry out gender impact assessments of the effects of their actions.

Emmerij *et al.* see the major accomplishment of Beijing as being

> [the] recognition of the need to shift the focus from women to the concept of gender, recognizing that the structure of society, and all relations between men and women had to be reevaluated. Only through such a fundamental restructuring of society and all its institutions could women be fully empowered to take their rightful place as equal partners. This change represented a strong reaffirmation that women's rights were human rights and that general equality was an issue of universal concern.[119]

In spite of this and the wide-ranging nature of the Program of Action, there were gaps in it (e.g. concerns of indigenous women were largely overlooked, even though they were well represented in the NGO Forum). In the conference's last negotiating session, there was an impassioned and unprecedented debate on sexual orientation. In the end, all specific references to disallowing discrimination on the basis of sexual orientation were removed from the Platform. Moreover, in the final plenary session, more than forty countries added interpretative statements or expressed reservations to particular passages in the Platform. Most focused on Paragraph 96 which established a woman's right to control her own sexuality and Paragraph 106k which calls on governments to consider reviewing abortion laws that punish women who had illegal abortions. The Vatican expressed a reservation to the entire health chapter and some additional paragraphs, but went along with the overall consensus.[120]

Critics contend that the areas of poverty, multilateral debt and structural adjustment were not adequately dealt with, the importance of which we have seen was repeatedly stressed at earlier global conferences. Even the critics agree, however, that the Platform did make

advances in terms of sexuality, reproductive health, and in acknowl-
edging the right of women to inherit property (but not equal to men,
owing to opposition by some Sub-Saharan and Islamic delegations).[121]

Much of what was accomplished in Beijing has been credited to the
work of women's NGOs and the delegates from the South, especially
Africans (who had coordinated prior to Beijing at the regional
PrepCom, regional ministerial meetings, sub-regional meetings and a
meeting sponsored by the OAU), but credit also belongs to many from
Latin America and the Caribbean and to an occasionally assertive US
delegation, including the pro-family addresses by First Lady Hillary
Clinton.[122] Shepard explains the NGOs' influence by the fact that
women's networks "had gained legitimacy by organizing and summa-
rizing the results of countrywide consultations with women's and other
civil society organizations." Moreover, "[m]any networks then became
part of the official negotiations and, in some cases, members of
country delegations."[123] Gertrude Mongella of Tanzania served as the
conference Secretary-General; the secretariat was responsible for the
drafting of the Platform for Action. Chen Muhua, vice-chairman of
the Standing Committee of the Eighth National People's Conference
of China and President of the Executive Committee of the All-China
Women's Confederation, was elected conference President.

Among the follow-up commitments of governments were the preparation of national plans to be submitted to the UN Division for the
Advancement of Women and what Charlesworth refers to these as
"conference of commitments." She sees this Australian initiative as
perhaps the most significant outcome of the Beijing Conference. It
allows governments to tailor commitments to their own local situations, providing for a greater likelihood of implementation. As of
October 2000, the Division had received 117 such plans. NGOs do the
documenting and monitoring of these commitments, as the UN was
not given those responsibilities. Some of the commitments were pretty
impressive such as the British commitment to remove many of its
debilitating reservations to CEDAW and the Austrian pledge to add to
its family and marriage law an obligation for spouses to share household, childrearing and childcare tasks.[124]

Four years after the Beijing Conference, governments were asked to
report to the ECOSOC Commission on the Status of Women on their
actions to implement the Platform for Action in the twelve critical areas
of concern. A review of those national reports—the Commission's
request netted an impressive 80 percent response rate—showed
"profound changes in the status and role of women [to have] occurred
in the years since the start of the United Nations Decade for Women in

1996, some more markedly since" the Beijing Conference. Despite the progress, two major areas—violence and poverty—were found to "continue to be major obstacles to gender equality." "Overall, the analysis of the national reports … revealed that there had been no major breakthrough with regard to equal sharing of decision making in political structure at national and international levels."[125]

These reports were part of the materials reviewed by the Ad Hoc Commission of the Whole of the Twenty-third Special Session of the General Assembly that met to discuss progress made in implementing the Beijing Declaration and Platform of Action and further actions and initiatives that could be undertaken to implement the Declaration and Platform. In virtually all the twelve priority areas, they found that progress had been made, but that obstacles had also been encountered. In many instances, progress was limited to having successfully raised the consciousness of key actors, for example, in the area of women and poverty, it was noted that "considerable progress" had been made "in increasing recognition of gender dimensions of poverty and in the recognition that gender equality is one of the factors of specific importance in eradicating poverty"; in the area of "women and health," programs were "implemented to create awareness among policy makers and planners of the need for health programmes to cover all aspects of women's health throughout the women's life cycle." The obstacles encountered were multiple (e.g. in explaining the widening economic inequality between women and men, explanations included income inequality, unemployment and the deepening of poverty levels of the most vulnerable and marginalized groups, "third world" indebtedness and the unfulfilled commitments of the rich to the official development assistance goals set decades earlier).

A number of "current challenges affecting the full implementation of the Beijing" documents were also identified. These were "challenges" not focused on in 1995, but which five years later were recognized as among the most serious obstacles to full implementation of the goals of the fourth women's conference. Chief among these was globalization. While recognizing some of the benefits that globalization afforded women, it was also seen as contributing to the feminization of poverty and "increased gender inequality, including through often deteriorating work conditions and unsafe work environments, especially in the informal economy and rural areas." Also noted were the hardships induced by economic restructuring in the economies in the transition to capitalism and the fact that women and girls were increasingly involved in internal, regional and international labor migration. Also among the new challenges were the HIV/AIDS pandemic's "devastating impact on women," the way in which current demographic trends were increasing the numbers of widows and single women, "often leading to their social isolation and other social challenges" and the growing drug and substance abuse among young women and girls. Thus, while recognizing that progress was being made in the area of women's rights, it was clear that there were ongoing and new challenges to meet, all of which required time, energy, creativity, money and commitment.[126]

United Nations Conference on Human Settlements (Habitat II)

The United Nations Conference on Human Settlements (Habitat II) was held in Istanbul from June 3–14, 1996, in accordance with a General Assembly resolution of December 22, 1992 (A/RES/47/180), although the seeds for it had been planted earlier. The President of Turkey Süleyman Demirel was selected as Habitat II President and Wally N'Dow (of the Gambia) served as conference Secretary-General.

The conference, also called the "City Summit," addressed two themes: adequate shelter and sustainable human settlements in an urbanizing world. The second theme was seen as one significant difference between the 1996 conference and its predecessor twenty years earlier: Habitat II was "not just a housing conference, it was importantly a debate about the cities, the urban challenge." Instead of focusing on cities as "static entities," the conference focused on the process of urbanization. In this context, conferees sought to understand rural–urban migrations, the growth of squatter slums and the informal sector economies that often drive growth and deterioration.[127] It has been argued that it was not possible in 1976 to "discuss such topics as the role of the private sector"; the world was "still in the grips of the Cold War" with the ideological confrontation making it unacceptable to discuss the private sector, who owned land and how it was managed, in a UN forum.[128] In Istanbul, however, those barriers were long gone. Moreover, the debate in Istanbul included not only national governments, that earlier had contended they were the only relevant voices and source of ideas and resources, but local authorities and especially mayors played a major role in Istanbul.[129]

The US delegation included three mayors and a city manager:

[this] emphasis on strong, democratic local authorities as key partners in implementing the Habitat Agenda was perhaps what most

markedly distinguished Habitat II from the UN conferences that preceded it. For the first time in the history of the United Nations, local officials were included in national delegations and given a voice and a seat at the negotiating table.[130]

The World Assembly of Cities and Local Authorities (WACLA) was held just prior to Habitat II and it appears to have had some influence on the intergovernmental gathering. The leitmotif of the WACLA meeting was the principle of subsidiarity, that is, that decisions should be taken at the level closest and most accountable to citizens, and only those tasks that local governments could not carry out efficiently would be referred to higher levels of governance. Thus, in seeking means to achieve adequate shelter for all, governments were urged to decentralize shelter policies and their administration to sub-national and local levels and to integrate shelter policies with macroeconomic, social, demographic, environmental and cultural policies.

But the degree of innovation should not be overstated. There was opposition to NGOs and local authorities participating in the PrepComs; they were instead allowed to sit in all of the sessions of drafting committees as observers and allowed to make presentations at the "public sessions."[131] Perhaps significantly, at the five-year review of Habitat II (in June 2001), none of the innovative stakeholder practices adopted at Istanbul appear to have survived.[132]

On June 14, 1976, conferees adopted the Istanbul Declaration on Human Settlements, which sought to go to the presumed root causes of the problems of human settlements. It contended that to combat the deterioration of human settlements a number of issues had to be addressed:

> unsustainable consumption and production patterns, particularly in industrialized countries; unsustainable population changes, including changes in structure and distribution, given priority consideration to the tendency towards excessive population concentration; homelessness; increasing poverty; unemployment; social exclusion; family instability; inadequate resources; lack of basic infrastructure and services; lack of adequate planning; growing insecurity and violence; environmental degradation; and increased vulnerability to disasters.[133]

Conferees also agreed that while the problems of the cities were a global phenomenon, there were particular needs of economically less developed countries and that these were exacerbated by the challenges of massive external debts, difficult terms for transfers of technology, inadequate development aid, and negative or declining terms of trade. In this context, one observer at the conference concluded that:

> There was an amazing degree of consensus at this conference.[134] Governments experienced common problems of pollution, violence, disease, unemployment, homelessness and poverty in their cities, particularly those that were growing rapidly. Developing countries were also battling with poverty, ignorance and illiteracy, plus civil strife and refugees.[135]

Also on June 14, conferees adopted the Habitat Agenda, which suggested that there were special human rights needs for people living in absolute poverty; displaced persons, including refugees; children and youth; indigenous people; women; people with disabilities; and older persons. The core of the Habitat Agenda was ten goals and principles: (1) equitable human settlements were those in which all people had equal access to housing, infrastructure, health services, adequate food and water, education and open spaces; (2) poverty eradication was essential for sustainable development; (3) sustainable development was essential for human settlement development; (4) the quality of life depends upon the conditions and spatial characteristics of villages, towns and cities; (5) as the basic unit of society, the family was entitled to receive protection and support; (6) all people had rights and also had to accept their responsibility to respect and protect the rights of others, including future generations; (7) partnerships among countries and within countries including public, private, voluntary and community-based organizations, the cooperative sector, NGOs and individuals were essential to the achievement of sustainable human settlements; (8) social cohesion is founded on solidarity with those belonging to disadvantaged and vulnerable groups; (9) human settlements of the present and future generations must be safeguarded; and (10) universal and equal access to quality education, the highest attainable standard of physical, mental and environmental health, and equal access of all to primary health.

Among the more innovative events at the conference was a selection of twelve out of 600 proposed "best practices" for improving the environment: initiatives by governments, local authorities, grass-roots organizations and community groups that had proved effective in solving pressing economic, social and environmental problems facing the urbanizing world. Another innovation was noted in the UN Secretary-General's report (A/51/384) on Habitat II. He drew attention to the promotion of new partnerships between the UN and civil society. Indeed, national committees included among their members representatives of local authorities. Significantly in his report, the Secretary-General noted that the UN system's role in shelter and settlements development is predominantly a "supporting one."[136] In part, this reflects the focus on subsidiarity and civil society involvement, but it also reflects institutional controversies and challenges evident at the conference and shortly thereafter. While it was agreed that the United Nations Center for Human Settlements (UNCHS) in Nairobi needed to be given more money and people to help it function better, other sections of the key documents indicated that the role of the UNCHS and of the Commission on Human Settlements that oversees Habitat only had to be reviewed. Moreover, there were references to other bodies being responsible for implementation. Perhaps even more revealingly, Gustave Speth, UNDP administrator, complained that financial assistance to the UNDP was declining: UNCHS activities were primarily funded by the UNDP. President Daniel Arap Moi of Kenya openly complained that too much aid was being directed to peacekeeping and democratization.

In June 2001, the UN General Assembly held a Special Session (informally dubbed Instanbul+5) to review and appraise progress toward meeting the goals of the Habitat II Agenda. Actually the official review process began before Istanbul+5 in October 1999. At that time, the UNCHS issued a set of "Guidelines for Country Reporting." The guidelines were developed through a "consultative process using broad-based, gender-balance national committees." Reports were to address twenty key commitments and strategies included in the Habitat Agenda, another example of the "conference of commitments" initiated at Beijing. The commitments were grouped under six themes: shelter; social development and the eradication of poverty; environmental management; economic development; governance; and international cooperation.

From these reports, it became evident that there were serious problems with implementation, especially in Africa. These stemmed from the challenges of globalization, HIV/AIDS, civil and regional war and the lack of capacity to implement the Habitat Agenda's recommendations. Moreover, in Africa the relationship between central governments and local authorities was poorly developed. Further, local authorities often had low management and administrative capacities and they lacked necessary resources. In Asia, on the other hand, there was a significant increase in partnerships with the private sector, although eviction remained a large threat for slum dwellers.[137]

While the Istanbul conferees had reached considerable consensus on an important global problem and had identified a variety of strategies to begin to address that problem, including some quite innovative ones, money was again a key stumbling block to implementation. Involvement of local authorities, especially in Africa, was found not to be a viable way around that particular obstacle.

The topics of the conferences of the 1990s were familiar; many were convened to revisit issues dealt with in earlier conferences: to assess what had been accomplished and to set new goals and select new strategies for the future. Most were able to identify successes as well as significant remaining challenges, that is, reconvening diplomats on the same topics was a valuable and appropriate strategy. Most were also able to find new and innovative ways to address the continuing and new problems. Often this took the form of drawing better connections between issues previously artificially separated and more innovative and comprehensive manners of civil society involvement, at conferences and in proposed conference follow-up. But the conferences also shared other common, less positive themes. In a world with one remaining superpower, the pressures on that superpower to be forthcoming had declined. And, at least as importantly, the preferences, proclivities and perceived salience of issues of that superpower significantly affected the success of the conferences, not least of all in terms of specific financial commitments and whether money was actually forthcoming to support the conferees' words. Or perhaps there were (again) just too many conferences in too short a period of time: all rightly identifying pressing global problems; all correctly noting the need for more resources; all seeing a limited number of sources of those resources. Conference fatigue was growing (again).

6 The twenty-first century UN global conferences

- **Millennium Summit**
- **Third United Nations Conference on the Least Developed Countries**
- **United Nations Conference on Illicit Trade in Small Arms and Light Weapons in All Its Aspects**
- **World Conference against Racism, Racial Discrimination, Xenophobia and Related Intolerance**
- **International Conference on Financing for Development**
- **Second World Assembly on Ageing**
- **World Summit on Sustainable Development (WSSD)**

As the new millennium began, few could deny that the world was unipolar and that the USA had become the global hegemon.[1] Indeed, many began to speak of it as an imperial power, some in a positive way and some critically. While earlier authors had somewhat persuasively spoken of a "unipolar moment," as the twenty-first century dawned, authors began to speak of the USA as a reluctant imperial power or in terms of a liberal empire, whose future partly depended on whether it would or could rein in its aspirations.[2] The implications of this for UN global conferences became evident quite quickly and throughout the early part of the century: hegemonic fatigue, frustration and disinterest had their costs. Of course, things did not turn around abruptly with the dawn of a new century. To understand the context requires that we backtrack a bit to US Congressional-executive discussions as the twentieth century was coming to a close.

As part of a compromise with the Republican head of the US Senate Foreign Relations Committee leader Jesse Helms to get funds to begin to end the US arrears with the UN, the Clinton administration agreed to place a moratorium on US participation at UN global conferences, with the long-in-preparation third anti-racism conference as the singular exception. The proposed moratorium by the world's only remaining superpower was something that the Clinton administration, particularly its first Secretary of State, Warren Christopher, had been talking about for some time. While the USA was most outspoken in its conference fatigue, however, it was hardly alone. Filling the void left by the mega conferences were a series of so-called +5 and even +10 follow-up conferences, the first of which has already been noted.

But at the urging of UN Secretary-General Kofi Annan, as part of his program to reform the UN, the new millennium began with a variant of the "traditional" UN global conferences, that is, while it shared the characteristics of a global conference, it was technically not one. This took the form of the Millennium Summit. This continued Annan's quest to reinvigorate the UN in spite of the inauspicious global environment. His innovations included the widely acclaimed and widely criticized Global Compact that he had announced at the World Economic Forum on January 31, 1999, and which had become operational just prior to the Millennium Summit (i.e. on July 26, 2000). The Global Compact seeks to engage

> the private sector to work with the UN, in partnership with international labor and NGOs, to identify, disseminate, and promote good corporate practices based on nine universal principles … drawn from the Universal Declaration of Human Rights, the International Labour Organization's (ILO) Fundamental Principles and Rights at Work, and the Rio Declaration on Environment and Development. Companies are challenged to move toward good corporate practices as understood by the broader international community, rather than relying on their often superior bargaining position vis-à-vis national authorities, especially in small and poor states, to get away with less.[3]

Critics claimed that this allowed companies to "bluewash" their image by wrapping themselves in the UN's flag. Perhaps as a counter-point to such naysayers, it should be noted that during the first Global Compact Leaders Summit, convened at UN headquarters on June 24, 2004, the Secretary-General announced the addition of a tenth principle, one against corruption. This contentious principle followed a long consultation process with all Global Compact participants. Its importance relates to the Global Compact participants' commitment to post on the Global Compact website at least once a year concrete steps taken to act on any of the Compact's principles.

Millennium Summit

On December 17, 1998, the UN General Assembly adopted Resolution 53/202, by which it decided to convene the Millennium Summit as an integral part of the Millennium (General) Assembly, all part of a process instigated by UN Secretary-General Kofi Annan: "It was a political risk he didn't have to take. But he did, and the UN is probably better off now than if none of this had occurred."[4] Summit meetings were held at the UN headquarters in New York City from September 6–8, 2000. It was the largest gathering of heads of state and government in world history. The Assembly agreed that Goh Chok Tong, Prime Minister of Singapore; Alexander Kwasniewski, President of Poland; Hugo Rafael Chavez Frias, President of Venezuela; and Abdelazia Boutefika, President of Algeria, would each chair one of the summit's four roundtables.

On May 15, 2000, the Secretary-General invited the heads of state and government to use the opportunity of the summit to express their support for various international legal documents that had been deposited with him, singling out a core group of twenty-five multilateral treaties where he was hoping for universal participation. These included the Optional Protocol on the Rights of the Child on the involvement of children in armed conflict; the Optional Protocol on the Rights of the Child on the sale of children, child prostitution and child pornography; the Optional Protocol to the Convention on the Elimination of All Forms of Discrimination against Women; the Rome Statute of the International Criminal Court; and the International Convention for the Suppression of the Financing of Terrorism. A total of eighty-four governments followed up on the Secretary-General's overture, a figure some deemed impressive.

Although the Millennium Declaration (Resolution A/55/2, dated September 8, 2000) was, "[f]or many, a vague menu of non-binding commitments, simply confirm[ing] people's worst stereotypes of the UN as a sterile and ineffective talking shop,"[5] it had a number of novel aspects worth underscoring. For example, one of the clear themes in speeches at the summit and in the Declaration itself was the need to "give greater opportunities to the private sector ... to contribute to the realization of the Organization's goals and programs," which can be seen as a logical follow-up to the Global Compact and a clear reflection of the evolving global ideological consensus on the virtues of classical liberalism or at least capitalism. But the most novel aspect of the Declaration was its goals, including the so-called Millennium Development Goals (MDGs). Based on the lessons learned from the conferences of the twentieth century and perhaps most specifically from a recognition that Agenda 21 had failed to serve as a useful guide to action, it had seemed clear to many that the more concrete and measurable the goals, the easier it would be to hold governments accountable.[6] Moreover, just the setting of the goals would likely allow the UN to present itself as reforming itself, moving beyond the vagaries of some of the earlier conferences that had led some to describe them as global talkathons. The Millennium Development Goals (see Box 6.1) mostly had deadlines of 2015.While these goals are laudable, a definitive answer on how valuable and feasible they were and indeed how useful the summit was will only be apparent in 2015.

Still, one set of observers has already concluded that, while "few would describe the results as pivotal, the summit did exceed the low expectations of many by producing a series of commitments … with specific goals and targets for achieving these goals."[7] While that might, in the end, prove to be the right judgment about the summit, it seems a bit premature. But some post-summit progress can already be reported. For example, to help track progress in meeting the goals, the UN Secretariat and the specialized agencies (including representatives of the IMF and the World Bank) and the Organization for Economic Cooperation and Development (OECD) have defined a set of time-bound and measurable goals and targets for combating poverty, hunger, disease, illiteracy, environmental degradation and discrimination against women. International experts have also selected relevant indicators to be used to assess the progress over the period from 1990 to 2015, when most of the targets are set to be met. Moreover, each year, the Secretary-General prepares a report on progress achieved towards implementing the Declaration's goals, based on data on the forty-eight selected indicators, aggregated at global and regional levels.[8]

The obvious question is the one bluntly posed by Lloyd Axworthy (Canada's former foreign minister): "are the goals to be acted upon, or is it just another masquerade?" Axworthy suggests that immediately "[a]fter the summit, it looked as if these were goals that were being taken seriously." He points to the Doha meeting of the World Trade Organization (WTO; in November 2001) in this regard. Of course, he goes on to note that it didn't take long for there to be setbacks in achieving the goals, including those relating to the US and EU's agricultural subsidies (for which a possible accord may be in the offing).[9]

Others have been more enthusiastic than Axworthy. The MDGs have been referred to as "an idea whose time has come" and have been portrayed as "propelling governments, aid agencies and civil society

Box 6.1 Millennium Development Goals

- Eradicate extreme poverty and hunger:
  - Reduce by half the proportion of people living on less than a dollar a day.
  - Reduce by half the proportion of people who suffer from hunger.
- Achieve universal primary education:
  - Ensure that all boys and girls complete a full course of primary schooling.
- Empower women and promote equality between women and men:
  - Eliminate gender disparity in primary and secondary education preferably by 2005, and at all levels by 2015.
- Reduce child mortality:
  - Reduce by two-thirds the mortality rate among children under the age of 5.
- Improve maternal health:
  - Reduce by three-quarters the maternal mortality ratio.
- Combat HIV/AIDS, malaria and other diseases:
  - Halt and begin to reverse the spread of HIV/AIDS.
  - Halt and begin to reverse the incidence of malaria and other major diseases.
- Ensure environmental sustainability:
  - Integrate the principles of sustainable development into country policies and programs; reverse loss of environmental resources.
  - Reduce by half the proportion of people without sustainable access to safe drinking water.
  - Achieve significant improvement in the lives of at least 100 million slum dwellers, by 2020.
- Create a global partnership for development:
  - Develop further an open trading and financial system that is rule-based, predictable and non-discriminatory.
  - Make commitments to good governance, development and poverty reduction both nationally and internationally.
  - Address the least developed countries' special needs. This includes tariff- and quota-free access for their exports;

enhanced debt relief; relief for heavily indebted poor countries; cancellation of official bilateral debt; and more generous official development assistance for countries committed to poverty reduction.

- Address the special needs of landlocked and small island developing states.
- Deal comprehensively with developing countries' debt problems through national and international measures to make debt sustainable in the long term.
- In cooperation with the developing countries, develop decent and productive work for youth.
- In cooperation with pharmaceutical companies, provide access to affordable essential drugs in developing countries.
- In cooperation with the private sector, make available the benefits of new technologies, especially information and communications technologies.[1]

Note

1 UN Millennium Development Goals (MDG), 2000. Available at http://www.un.org/millenniumgoals/ (accessed July 4, 2004).

organizations everywhere to reorient their work."[10] They have also been described as

[having] gained tremendous currency, primarily in development circles but increasingly in related trade and finance circles. Many actors are now counting on the goals ... to galvanize disparate and sometimes competing development agendas and are imagining how they might become a powerful political tool to hold governments and international institutions accountable.[11]

Of course, that is the key point. A recent study using World Bank data put it this way:

Many developing countries are making substantial progress toward the MDGs as a result of improved policies, better governance and the productive use of development assistance. But they could do more with the right mix of policy reforms and additional help ... Without greater impetus, there is a serious risk that many countries will fall short of many of the goals.[12]

What seems to be helping, however, is the political autonomy that the MDGs allow economically less developed countries to have in "defining their own strategies." That appears "fundamental to ensuring appropriate and high impact development efforts." The notion that "one size does not fit all" is key[13] and works with the MDGs in a way that it has not with the recommendations from earlier UN conferences.

The UN General Assembly and especially the UN Secretary-General, however, are not leaving anything to chance. The General Assembly scheduled a follow-up meeting in September 2005, in spite of members' calls for not making +5 conferences routine anymore. More specifically, the Secretary-General, along with UNDP Administrator Mark Malloch Brown, launched the Millennium Project in 2002, aimed at recommending the best strategies for achieving the MDGs. The Project is directed by Professor Jeffrey Sachs of Columbia University, who serves as Special Advisor to the Secretary-General on the MDGs. It is overseen by a UN Experts Group, comprised of senior representatives from UN agencies whose role is to ensure that the Project's ten task forces comprised of academics, and representatives of civil society organizations, the public sector and the UN—poverty and economic development; hunger; education and gender equality; child health and maternal health; HIV/AIDS, Malaria, TB, and Access to Essential Medicines; Environmental Sustainability; Water and Sanitation; Improving the Lives of Slum Dwellers; Open, Rule-based Training Systems; Science, Technology, and Innovation—have access to and make full use of the knowledge, experience, and capacities of the UN system. The Project's research, which is conducted mostly by the ten task forces, focuses on identifying the operational priorities, organizational means of implementation, and financing structures necessary to achieve the MDGs. The Project is scheduled to make its recommendations to the Secretary-General in January 2005 and to conclude its work in June 2005, that is prior to the September 2005 General Assembly meeting celebrating the UN's sixty-year anniversary. The importance of the success of the project, and the reinvigoration of the UN more generally, became even clearer to Annan as time from the Millennium Summit and the consensus represented there passed. Especially noteworthy in this context is Annan's September 23, 2003, speech to the

UN General Assembly in which he spoke of the UN coming "to a fork in the road ... a moment no less decisive than 1945 itself, when the United Nations was founded." Thus, a lot of weight was placed on success in the achievement of MDGs, but Annan also set up a High Level Panel on Threats, Challenges and Change to help shoulder that burden, to develop recommendations to try and re-forge the "vision of global solidarity and collective security, expressed in the Millennium Declaration."[14]

Third United Nations Conference on the Least Developed Countries

On December 18, 1997, the General Assembly decided (Resolution 52/187) to convene in 2001 the Third United Nations Conference on the Least Developed Countries. The conference mandate was: (1) to assess the results at the country level of the Program of Action for the 1990s; (2) to review the implementation of international support measures, particularly in the areas of official development assistance, reducing debt, and increasing foreign investment and trade; and (3) to consider the formulation and adoption of appropriate national and international policies and measures for sustainable development of the least developed countries as well as their progressive integration into the world economy. In its Resolution 53/182, the General Assembly accepted the EU's offer to host the conference (in Brussels, May 14–20, 2001) and designated UNCTAD Secretary-General Rubens Ricupero as the conference Secretary-General. It asked that the UNDP Round Tables and the World Bank Consultative/Aid Groups make substantive contributions to the preparation for the conference and requested the UNDP Administrator Malloch Brown, in his capacity as the convener of the UN Development Group, to ensure the full involvement of the UNDP resident (country) coordinators and country teams in the least developed countries. The General Assembly further called upon the conference Secretary-General to organize well-focused sectoral, thematic and country-specific round table meetings during the conference. It also "invited" the conference Secretary-General to facilitate the involvement of civil society, including NGOs and the private sector, in the preparatory process. In its Resolution 54/235, the General Assembly decided to convene PrepComs in two parts, in New York City. The conference secretariat also convened three regional-level preparatory meetings in Addis Ababa (Ethiopia) in March 2000; Kathmandu (Nepal) and Niamey (Niger) in April 2000.

In his opening address to the conference, UN Secretary-General Kofi Annan set the context:

> This is the third such conference in 20 years. In that time the list of Least Developed Countries has grown longer, not shorter. Only one country has ever graduated from the list, and by a cruel twist of fate that country, Botswana, now sees its prospects blighted by HIV/AIDS. It has the highest rate of infection in the world. Clearly, this Conference has to be different from the previous ones. And it is. It has been carefully planned to ensure that no source of ideas is neglected, and that people with different roles and different viewpoints have to listen to each other.

What could also be added is that in the twenty-first century the USA and its variant of capitalism seemed ascendant (i.e. a strong commitment to a freer market, democratic governance and a facilitating role for government in the economy). This was, of course, reflected in the role that the private sector was expected to play during and after this particular global conference.

As has become the pattern, the major outcomes of the conference were two-fold: the Brussels Declaration, and the Program of Action for the Least Developed Countries. While the Declaration's commitment to the eradication of poverty was familiar, its stress on "good governance" at the national *and* international level (including the rule of law), respect for internationally recognized human rights (including the right to development), gender equality, and democracy were not as traditional. Not surprisingly stress was placed on the need to address the HIV/AIDS pandemic, the decline in official development aid and countries' external debts, as was the need to improve preferential market access.[15]

The Program of Action was as blunt as were the UN Secretary-General's remarks, starting out with a clear statement that it was being written "against the backdrop of a lack of progress in socioeconomic development" in the least developed countries and a lack of progress in terms of the implementing the Program of Action for the 1990s. Still, it was ambitious in its overarching goal: "to make substantial progress toward halving the proportion of people living in extreme poverty and suffering from hunger by 2015 and to promote the sustainable development" of the least developed countries. The means for achieving this was identified as requiring a 7 percent per year GDP growth and an increase in the ratio of investment to GDP to 25 percent per year. Then comes what is most innovative (and in a historical sense, most remarkable): to achieve these goals, "civil society, including the private sector, is an important participant." The Program of Action speaks of a "framework for partnership" and in each of the commitment areas, which are often quite familiar (e.g. building productive and institutional capacities, enhancing the role of trade in development), the document identifies actions to be taken by the least developed countries *and* those by their "development partners." But the Program makes it clear that even this liberal agenda will not suffice, without military stability,[16] again an unusual statement for a document coming out of a UN global conference.

While the Program speaks at length about accountability, transparency and the rule of law, the World Bank President, James Wolfensohn, was even more direct in his address at the conference. He called for a "new compact" between rich and poor countries, i.e. the least developed countries cannot be expected to reduce poverty on their own, nor is the reduction of their poverty only in their interest. It is a global problem, needing a global solution and with potential global benefits. (Of course, the massive reconstruction needs and priority of Iraq makes the future look a bit bleak in terms of increased assistance and foreign investment from the OECD countries.) But then Wolfensohn pointedly noted that while "[the least developed] countries can certainly benefit from advice and technical assistance ... ultimately it is up to them to reform institutions, implement regulation and fight corruption."[17] Yes, he used the "c" word.

Clearly, those attending the third conference tried to take seriously the UN Secretary-General's warning and suggestion: the third conference had to be different if the needs of the least developed countries were to be addressed. The call for working with the private sector and bluntly addressing the obligations of the least developed countries seemed consistent with that warning and suggestion. Unfortunately, achievement of the conference's goals was thwarted by unpredictable events, most notably the wars in Afghanistan and Iraq and the expensive and ongoing rebuilding efforts in both of those countries. Parliaments in the most likely donor countries were hardly anxious to expend much more on development challenges elsewhere, even if the potential recipient countries were ready to fulfil their end of the bargain.

United Nations Conference on Illicit Trade in Small Arms and Light Weapons in All Its Aspects[18]

Considerable attention needs to be devoted to the UN Conference on Illicit Trade in Small Arms and Light Weapons in All Its Aspects because its focus differed from most, if not all, of its predecessor conferences. Although obviously with implications for development, economics, the environment, etc. (elements of *human* security), its focus was on an aspect of *military* security. Moreover, this conference is in many ways emblematic of the conferences of the world order that has come to characterize the twenty-first century, i.e. a hegemonic world order in which the constraints on the hegemon are limited.

The context that gave almost simultaneous rise to UN and NGO interest in the issue of small arms included the rise of narco-trafficking, especially in Latin America; the proliferation of ethnic and secessionist warfare in the post-Cold War era; the evolution of so-called new wars, where small arms "exacerbate" a "culture of violence" and can "obstruct international relief and reconstruction efforts"; the expansion of black market operations of weapons (i.e. "gun running") facilitated by the breakdown in bipolarity that had controlled and rationalized conflicts in the Cold War and by increased globalization (including increased economic interdependence and the global spread of the ideas of neo-liberalism and thus a decrease in government regulatory predilections); the success of the Convention on the Prohibition of the Use, Stockpiling, Production and Transfer of Anti-Personnel Mines and on Their Destruction (the so-called Ottawa Treaty or Landmines Treaty, which was developed with collaborative work with NGOs), and some movement on the traditional arms control agenda.[19]

While the International Relations literature often emphasizes the role of civil society, especially NGOs as "norm entrepreneurs," in the small arms case, it was governments and intergovernmental organizations, not NGOs, that first seized upon this issue. The government of "Mali's October 1993 request for UN assistance in controlling small arms, and UN Secretary-General Boutros-Ghali's inclusion of the issue in his January 1995 *Supplement to an Agenda for Peace*, were key markers in the emerging discussion."[20] Indeed, Boutros-Ghali has been described as the "first major world figure to sound the alarm in relation to the spread and misuse of small arms and light weapons."[21] He reportedly included small arms in the *Agenda* because of the failures of arms embargoes, including in Somalia and Serbia.[22]

Following his precedent-setting statement, on December 12, 1995, the UN General Assembly requested that the Secretary-General,

> within the existing resources to prepare a report, with the assistance of a panel of qualified governmental experts to be nominated by him on the basis of equitable geographical representation, on:
> (a) The types of small arms and light weapons actually being used

in conflicts being dealt with by the United Nations; (b) The nature and causes of the excessive and destabilizing accumulation and transfer of small arms and light weapons, including their illicit production and trade; (c) The ways and means to prevent and reduce the excessive and destabilizing accumulation and transfer of small arms and light weapons, in particular as they cause or exacerbate conflict; with particular attention to the role of the United Nations in this field and to the complementary role of regional organizations, and taking into account views and proposals of Member States and all other relevant information for submission to the General Assembly at its fifty-second session.[23]

The resultant report was shared with the General Assembly on August 27, 1997. Its Foreword by the Secretary-General began:

Readily available and easy to use, small arms and light weapons have been the primary or sole tools of violence in almost every recent conflict dealt with by the United Nations. In the hands of irregular troops operating with scant respect for international and humanitarian law, these weapons have taken a heavy toll on human lives, with women and children accounting for nearly eighty per cent of the casualties.

The report was described as "pragmatic and results-oriented" with a "set of practical measures to reduce the weapons already in circulation and to prevent further accumulation." Among its recommendations was one that the UN "consider the possibility of convening an international conference on the illicit arms trade in all its aspects, based on the issues identified" in the report.[24]

Government support for such a conference was for reasons similar to earlier UN global conferences, namely the belief that such a conference was a way to raise awareness of the issue, develop norms where none existed and, perhaps, to develop some action plans to which governments would formally commit themselves. Some also saw a conference as the only way to broaden the issue of illicit arms beyond a narrow arms control focus.

Some governments, however, thought it was premature to hold a conference: more work had to be done on the small arms issue. Some feared that the conference could be hijacked by the pro-arms lobby. The US government objected to the convening of the conference, objecting to its cost, claiming it overlapped with other multilateral issues under discussion and—aside from the criminal aspects of the issue that were being dealt with in the UN Protocol against the Illicit Manufacturing of and Trafficking in Firearms, Their Parts and Components and Ammunition, supplementing the United Nations Convention against Transnational Organized Crime—that could basically be dealt with on the regional level.[25] "Some states were also concerned about putting the small arms issue into the orbit of the UN disarmament system, given the success [that had been] achieved on the landmines issue outside the UN system," that is, they thought it best that the UN, whether through a global conference or other means, not handle this issue.[26] On the other hand:

> [t]he UN bureaucracy and those states which relied on the UN to solve problems were very concerned that the *Ottawa Treaty* would set a precedent that would see more and more disarmament issues go outside the UN for solution, and were thus intent on keeping the small arms issue within the organization. They were well aware that the International Campaign to Ban Landmines (ICBL) and supportive governments felt that the UN process had failed them.[27]

Perhaps the controversy over convening a possible conference can be explained in part at least by the fact that UN conferencing was now stepping into the realm of the highest of high politics: issues of military security.

In any event, on December 4, 1998, the General Assembly agreed (Resolution 53/77E) to hold an international conference on the subject and accepted the Swiss invitation for them to host it in Geneva (although, in the end, the conference was held in New York City). Some understood this to be an implicit admission that the extant institutional machinery, the regional organizations but also the UN General Assembly and the UN Security Council, were insufficient and inadequately coordinated to meet the challenges of the day. In a slightly different vein, the decision to convene a conference meant that governments that had previously not expressed interest in the issue, or had thought it was sufficient to handle it as a national—or at most regional—issue had to take note, as the UN began to query them as to what should be addressed.

Moreover, the decision to convene the conference, where Camillo Reyes of Colombia would serve as President, led to a vast increase in the number of NGOs concerned with the issue.[28] Actually, the NGO focus on the small arms issue began in the mid-1990s (i.e. after Boutros-Ghali's precedent-setting statement) initially involving humanitarian and human rights NGOs. They began by producing "empirical evidence of a link between increased small arms proliferation and such negative effects as increased violence and loss of life—especially amongst civilians." The key non-human rights-focused NGOs included the International Action Network on Small Arms (IANSA) that was founded in 1999 but actually had its origins in a virtual, Internet-based organization that was established a year earlier. Many of the 320 organizations in seventeen countries that joined IANSA had had experience in the international campaign to ban landmines.[29] Prior to the conference, NGOs focused on generating concrete proposals for controlling the legal and illicit trade in small arms as well as highlighting the humanitarian impacts of the proliferation, availability and misuse of small arms. Significantly, the World Forum on the Future of Sport Shooting Activities (WFSA), which is the international arm of the US-based, pro-gun ownership National Rifle Association (NRA), was also formed in the late 1990s with the aim of mobilizing firearms groups in anticipation of the UN conference. The WFSA, which represents thirty organizations, including hunting, sport shooting, firearms, and ammunition manufacturing associations in thirteen countries, focused on limiting global gun control efforts that might restrict the legal (legitimate in their preferred language) trade in small arms or infringe on the "rights" of private individuals in various countries. Their goal was to get governments and intergovernmental organizations to do very little in this area, i.e. to stick with the status quo, not to introduce new legislation, much less binding international treaties. The NGOs were particularly active in lobbying delegations during the conference's PrepCom meetings, especially those relating to the drafts of the Program of Action. This was because NGOs were excluded from the formal negotiations sessions, although they did serve as advisors to governmental delegations, critical observers in open sessions, commentators and, of course, lobbyists.[30] Thus, what we see here is a different sort of pattern than that observed at most of the previous conferences. Unlike with environmental, women's, human rights and development NGOs which lobbied for global conferences and helped shape the initial agendas, here the initiative rested with governments and the UN itself, but civil society quickly mobilized to try to affect the conference outcomes.

For the July 9–21, 2001 conference, the Group of Experts had recommended that "[t]he primary focus of attention should be on small arms and light weapons that are manufactured to military specifications." More specifically, they recommended that the "objective of the Conference should be to develop and strengthen international

Box 6.2 Aims of the Small Arms Conference

- Strengthen or develop norms at the global, regional and national levels that would reinforce and further coordinate efforts to prevent and combat the illicit trade in small arms and light weapons.
- Develop international measures to prevent and combat illicit arms trafficking in and manufacturing of small arms and light weapons and to reduce excessive and destabilizing accumulations and transfers of such weapons throughout the world, with particular emphasis on the regions of the world where conflicts are ongoing and where serious problems with the proliferation of small arms and light weapons have to be dealt with urgently.
- Mobilize the political will to prevent and combat illicit transfers in and manufacturing of small arms and light weapons.
- Raise awareness of the problems associated with illicit trafficking in and manufacture of small arms and light weapons and the excessive and destabilizing accumulation of these weapons.
- Promote government responsibility with regard to the export, import, transit and retransfer of small arms and light weapons.

efforts to prevent, combat and eradicate the illicit trade in small arms and light weapons in all its aspects" (see Box 6.2).

The conference itself had an inauspicious beginning in the form of US Under-Secretary of State John Bolton's July 9 address, which had a significant impact (see Box 6.3).

Aaron Karp suggests that Bolton's speech came as a "complete surprise" to many of the conference delegates:

> The shock … was the result of the tone, not the message. Staking out an extreme position, almost gleeful in his repudiation of the conference he was addressing, Bolton was joining in the global tide of sovereign reassertion. The fate of the Small Arms Conference was incidental to this larger trend.

Karp goes on to note that "a number of other governments, ranging from China to Switzerland had been discretely expressing similar

Box 6.3 Secretary Bolton's address to the Small Arms Conference

Small arms and light weapons, in our understanding, are the strictly military arms—automatic rifles, machine guns, shoulder-fired missile and rocket systems, light mortars—that are contributing to continued violence and suffering in regions of conflict around the world. We separate these military arms from firearms such as hunting rifles and pistols, which are commonly owned and used by citizens in many countries. As U.S. Attorney General John Ashcroft has said, "Just as the First and Fourth Amendments secure individual rights of speech and security respectively, the Second Amendment protects an individual right to keep and bear arms." The United States believes that the responsible use of firearms is a legitimate aspect of national life. Like many countries, the United States has a cultural tradition of hunting and sport shooting. We, therefore, do not begin with the presumption that all small arms and light weapons are the same or that they are all problematic. It is the illicit trade in military small arms and light weapons that we are gathered here to address and that should properly concern us.

… Some activities inscribed in the Program are beyond the scope of what is appropriate for international action and should remain issues for national lawmakers in member states. Other proposals divert our attention from practical, effective measures to attack the problem of the illicit trade in SA/LW [small arms, light weapons] where it is most needed. This diffusion of focus is, indeed, the Program's chief defect, mixing together as it does legitimate areas for international cooperation and action and areas that are properly left to decisions made through the exercise of popular sovereignty by participating governments:

- We do not support measures that would constrain legal trade and legal manufacturing of small arms and light weapons. The vast majority of arms transfers in the world are routine and not problematic. Each member state of the United Nations has the right to manufacture and export arms for purposes of national defense. Diversions of the legal arms trade that become ``illicit" are best dealt with through effective export controls. To label all manufacturing and trade as "part of the problem" is inaccurate and counterproductive. Accordingly, we would ask that language in Section II, paragraph 4 be changed to establish the principle of legitimacy of the legal trade, manufacturing and possession of small arms and light weapons, and acknowledge countries that already have in place adequate laws, regulations and procedures over the manufacture, stockpiling, transfer and possession of small arms and light weapons.

- We do not support the promotion of international advocacy activity by international or non-governmental organizations, particularly when those political or policy views advocated are not consistent with the views of all member states. What individual governments do in this regard is for them to decide, but we do not regard the international governmental support of particular political viewpoints to be consistent with democratic principles. Accordingly, the provisions of the draft Program that contemplate such activity should be modified or eliminated.

- We do not support measures that prohibit civilian possession of small arms. This is outside the mandate for this Conference set forth in UNGA [United Nations General Assembly] Resolution 54/54V. We agree with the recommendation of the 1999 UN Panel of Governmental Experts that laws and procedures governing the possession of small arms by civilians are properly left to individual member states. The United States will not join consensus on a final document that contains measures abrogating the Constitutional right to bear arms. We request that Section II, para[graph] 20, which refers to restrictions on the civilian possession of arms, be eliminated from the Program of Action, and that other provisions which purport to require national regulation of the lawful possession of firearms such as Section II, para[graph]s 7 and 10 be modified to confine their reach to illicit international activities.

- We do not support measures limiting trade in SA/LW solely to governments. This proposal, we believe, is both conceptually and practically flawed. It is so broad that in the absence of a clear definition of small arms and light weapons, it could be construed as outlawing legitimate international trade in all firearms. Violent non-state groups at whom this proposal is presumably aimed are unlikely to obtain arms through authorized channels. Many of them continue to receive arms despite being subject to legally-binding UNSC [United Nations Security Council] embargoes. Perhaps most important, this proposal would preclude assistance to an oppressed non-state group defending itself from a genocidal government. Distinctions between governments and non-governments are irrelevant in determining responsible and irresponsible end-users of arms.

- The United States also will not support a mandatory Review Conference, as outlined in Section IV, which serves only to institutionalize and bureaucratize this process. We would prefer that meetings to review progress on the implementation of the Program of Action be decided by member states as needed, responding not to an arbitrary timetable, but specific problems faced in addressing the illicit trade in small arms and light weapons. Neither will we, at this time, commit to begin negotiations and reach agreement on any legally binding instruments, the feasibility and necessity of which may be in question and in need of review over time.[1]

Note

1   John R. Bolton, "Statement to the UN Conference on the Illicit Trade in Small Arms and Light Weapons in All Its Aspects," USUN Press Release # 104(01), US Mission to the UN, July 9, 2001.

views. A few, especially ... among the Arab block, would become just as outspoken later on, while others grew quieter, safe behind US brazenness."[31] But, as Karp also argues, Bolton's position was not the result of a major new policy initiative. Indeed, the conference does not appear to have been a high administration priority or even a high priority for Bolton. Moreover, the Clinton administration policy on the small arms issue had already "become cautious in the extreme. Determined to contribute, but fearful of domestic criticism, it [had] stressed domestic reforms minimizing the danger of US involvement in the illegal gun trade. The United States [had] supported international action, but refused to lead."[32] Even more specifically, focused as it was on "growing the economy," the Clinton administration was concerned with boosting the competitiveness of the US arms industry.[33] Not only did this push in the opposite direction of the conference supporters, but it contributed to the growth of a strong lobbying force against restricting such trade. "The Bush administration did not change the essence of this conventional arms transfer legal framework, though it opposed more openly domestic and international initiatives for further controls."[34]

In this context, the fact that a Program of Action could be agreed to is probably an important accomplishment itself. Actually consensus was reached only after African delegates, in late-night discussions, agreed to give in to US demands and abandon attempts to have the Program of Action include references to the need to regulate the civilian possession of weapons and to restrict weapons transfers to non-state actors.[35] Before that key concession, debates at the conference had focused on: (1) the linkage of small arms to human rights violations; (2) excessive and destabilizing accumulation of both legal and illicit small arms; (3) transparency; (4) commitments to negotiate legally binding instruments on arms brokering and the marking and tracing of weapons; (5) national regulation of civilian possession of military weapons; (6) export and re-export control criteria; and (7) the supply of arms to governments only.[36]

The Program of Action commits governments to implement a wide range of measures at the national (e.g. enacting and enforcing relevant laws, establishing national coordination agencies, identifying groups and individuals engaged in illegal small arms-related activities, taking responsibility for all small arms held and issued by the state), regional (e.g. encouraging negotiations for binding agreements[37] and establishing regional and sub-regional law enforcement agency information-sharing arrangements) and global (e.g. enhancing cooperation with INTERPOL) levels affecting the trade (legal and illegal), production, and holdings of small arms and light weapons. The measures included strengthening national regulation of the production and transfer of small arms, ensuring that manufacturers mark all weapons (and keep appropriate records); allowing the tracing of seized weapons and improving the system of end-user certification to reduce the risk of diversion and illicit trafficking; encouraging the destruction of weapons seized in criminal investigation, collected in post-conflict disarmament programs, or surplus to national requirements (while there was extensive discussion at the conference on the importance of reducing surplus stocks, the consensual Program of Action does not insist on their destruction); and increasing the security of small arms stocks.

But the Program of Action also included a lot of room for maneuver and loose language, allowing governments a wide margin to exercise discretion in interpreting various clauses and commitments. Moreover, many important issues were dropped from earlier drafts, such as commitments to negotiate an international mechanism to trace illicit small arms (only a UN feasibility study was agreed to); initiatives to regulate the civilian possession of weapons (something the Bush administration couldn't fathom allowing to be included); increased transparency in the production, stockpiling and trade in small arms; specific criteria (such as a code of conduct) governing authorized exports, and greater regulation of arms brokering.

In spite of all of this, *during* the conference, US Republican Congressman Bob Barr of Georgia, a member of the official US delegation to the conference, offered amendments to two US House of Representative appropriations bills to bar all funding for implementation of the conference's Program of Action. While at the conference itself, the US delegation worked to delete requests for financial support of conference initiatives and to allow for only a limited role for the UN in follow-up activities. And from Bolton's speech onward, the USA fought—unsuccessfully in the end—to block the convening of any follow-up conferences.[38]

While the conference outcome disappointed some (e.g., because there were no concrete measures or monitoring or early warning system agreed to; no references to the need to regulate the civilian possession of weapons or to restrict weapons transfer to non-state actors; no commitment to negotiating a legally binding treaty on the topics; no movement to better regulate the "legitimate" trade in arms;[39] and the Program of Action, having been developed largely within an arms control and disarmament framework, did not address some key human rights, humanitarian, developmental or crime prevention dimensions associated with small arms and light weapons), the Program of Action appears to have been significant in meeting at least one of the conferees' goals. It contributed to the creation of norms because of its sheer breadth of scope.[40]

The conference also met a number of additional goals of its supporters and initial proposers. It raised popular and elite consciousness about the issue, forced governments to go on record with their views, created and disseminated knowledge about the small arms issue, helped build partnerships between governments and civil society, and resulted in the construction of specific proposals to confront the problem.[41]

The reasons why it failed to meet conferees' highest expectations go well beyond the position of the Bush administration. One needs to build into the explanation the inherent intractability of the issue; the fact that "most developing countries" opposed anything that would take away their right to acquire weapons; the Chinese opposed transparency and a comprehensive program, especially one covering legal small arms transfers; Arab states opposed transparency, and global standards for weapons destruction and favored national, not even regional, decision-making; the relative absence of gun control and anti-violence activists (while the NRA's voice was heard, they weren't that active in the conference either, once it became clear that their biggest concern had been met, i.e. there wasn't going to be a prohibition against domestic laws permitting the use of arms).[42]

As with any UN global conference, however, what is most important is not the gloom or glee at the end of the conference, but rather its impact some years on. Although there has not yet been the +5 review conference—it is scheduled for 2006—there was a week-long biennial meeting of states (BMS) held in July 2003. That meeting was not without controversy, as there were tensions between those who wished the meeting to restrict itself to its reporting mandate and those who saw this as a forum to present new ideas and reopen those which had been discussed, but rejected in 2001. (In spite of its name, many NGOs were there as observers.) Batchelor makes a strong case for why the BMS, even separate from what countries reportedly had accomplished or not, was a success:

> It was an important confidence-building measure for states on an issue that until recently was regarded as a highly sensitive "national security" issue; it helped to sustain, build, momentum for global action on the topic; and, last but by no means least, it reaffirmed the importance of partnerships between governments, international organizations and civil society for the effective implementation of the Programme of Action.[43]

But even before the BMS, there were some positive impacts of the 1991 conference. There were quite a few follow-up meetings convened by existing regional structures, with a goal of regionalizing the Program of Action. UNDP established a Trust Fund for Support Prevention and

Reduction of the Proliferation of Small Arms for those working on building the capacity for small arms removal and related training. UNICEF focused on the role of small arms and children in armed conflict, initially focusing on Angola, Colombia and Sri Lanka. In this context, Laurence and Stohl's overall judgment is an upbeat one:

> individual states are enacting new laws, building needed capacity, and funding projects in affected states. UN agencies are engaged in various activities in support of the *Programme*, while the UN Secretariat is carrying out the tasks assigned to it in this document. At the same time, regional IGOs [including the Organization of American States (OAS) and the Organization for Security and Cooperation in Europe (OSCE)] are taking action loosely based on the *Progamme*. And NGOs, both global and local, have embarked on specific programmes and awareness-raising initiatives, empowered by the mandate contained in the *Programme*.
>
> In just a few years, a marked indifference to, or denial of, the global nature of the small arms problem has given way to a situation where the generation of policy involves a process not unlike the political bargaining one finds within states.[44]

Two years on, there was evidence that many governments had taken steps to review and enhance the controls they already had in place. Where there were none in place, some countries had begun to develop controls and measures. There were also regional "strategic partnerships" being formed, connections between civil society organizations and governments were being forged and increased financial assistance for these purposes was evident.

On the other hand, a number of ominous signs were also present. For example, a "worrying number of governments" appeared complacent about the laws and regulations that they had in place. Some countries lacked cooperative arrangements between different relevant bureaucracies and others lacked good working relationships between governments and relevant actors in civil society. Mechanisms for identifying and spreading "good practices" internationally were deemed to be poorly developed, and in "some regions, including North Africa, the Middle East, and parts of Asia, progress toward implementing any aspect of the Program of Action appear[ed] to be the exception rather than the rule." Moreover, 9/11 appears to have set the agenda back, or at least in some countries.[45] Perhaps the most worrisome sign of all is the real "bottom line" in terms of the conference's impact. Although recognizing that it is too soon to throw in the towel, the concise judgment from the IANSA makes the challenge quite vivid:

> There is little evidence to suggest any overall success so far in reducing the scale and impacts of small arms and light weapons trafficking and proliferation. Throughout much of the world, the excessive availability and misuse of small arms and light weapons continue to contribute to create suffering and insecurity, with grave implications for poverty, underdevelopment, crime, violent conflict and abuse of human rights. Over 500,000 people continue to be killed each year and millions more by small arms and light weapons as combatants or civilians in wars or as victims of crime, oppression, suicide, accidents and societal or domestic violence.[46]

Thus, while there appears to have been significant progress in terms of consciousness-raising, norm creation, and institution-building at all levels of governance, there has not been progress where it really counts, namely in the saving of lives, i.e. the reason for the undertaking in the first place. As in the past, in even less high priority issue-areas, the small arms and light weapons conference demonstrated that there are clear limits to what global conferences can achieve when the global hegemon has staked out a position largely opposed to significant changes in the status quo.

World Conference against Racism, Racial Discrimination, Xenophobia and Related Intolerance

The August 31–September 8, 2001, World Conference against Racism, Racial Discrimination, Xenophobia and Related Intolerance, the UN's third global conference on the race issue, was intended to be something of a celebration. Formally agreed to by the General Assembly on December 12, 1997 (Resolution 52/111), it was sited in Durban, in post-apartheid South Africa. UN Secretary-General Kofi Annan opened the conference with the following rhetorical question: "Who better to teach the international community to overcome racism, discrimination and intolerance than the people of South Africa?" In addition, it was the first of the race conferences to be convened after the UN General Assembly had revoked the infamous "Zionism" as Racism resolution.[47] That is, the main foci of the previous conferences and the reasons for boycotts, walkouts, acrimonious debate and a general lack of consensus were things of the past. Moreover, the UN had its first black African Secretary-General and the USA, which had boycotted the previous two racism conferences, had its first African-American Secretary of State. Further, Mary Robinson, the outspoken and high profile UN High Commissioner for Human Rights, was named the conference Secretary-General. Dr. Nkosazana Dlamini Zuma of South Africa was elected as conference President. The US government volunteered $250,000 to the Conference budget of $12 million, a sharp contrast to the contribution of $5,000,000 to the Beijing Conference, but also a break from the evolving tradition of opposing all such mega conferences.[48] Further, both President George W. Bush and US Secretary of State Colin Powell had discussed the impending conference at meetings of the G-8 and US–EU Summit.[49]

But the conference was also being convened in the context of

> [a] lack of interest, support and financial resources for the Third Decade [to Combat Racism and Racial Discrimination] and its related Programme of Action, reflected in the fact that very few of the activities planned for the period 1994–1997 were carried out.

Also, in light of the minimal and less than required "contributions made by the international community to the Trust Fund for the Program of Action"[50] and, of course, the Palestinian quest for a sovereign homeland, which was the subject of an ongoing political and military conflict.

In addition to 2,300 government representatives from 163 countries, including sixteen heads of state, fifty-eight foreign and forty-four other ministers, some 3,000 accredited NGO representatives went to Durban to publicize the injustices they had suffered and their struggles to overcome them. Three-quarters of those seeking accreditation, however, were from the USA and "many of the organizations going from the USA and Europe are, at this point, due to financial issues and other considerations, white-led."[51] In addition, over 1,000 accredited media representatives were present to cover the conference, which was preceded by a Youth Summit (August 26–27) and the NGO Forum (with 7,000 NGO representatives, August 28–September 1).

The goal of the intergovernmental conference was as ambitious as it was straightforward: to get governments to commit themselves to remedying and ultimately eliminating racism and related violations. The "significant push for the expansion" of the agenda beyond the previous two conferences (i.e. to include "xenophobia and related intolerance") had come from Europe "where groups lobbied to ensure that ethnic cleansing and Anti-Semitism made it to the mix. Groups working on Anti-Semitism united with those from Eastern Europe to form almost 80 percent of the region's World Conference preparatory meeting participants." Indeed, this broadening had precursors in 1993, when the UN Commission on Human Rights had appointed a Special Rapporteur on contemporary forms of racism, racial discrimination, xenophobia and related intolerance. Plus the Third Decade to Combat Racism and Racial Discrimination (1994–2003), which had been declared by the UN General Assembly on December 20, 1993 (A/RES/48/91) included a broadened view of racism. "By necessity, ethnic cleansing and genocide [had] come under special consideration, as well as the institutionalization of xenophobia, as some States implement measures against migrant workers."[52] It has also been argued that, in part at least, the term "xenophobia" was added because race is often thought of in black–white terms, yet many of those suffering marginalization and discrimination are not black or at least not considered black in all contexts, as race is socially constructed.[53]

The key issues on the conference's initial agenda included reparations, environmental racism, race and health, race and education, race and poverty, race and criminal justice, and migrants' rights. The preparatory process significantly broadened the scope to include discussions of hate speech, hate crimes, and hate sites on the Internet, and to include draft texts on globalization, indigenous issues, and the impact of multiple discriminations, especially for women. In the last regard, attention was drawn to the link between racial and social marginalization of the women and girls being trafficked (i.e. the issue was presented as not "simply" gendered as often characterized in the past). The USA, in particular, worked "hard to introduce principles in the declaration on a host of issues, including: treatment of immigrants and refugees; equal opportunity for people with disabilities; and programs that support civil society in combating racism, poverty and intolerance."[54] Its chief concerns, however, focused on language in the drafts relating to the Middle East that it deemed "inflammatory" and seemed to have the same intent as that in earlier conferences. In fact, President Bush made conditional US participation in the conference on the removal of language from the documents that unfairly singled out and criticized Israel.[55] The US delegation also expressed concern about other language that it believed had the effect of "diminishing the historically unique tragedy of the Holocaust in Europe." The other "hot button" issue for the US related to reparations. The US position was that it was willing to express its "regret of historical injustices, such as slavery and the slave trade" and it seemed willing to accept calls for recourse and remedies for "victims of contemporary racism."[56] The focus on "contemporary" was seen by some as a way to sidestep the reparations issue.

Serious problems emerged as early as the first PrepCom (in Geneva in May 2000). The committee invited the conference Secretary-General to draw up a draft declaration and Program of Action. These drafts proved so contentious that delegates spent five days debating whether they could even be used as a basis for negotiations. Second, the PrepCom ran into a kind of buzz saw as it tried to identify conference themes. The first big debate was on the reparations issue. The Western Europe and Others group, which included the USA, Canada, Australia, New Zealand and Japan, argued for using the objectives in the authorizing General Assembly resolution (52/111). The Africa group, supported by Latin America and the Caribbean, demanded that the conference go further, that an item be included covering national, regional, and international compensation measures. While compromised language was agreed to, the Western states remained worried that the conference might adopt a demand for redistribution of wealth away from those states "responsible" for past injuries and toward purported modern-day victims of the past.

Delegates at the PrepCom also agreed to convene four regional conferences, in Strasbourg, Santiago, Dakar and Tehran. In Santiago, the Canadians and Americans objected to the Report's treatment of reparations. The Dakar Programme of Action recommended the establishment of an "International Compensation Scheme" for victims of the slave trade and "any other transnational racist acts" as well as a "Development Reparation Fund" for countries affected by colonialism. But actually the most controversy came out of the Tehran meeting. According to the Tehran Declaration, war and racial policies of an occupying power had forced Palestinians to leave their homes and prevented them from returning. While potentially inflammatory, the language could also be seen as the basis for subsequent negotiations. But it remained unchanged throughout the Preparatory meetings. In this context, the USA chose to send a mid-level delegation (headed by Ambassador Michael Southwick, Deputy Assistant Secretary of State for International Organizations) to the conference in the hope that it could get the offensive language removed from the texts. German officials reportedly criticized the Bush administration's decision not to send the Secretary of State, but rather a lower-level delegation with much less muscle to negotiate.[57] While the US Congressional Black Caucus, members of which went to Durban, urged Powell to attend, the Anti-Defamation League (ADL) had urged him to stay away.[58] But, of course, no single decision or set of decisions can explain the problems besetting the Durban conferees. Some explain it by the failure of the White House to get views from civil society prior to the conference.[59] Others point the finger at Robinson, her lack of mediating and bureaucratic experience and thus her inability to resolve sensitive issues, seemingly one of the reasons later on that the USA didn't support her continuation as UN High Commissioner for Human Rights.[60]

But the context was more complicated and even more ominous. While the Youth Conference was successful, the NGO Forum had ended in discord, with several delegates walking out in disgust to the jeers of their colleagues. The final NGO document included offensive references to Israel and Jews; several prominent NGOs, including Amnesty International, Human Rights Watch and the Lawyers' Committee for Human Rights, disassociated themselves from the offensive language. The conference Secretary-General refused to present the document to the official conference. All of this had an unfortunate and unintentional side effect as the NGO Forum's Declaration and Program of Action had also contained strong and innovative language on other themes including the plight of the Roma.

At the conference itself, attention focused on the anti-Israeli language. After four days of intense efforts to reach an agreement to remove anti-Israeli language from the document, the US and Israeli delegations gave up. In spite of mediation using Norway as the mediator, no compromise with the Arab delegates, at least this early in the conference, proved possible. As a consequence, on September 3, both the US and Israel withdrew their delegations and ended their participation in the conference. Among the most dismayed by their departure were many in the NGO community and the host South Africans. Christopher Camponovo puts the US departure in perspective:

> It is difficult to gauge the effect of the departure of the United States from the Conference. The language eventually adopted regarding the Middle East would have been unacceptable to the United States and Israel [it amounted to two paragraphs: one paragraph in the Declaration and one in the Program of Action, focusing on the rights of the Palestinians to their own state], just as it was to Canada, which made a strong statement in opposition at the end of the Conference.[61] Some would argue that had the United States stayed in Durban and delayed its threats of departure, it would have been in a stronger position to negotiate acceptable language on this issue. The departure of the United States, on the other hand, provided something of a wake up call to hard-liners, as well as to the South African host, that a compromise

was necessary or they would risk Canada and the European Union walking out.[62]

Some claim that senior officials should have been deeply involved in the rewriting of sensitive language before the conference began, rather than after the US and Israeli walkout. The Europeans reportedly stayed on at the conference to help the South Africans salvage the meeting.[63]

The handling of the reparations issue proved creative especially given the fight by the USA against slavery being described as "a crime against humanity," fearing that that language might result in lawsuits by the slaves' descendants, and some European countries' objections to the notion that they should apologize for colonialism.[64] The conferees first affirmed that:

> victims of human rights violations resulting from racism, racial discrimination, xenophobia and related intolerance ... be assured of ... justice ... including the right to seek just and adequate reparation or satisfaction for any damage suffered as a result of such discrimination.

Then, rather than attempting to set up a reparation scheme for past injustices, the conferees compromised by expressing support for existing initiatives designed to promote African development.

One of the significant omissions from the final document related to the Dalit; indeed, there is no discussion of "caste-based discrimination," even though it was among the issues raised most pointedly in Durban, especially by NGOs from India. The Indian government was able to have the relevant paragraph (73) deleted from the draft Declaration, arguing that the traditional Hindu caste system, in which the Dalits are considered the untouchables, have been formally outlawed for years in India and that whatever continuing problems exist, there are internal matters.[65]

Migrants and refugees, on the other hand, were among the victim groups that fared relatively well in the language of the final Declaration and Program of Action. The Declaration states that "xenophobia against non-nations, particularly migrants, refugees and asylum-seekers, constitutes one of the main sources of contemporary racism." The final Declaration also contains a number of paragraphs relating to the rights of indigenous peoples and the particular discrimination they face.

Given what happened at the conference, the reactions of participants are hardly surprising. Putting the best face on it, the UN Secretary-General welcomed the final documents, but expressed disappointment over the disagreements. The US National Security Advisor, Condoleezza Rice, said it was too focused on the past and that debates about reparations would have been better avoided. The Canadian Foreign Minister, John Manley, said: "It hasn't been a good experience for the world community … It has not been a good experience for the United Nations and I hope we don't have to see this happen again."[66] While such judgments are certainly understandable and not without merit, they also seem a bit narrowly focused. As Marable reminds us, some of the immediate objectives of the conference and the mass mobilization behind it "were to strengthen networks involved in anti-racist activities, both in individual states and internationally, and to bring human rights activities in closer coordination with each other," for, as Marable suggests, the dismantling of racial inequality requires actions by civil society and not simply governments.[67]

Plus, of course, as Robinson stressed in her closing statement at the conference, Durban was to be a beginning and not an end (although it's hard to believe that the USA will be supportive of another anti-racism conference in the near term). In line with this sentiment and as is traditional in such global conference documents, the Program of Action included provisions for follow-up mechanisms. For example, it calls on governments to provide the Office of the High Commissioner for Human Rights with reports on national actions relating to implementing the Program of Action's recommendations. It also proposed that the UN Secretary-General appoint an expert body to follow up on implementation and called for the establishment of a comprehensive database containing information on practical means to address racism, racial discrimination and related intolerance (e.g. of anti-discrimination legislation). The Program of Action also notes that NGOs will be essential to the successful achievement of the conference's goals, in line with Marable's observations about the importance of civil society in coping with this particular issue.

Significantly, however, there was no formal accord on a +5 review conference.[68] However, an Intergovernmental Working Group on the Effective Implementation of the Durban Declaration and Program of Action was established by Commission on Human Rights Resolution 2002/68 and approved by the Economic and Social Council in its decision 2002/270. It held its first meeting in late January 2003; but it meets on an *annual* basis. However, even this should be seen as progress, especially in light of the fact that 9/11 happened almost as soon as the conference concluded and the globe's attention shifted dramatically, if not permanently, at least for an extended period of time.

International Conference on Financing for Development

On March 21, 2001, the UN General Assembly (Resolutions 55/245A and 55/245B) called for the convening of the International Conference on Financing for Development. Mexican President Vincente Fox served as the conference President as it was convened in Monterrey, Mexico. The six plenary sessions met March 18–22, 2002.

The Monterrey conference can be understood as building, at least in a procedural sense, on the Brussels Conference and as a vivid contrast to the ill-fated gathering in Durban. As was noted above, the Brussels Conference began with the UN Secretary-General praising the conferees for their careful preparatory work, a vivid contrast to Durban where some suggest that that conference's problems were exacerbated by a lack of preparatory work, including by and in the United States. The contrast couldn't be starker.

> The actual Monterrey Conference was more of a formal gathering, than a debate on the way to implement Financing for Development policies and goals. There was no debate because the United States wanted a consensus document finalized before the start of the Conference with no changes so they would know what exact elements were in it … Latin American countries also wanted to know what was in the Consensus Document to determine if they wanted to participate with the goals and policies in order to receive development aid.[69]

The ideological frame of the Monterrey Conference was quite similar to that in Brussels (i.e. neo-liberal economics). Accordingly, the so-called Monterrey Consensus document spoke of the need to increase the flow and broaden the reach of private international investment; to open access to the market and to ensure a fair and equitable trade regime; to accelerate the mobilization of economic resources within economically less developed countries, and to improve global and regional financial structures. There were also a number of longer-standing, very familiar topics included in the document, such as the need to increase official development assistance, to solve economically less developed countries' debt problems, and to promote fair representation of economically less developed countries in international decision-making (meaning at the international financial institutions, especially the World Bank and the IMF).

On the other hand, in vivid contrast to Durban (and Brussels), not simply was the USA an active author-participant prior to the conference, but US President Bush was its featured speaker. Interestingly, this is where the careful conference choreographing was a bit less evident. Before the conference, it was believed that there would be no firm commitments made on financial assistance for the economically less developed countries. But at the conference, both the United States and the EU confirmed increased financial assistance for development. This, of course, underscores one of the reasons why such conferences are convened and why world leaders are invited. Major world figures usually want to have something positive and newsworthy to say at such conferences; indeed that's why the appearance of President George H.W. Bush at Rio got so much negative publicity and indeed why some suggested that he and the USA would have been better off had he skipped that conference rather than make the sort of widely reported statement that he did there, and why there was massive disappointment that neither President Bush nor Secretary of State Powell showed up in Durban.

While President George W. Bush's statement at Monterrey was positively received including his announcement of "a new compact for development" which involved "new accountability for both rich and poor nations alike," what was less clear initially was the magnitude of the US commitment and whether in fact these were new funds that the US President was offering. Subsequently, the President made it clear that in fact they were additional funds and he would do everything he could to get the US Congress to appropriate the funds. His pledge was to increase US core assistance to developing countries by 50 percent over the following three years, resulting in a $5 billion increase over the then current levels of about $10 billion. These funds were to go to a new "Millennium Challenge Account" (MCA) aimed at countries that demonstrated a strong commitment to good governance (including rooting out corruption, upholding human rights and adherence to the rule of law), health and education, and sound economic policies that foster enterprise and entrepreneurship, including more open markets and sustainable budget priorities.

The EU, on the other hand, made it clear that it would work to get governments below the previously agreed - to figure of 0.7 percent of the GDP level in the form of ODA to increase the level of their contribution by roughly 15 percent. That actually would mean an increase from approximately 0.33 to 0.39 percent of GDP, well short of the long-standing commitment or what the economically less developed countries sought. That, however, may have been realistic, given that the terrorist attacks of 9/11 had led to slower than expected economic growth in the developed countries and that countries were having trouble fulfilling their MDGs.[70]

Prior to the Conference, NGOs gathered for a three-day Global Forum: Financing the Right to Sustainable and Equitable Development. The Forum was attended by 2,600 persons, representing 700 organizations. The participants crafted a set of common proposals for an "alternative economic model intended to place people at the centre of development." Not surprisingly—given the lack of debate in Monterrey and the Forum's focus on equitable development—NGO representatives were generally dissatisfied with the Monterrey Consensus document. Still they wanted to stay engaged with follow-up activities. Much of the NGO (and business) post-Monterrey participation has, in fact, been through ECOSOC.

Paragraph 72 of the "Monterrey Consensus" called on the UN Secretary-General to submit annual reports on the follow-up efforts to the conference, undertaken by the UN system and other major stakeholders. In addition to speaking hopefully of the increased promises of bilateral aid, especially from the USA—the first report was written before the magnitude of the Iraqi reconstruction effort was clear—the Secretary-General wrote of the intentions of the World Bank and the IMF to scale up and increase their efforts, including catalytic promotion of policy, governance and institutional reforms; leveraging and enhancing the effectiveness of all aid resources; and by supporting market opening and capacity building. The report also took note of UNCTAD's efforts in terms of multilateral assistance in the area of commodities, always a high priority area.[71]

Second World Assembly on Ageing

Unfortunately for any observer of UN global conferences, or for that matter any reader of this book, the events at the Second World Assembly on Ageing, convened in Madrid April 8–12, 2002, were predictable or at least familiar. While the topic was an urgent one, attendance was large, thoughtful documents with clearly articulated recommendations were produced, and a well-attended NGO Forum on Ageing was convened (April 5–9, 2002), conferees framed the issue in terms of the need for further development and development assistance, politicization occurred but specific financial commitments were not forthcoming.

The primary purpose of the Second World Assembly, as noted in the UN General Assembly resolution (A/RES/54/262, dated June 16, 2000) that called for it, was to sustain the momentum of the International Year of Older Persons (1999) by addressing the "challenges of ageing and the concerns and contributions of ageing and older persons." More specifically, the Assembly sought to assess progress made on the Vienna Program of Action from twenty years earlier and to seek action on "three priority directions: older persons and development; advancing health and well-being into older age; and ensuring enabling and supportive environments."[72] The need to address these "priority directions" was clear to all 160 national delegations. By 2050 the number of persons aged 60 years or over was expected to increase from 600 million to almost two billion and the proportion of persons aged 60 years or older was expected to double from 10 to 21 percent. Moreover, the increase was expected to be greatest and most rapid in economically less developed countries where the older population was expected to quadruple by 2050.[73] In this context, Article 7 of the Assembly's Political Declaration stated:

> Unless the benefits of social and economic development are extended to all countries, a growing number of people, particularly older persons in all countries and even entire regions, will remain marginalized from the global economy. For this reason, we recognize the importance of placing ageing in development agendas.[74]

Interestingly, Article 14 of the same Declaration committed Assembly delegations "to providing older persons with universal and equal access to health care and services, including physical and mental health services."[75]

The central themes running throughout the International Plan of Action on Ageing 2002 included: (1) the full realization of all human rights and fundamental freedoms of all older persons; (2) the achievement of secure aging; (3) empowerment of older people to be full participants in society, "including through income-generating and voluntary work"; (4) provision of opportunities for individual development and self-fulfillment; (5) ensuring all human rights, including elimination of discrimination against older people; (6) commitment to genuine equality among older people; (7) recognition of the importance of families and intergenerational interdependence; (8) provision of health care; (9) facilitating partnerships amongst all agents of governance to effectuate the Plan of Action; (10) harnessing scientific research on the social and health implications of aging "in particular in developing countries;" and (11) recognizing the special circumstances of aging indigenous persons.[76] While the Plan of Action was agreed to unanimously, this was only after "four days of heated debate" in which wealthier countries resisted the demands of economically less developed countries and NGOs to establish a special agency to effectuate the plan. Moreover, while referring to the often repeated demand for an increase in ODA, the Plan contained no specific financial commitments by the wealthier delegations.[77]

One of the areas emphasized at the NGO Forum that was less central to the government delegates was the consequence of HIV/AIDS for older persons. The HIV/AIDS pandemic, especially in Africa and Asia, has meant that there are new responsibilities for older people "at a point in life when health and income are both in decline."[78]

One news reporter's comment on the summit's politicization summarizes the situation well: "It may be getting old, but Israel-bashing at UN meetings doesn't let up even when the topic is as innocuous as aging." With the US and Israeli walkout in Durban clearly in everyone's memory, the Israeli delegation issued a plea that the summit not "be hijacked by those with a narrow and hostile political agenda." Both sides of the "debate" recounted instances of deaths of older people in the ongoing Israeli–Palestinian conflict. In the end, the Plan of Action contained no explicit mention of Israel and Arab delegates agreed to drop one of the three references to "foreign occupation."[79]

Putting the best face possible on the Summit, Nitin Desai, the UN Under-Secretary-General for Economic and Social Affairs, declared that the summit was aimed at raising awareness of the issue of aging and "Now pressure groups will have a much stronger voice to ensure governments stick to these commitments."[80]

World Summit on Sustainable Development (WSSD)

Pursuant to UN General Assembly Resolution 55/99 (dated December 20, 2000), entitled "Ten-Year Review of Progress Achieved in the Implementation of the Outcome of the United Nations Conference on Environment and Development," the World Summit on Sustainable Development (WSSD) was convened in Johannesburg August 26–September 4, 2002. Nitin Desai, the UN Under-Secretary-General for Economic and Social Affairs served as the summit's Secretary-General.

It was one of the most eagerly anticipated of the UN global conferences. That may have been its problem: too high expectations to possibly fulfill, especially given that when the UN General Assembly authorized the WSSD it was indisputable that progress in achieving sustainable development in the post-1992 Rio conference era had been extremely disappointing (what some had termed a "crisis of implementation"). Poverty was deepening and environmental degradation was worsening. OECD bilateral and multilateral aid levels were at an all-time low as a percentage of GDP. The GEF remained "at best a designer niche in the development business."[81]

In this context, what the General Assembly wanted was a summit of action and results. The summit mantra was specific commitments, targets and timetables.[82] To help achieve this and as a part of two years of intensive preparatory work for the conference, regional meetings were convened in Geneva, Nairobi, Rio, Cairo and Phnom Penh and there were also four PrepComs, with the tenth session of the CSD serving as the first. Moreover, UN Secretary-General Kofi Annan suggested a ten-point plan for *action* (see Box 6.4).

Also to provide the summit with focus and an impetus to action, the Secretary-General provided five thematic areas for which papers were commissioned. The five themes of the so-called WEHAB initiative were: water, energy, health, agriculture and biodiversity (and ecosystem management).

Approximately 22,000 people attended the Johannesburg summit, including eighty-two heads of state or government (neither the Russian President nor US President George W. Bush attended; the US delegation was headed by US Secretary of State Colin Powell), thirty vice-presidents and deputy prime ministers (for the "high-level segment" of finalizing negotiations over the Plan of Implementation), seventy-four ministers, royalty and other senior officials. Some 8,000 representatives of major organizations (NGOs, businesses, trade unions, etc.) and 4,000 media representatives were accredited to the summit. In addition a large number of NGOs and other civil society representatives were in Johannesburg to attend

[the] literally hundreds of side events and parallel events [including the Civil Society Global Forum, the Business Action for Sustainable Development Forum, the Local Government Session, the Ubuntu Village and Exhibit, the Indigenous Peoples' Summit, the Youth Summit, the EnviroLaw 2002 Conference, the Stakeholder Forum Implementation Conference, the Trade Union Summit, the Water Dome, the World Conservation Union Environment Center, the Forum on Science, Technology and Innovation for Sustainable Development, Global Exchange, Center for Environmental Health, and Rainforest Action Network], some officially sanctioned and others surreptitiously organised, some intended to support the U.N. process and others to challenge it. Attendance was not consistently high at these events and the mood there seemed much more subdued than in Rio. All of them, however, in one way or another occurred

Box 6.4 Secretary-General Annan's ten-point plan for action for sustainable development

1 Make globalization work for sustainable development. Because benefits of globalization have been distributed unevenly and the world's poorest countries have been left behind, there is a need to eliminate trade-distorting subsidies and to improve access for products and services from developing countries to the markets of developed countries, particularly in areas such as agriculture and textiles.

2 Eradicate poverty and improve livelihoods in rural and urban areas. Large numbers of very poor people live in areas facing severe ecological stress. Thus, efforts to improve conditions and opportunities for the poor, such as through land tenure, sustainable livelihoods, credit, education, agricultural improvements, and efforts to minimize waste and encourage recycling are called for.

3 Change unsustainable patterns of production and consumption, including by increasing energy efficiency four-fold over the next two to three decades, enhancing corporate responsibility, and providing incentives for cleaner production.

4 Improve health through safe and affordable access to fresh water and a reduction in lead in gasoline and improved indoor air quality.

5 Provide access to energy and improve energy efficiency by developing and using more renewable and energy-efficient technologies and changing unsustainable energy consumption patterns.

6 Manage ecosystems and biodiversity on a sustainable basis, addressing the problems of over-fishing, unsustainable forestry practices and land-based marine pollution.

7 Improve freshwater supply management and arrange more equitable distribution of water resources.

8 Provide financial resources, through increases in official development assistance and private investment, and by the transfer and sharing of environmentally sound technologies.

9 Support sustainable development in Africa through new and extensive programs that can address hunger, health and environmental protection and resource management.

10 Strengthen international governance for sustainable develop-
    ment to promote an integrated, global approach, rather than
    a compartmentalized approach.[1]

Note

1 United Nations, General Assembly, Fifty-Sixth Session,
   Agenda Item 98 (a), Environmental and Sustainable
   Development: Implementation of Agenda 21 and the
   Programme for the Further Implementation of Agenda 21,
   *Progress in Preparatory Activities for the World Summit on
   Sustainable Development, Report of the Secretary-General*,
   A/56/379 (September 19, 2001).

because of the Summit; therefore, their outcomes could also be
attributed to the U.N. process.

This further complicated any assessment of the impact of the
summit.[83]

Most notable of the side and parallel events was the Global People's
Forum. The Forum, which was located at the Johannesburg Expo
Centre, about a 30-minute drive from the official conference venue,
concluded with the adoption of a Global People's Forum Civil Society
Declaration entitled "A Sustainable World is Possible." Its emphasis
was on the equality of all humans; it also called for rich countries to
reduce their "excessive" consumption of the world's resources, legally
binding regulations for multinational corporations, ratification of the
Kyoto Protocol and the phasing out of the fossil fuel industry. Forum
participations also passed a program of action that was mostly
addressed to governments.

Meeting for ten days—including the plenary sessions where there
was little interaction between the governmental participants, but rather
a series of short speeches, including frequent calls on the USA to do
more in the area of sustainable development including supporting the
Kyoto Protocol—resulted in three major outcomes. The first was the
Johannesburg Plan of Implementation. This accord, negotiated among
governments, reaffirms a wide range of commitments and targets
(including those in Agenda 21 and the Millennium Development

Goals and some that went beyond the MDGs) in working toward achieving sustainable development (i.e. it went well beyond the narrower environmental focus of Rio and Stockholm). It includes an agreement to a significant reduction in the rate of loss of biological diversity by 2010; this was actually weaker language than contained in the CBD that makes *no* allowance for further loss. On the other hand, it expanded upon Agenda 21 in the areas of energy, sanitation (where it also went beyond the MDG), corporate responsibility and account-ability. Further, it called for the establishment of a *voluntary* "world solidarity fund" to eliminate poverty and promote social and human development in economically less developed countries. It also included a call for steps to improve access to environmentally sound energy services and resources and to increase the use of "renewables, cleaner liquid and gaseous fuels and enhanced energy efficiency," all phenomena earlier anathema to oil-exporting countries. The Plan also calls for the WTO's Agreement on Trade-Related Aspects of Intellectual Property (TRIPS) to "be interpreted and implemented in a manner supportive of WTO members' right to protect public health and in particular to promote access to medicines for all," language hardly soothing to the ears of major pharmaceutical companies. It set target dates relating to over-fishing (e.g. by 2015 for maintaining or restoring stocks to levels that can produce maximum sustainable yield; by 2005 developing and implementing national and, where appro-priate, regional plans of action for the management of fishing capacity). It acceded to the US demand that the word "fully" not be included in the call for implementation of the Third Law of the Sea Treaty. Moreover, the Plan called upon the General Assembly to convene a global conference on the Sustainable Development of Small Island States and to apply a precautionary "approach" to preventing environmental damage rather than the more contentious (and clearer) precautionary "principle," which some believed (and feared) was gaining currency as binding customary international law.

Comprehensive as the Plan sounds, it disappointed some, including the World Fund for Nature, which pointed fingers at the USA, with the help of Canada and Australia among others, for not including a comprehensive timetable for implementation.[84] The Plan's section on implementation opens with the assertion that achievement of the goals will require a "substantially increased effort." It also restates the contentious concept of "common but differentiated responsibilities," which includes the responsibility of developed countries "in view of the pressures their societies place on the global environment and of the technologies and financial resources they command."

The Johannesburg Declaration on Sustainable Development was the second major document coming out of the conference. It lists numerous threats to sustainable development, including chronic hunger; malnutrition; foreign occupation; armed conflicts; illicit drug use; organized crime; corruption; natural disasters; illicit arms trafficking; trafficking in persons; racism and xenophobia; communicable and chronic diseases, especially HIV/AIDS, malaria and tuberculosis. The Declaration includes an agreement by heads of state and government to "assume a collective responsibility to advance and strengthen the interdependent and mutually reinforcing pillars of sustainable development—economic development, social development and environmental protection—at local, national, regional and global levels." The Declaration was described by some as lacking any innovations because of the contentious drafting process that had ensued.[85]

The third major outcome was the "Type 2" partnerships and initiatives, clearly the most innovative procedural outcome of the summit. The purpose of these partnerships was to implement Agenda 21 by tying together different stakeholders, including governments, intergovernmental organizations, civil society and businesses, that is, a kind of "new multilateralism" as contrasted to "old" solely intergovernmental multilateralism. These are meant to supplement so-called "Type 1" outcomes, the intergovernmentally negotiated commitments. The summit Secretary-General spoke of civil society organizations being more than just advocacy groups trying to influence governments, but rather as genuine "partners" in the implementation of Agenda 21 and other initiatives.[86]

Over 220 "Type 2" partnerships were identified leading up to the summit and sixty were announced at the summit itself. By the time the summit came, however, so much emphasis had been placed on the partnerships that "some major groups, NGOs, women, and indigenous people in particular, cautioned against this development as a potential distraction from the central role of governments and the increased power and influence they felt that this approach might accord to corporations and the private sector". The summit Secretary-General stated that the Type 2 partnerships were not intended to be a substitute for strong commitments between governments. Some UN member states also "expressed concern about the meaning and implications of this radically new departure in conducting UN business."[87] But, as the most careful study of the Type 2 partnerships has evidenced, they have not turned out to be much of a radical departure. Of those that actually have been operative, post-Johannesburg, most are dominated by rich countries, intergovernmental organizations or large Northern-based NGOs[88] The reason that the *limited* success of the Type 2 partnerships is so important is that so much hope was placed in them. This summary judgment on the summit is exemplary:

> The Summit succeeded in achieving some of its goals, such as setting a time-bound sanitation target [i.e. halving the proportion of people unable to reach or afford safe drinking water or without access to basic sanitation by 2015] and recognizing the rights of communities in natural resource management [including the reaffirmation of the vital role of indigenous peoples in sustainable development]. Yet it also had its share of failures, including the failure to address climate change and to reform global environmental governance. Finally, and perhaps most significantly, the extent and diversity of civil society engagement in the process set forth the challenge of overcoming divisions among governments, within civil society, and between governments and civil society to find a path to common solutions.[89]

One of the other unique aspects of the Plan of Action relates to ethics. In the plan, governments emphasized the need to consider ethics in the implementation of Agenda 21; this has been described as the first time that an explicit reference to ethics was made in any official UN environment or development document.[90]

Much of the criticism of the WSSD seems to have been due to the unrealistic expectations that some had for it. It was never really intended to develop new conventions or to renegotiate Agenda 21. Indeed some think the UN would have been better off having referred to it as Rio+10. Some of its problems, however, appear to have been due to a run-up process that lagged behind schedule, with the UN secretariat unable to muster support for its draft documents and government delegations dragging their feet.[91]

More specifically, "[t]he failure of governments to adopt and agree on effective means for implementation (including financing issues) and institutional mechanisms, make it likely that the successes of the summit could be rendered meaningless."[92] While it is too early to see whether that pessimism will ultimately prove justified, it should be noted that the first session of the CSD, held in New York, April 28–May 9, 2003, agreed to establish a work program for the implementation of the Johannesburg Plan and Agenda 21. "By many accounts," the CSD lived up to its tasks by creating a "New CSD" and maintaining the momentum of the Johannesburg Summit.[93] On the other hand, there was less evidence of the CSD putting multi-stakeholder partnerships high on its post-summit priorities.

As expected, the pace of UN world conferences has slowed in the first decade of the twenty-first century. Of course, the reasons for the alteration in the pace could only be partly anticipated at the outset of the century: no one had anticipated the war on terrorism that came to consume the world's only remaining superpower and few expected that superpower to be engaged in an extended war in Iraq. But, as suggested at the outset of the chapter, the UN Secretary-General knew that he would have to be extraordinarily creative if there were any hope for conferences and summits to engage the world's rich with the problems of the poor. And even though the demonstrable impacts of the summits and conferences seem limited or a long time in coming, we should not be too dismissive too quickly. Even if the outcomes were less than their conveners had hoped them to be, critical topics were addressed, including a return to issues of racism, aging, the plight of the poorest and sustainable development. Moreover, for the first time, a UN world conference was convened specifically to address a pressing military security issue. There, as at other recent conferences, the USA dominated and the ability to resist US wishes as minimal (e.g. by scheduling a follow-up conference). But there also, as at other recent conferences, the issues need to be addressed: the world's attention needs to refocus on these pressing global problems until significant progress, with the money to make it, is forthcoming. Indeed, in some ways the anti-racism conference evidences both the importance of global conferences and its limitations. This was a conference on a problem that affects people throughout the globe and for which there are no effective UN bodies to cope. Yet, as seen in the past, conferees found it impossible to make much headway, even when all interested parties actually showed up to negotiate. The problems were familiar: politicization, weak secretariat leadership including ineffective coordination between civil society and government delegations, and hegemonic opposition to key items on the conference agenda. And, of course, any serious follow-up to the conference was deflected by 9/11 and its consequences.

7 Conclusion

UN global conferences mirroring the evolving world order

As noted at the outset of the book, attributing particular outcomes to UN global conferencing, much less particular UN global conferences, is very tough. As Michael Zammit-Cutajar, who attended many of the conferences suggested and as this volume's various accounts evidence, their "utility is very uneven."[1] Still, Juan Somavia, the Chilean Ambassador to the UN who chaired the PrepComs for the World Summit for Social Development had a point when he argued that such conferences have made a difference in the world whether one agrees or not with his bold assertion that "they are the only common response of the world community to a disorderly process of globalization that runs the risk of spinning out of control."[2]

When the first world conference on the environment was convened in Stockholm in 1972, concern for the Earth was still a peripheral issue in most political and economic circles. While the globe's ecological threats are perhaps even greater now than they were in the 1970s, most agree that they would be even worse than they are had there been no UN global conferences. Even less controversial is the assertion that it is inconceivable now for any major development project to be initiated without someone arguing that consideration has to be given to the ecological impact. The so-called greening of the World Bank, partly a consequence of the conferences discussed above, is emblematic of this. Similarly, when the first World Conference on Women was held in Mexico City in 1975, gender issues were of little significance in political decision-making, much less considered appropriate topics for discussion by global institutions. Now, no serious discussion of social policies can avoid taking account of gender issues[3] and such issues are raised at practically all UN conferences, including those dealing with the environment, human settlements, armed conflict and human rights. The World Bank regularly requires studies of the impacts of its projects on women (as well as on the environment and indigenous peoples) and the

UN itself has worked hard to increase the number of women in higher administrative and visible positions. This, of course, is not meant to suggest that the conferences have been an unqualified success in terms of sexual, much less gender equality. Hilary Charlesworth's contention clearly has some justification: "The summits [and conferences; her article refers to both] have certainly produced benefits for women, but they have also allowed grand rhetoric to disguise global and local problems. They have not challenged gendered forms of power and knowledge."[4] Such a contention, of course, resonates with critics of other conferences, including the environmental ones and those directed to helping the economically least developed countries, for being longer on rhetoric than on action. Charlesworth, of course, also underscores another of the criticisms noted at the outset of this volume, namely that many of the conferences fail to deal with the fundamental sources of problems, including, in this instance global patriarchy, but more generally the global economic system. But as this most comprehensive-to-date review of UN conferences evidences, one needs to be a bit wary of generalizations like that. Over time, discussions of root causes of major problems have begun to be discussed at UN global conferences, even including global patriarchy, consumption patterns and energy use in rich countries, and the problems of corruption plaguing the least developed countries. And with the airing of such topics come an answer to another of the criticisms recounted at the outset of this volume, namely that the conferees equivocate and conferences are a way to avoid radical solutions. Such critical generalizations are less defensible after one has viewed the evolution of the conferences over time.

Emmerij *et al.* raise a related, but perhaps even tougher issue, namely whether the UN conferences were "ahead of the curve"—in formulating and nurturing ideas and political will. But even with this standard, they and the cases in this book suggest that there is some good news. For example, UN conferences have seemingly helped in the continual redefinition of the contents of development and human rights, including the assertion at numerous conferences of development as a human right and the contentious notion of reproductive health, something not spoken of at the first intergovernmental population conference, but often thereafter. Emmerij *et al.* also contend that "conferences are one of the main devices—some would say 'gimmicks'—that are used to spawn, nurture, and massage new ideas as well as to nudge governments, international secretariats, and international civil service to alter their conceptions and policies."[5] The discussion of the redefinition of desertification and the role that the

UN conferences played in that is an interesting case in point. Of course, what many of the conferences discussed in this volume show is that merely the agreement to convene a conference begins the "nudging" process, as governments and intergovernmental organizations have to gather data and develop policy documents and statements. This has proven true even at the most controversial of conferences, namely those addressing issues of racism. But, of course, the follow-up accords to the Millennium Summit are the best example of how conferees can nudge governments and intergovernmental organizations. Monitoring is essential.

Emmerij *et al.* conclude that "UN world conferences have been one means through which ideas are translated into action."[6] Of course, Rio's publicizing of sustainable development is only the most frequently cited example of this. But this volume abounds with similar examples, including the Beijing conference's promulgation of rape as a war crime and domestic abuse as a legitimate issue for international "legislation," the value of subsidiarity in dealing with problems of urbanization as stressed in Istanbul, and women's reproductive rights perhaps articulated most clearly in Vienna. Less successful from the perspective of its advocates, but of a similar vein, was the Durban conference's discussions of reparations and multiple conferences' focus on the rights of the Palestinian people.

Indeed one of the reasons why it is so difficult to assess the specific substantive impacts of UN global conferences (e.g. how much credit does the Beijing conference get for its efforts in the area of rape as a war crime, something formally applied by the International Criminal Tribunal for the former Yugoslavia and the International Criminal Tribunal for Rwanda) is because one of their major outcomes has been institution building. This takes the form of direct institution building (such as the agreement to set up IFAD, UNEP, the WFC, UNIFEM, INSTRAW, the High Commissioner for Human Rights or the CSD) or, even more often, by indirectly contributing to the building of civil society organizations, including NGOs, but also transnational elite networks as have evolved after each of the women's conferences and links to local governments and businesses after Habitat II and Johannesburg. All of these institutions, networks and linkages, in turn, have helped contribute to meeting the conferences' goals, whether it is in terms of seeking equal pay for equal work for women, cleaning up the Mediterranean Sea, or improved agricultural productivity and decreased economic stratification by providing the sort of loans to small farmers that the World Bank failed to do owing to "economies of scale." But how much credit for those achievements belongs to the conferences, much less any particular women's or environmental conference, and how much to UNIFEM, DAWN, UNEP or IFAD is less clear and perhaps impossible to know. Thus, while it is clear that "Global, ad hoc conferences have opened the door to a growing pluralization of international dialogue and institutionalized participation by NGOs, whereas previously it has been circumscribed,"[7] it is less clear how much credit for what has been achieved in various issue-areas is a consequence of the conferences *per se* or the growing pluralization they spawned. These spawned institutions do not simply provide the world with monitoring and advocacy groups (at all levels of governance and especially in the human rights field as evidenced by the rise of Amnesty International beginning with the 1968 Vienna Conference) but also with much-needed legitimacy and, as noted with the women's movement, help empower them.

While it is tough to quantify the impact of UN global conferences in general or even singly, this book has provided some insights into the factors that must be considered in such assessments. It has, for example, argued consistently as to the necessity to contextualize UN global conferences. Their success or failure is as much a consequence of structural conditions as anything specific to any one conference or another. The importance of the Cold War, the rise and fall of détente, the ending of the Cold War and the implosion of the Soviet Union, the ending of colonialism, the rise and decline of the G-77 as a unified actor in world politics, global prosperity, recession, the war on terrorism and especially 9/11, the global spread of ideas of neo-liberal economics, the timing of conferences relative to drought cycles, or the rise or fall of conservative or liberal administrations in major and superpower states cannot be overestimated in explaining conference success or failure.

How much different conferences were when Ronald Reagan was President than under his predecessor or successor. But, of course, the differences are not simply the ideological predilections of the leader of the global hegemon, they are also significantly affected by the economic situations in the wealthiest countries in the world, as the follow-up or lack thereof to the Monterrey Consensus and to the third Conference on the Least Developed Countries attests. As the cases in this volume suggest, ideological predilections often affect tone more than substance. And substance, particularly whether the funds necessary to effectuate the programs of action are forthcoming, turns as much on the global financial situation as anything else.

While conferences continued to be plagued by politicization in the post-Cold War, post-apartheid era, the atmospherics improved when time was not consumed by bickering between US and Soviet or Soviet and Chinese delegates, and the former colonial powers with representatives from former colonies. How much more productive would the conferences have been if either the Arab–Israeli conflict were not repeatedly placed on the agenda or, much better yet, were that conflict resolved? While the lack of significant progress at the racism conferences is only partly a consequence of the Arab–Israeli conflict, it surely worsened the atmosphere and diverted attention from the really hard and important issues that had been the reason for convening these conferences in the first place. Perhaps, as with the women's conferences, over time, progress will be made. What, of course, the women's conferences suggest is that progress is possible, but only if transnational advocacy networks are plentiful, strong and global. That, of course, is the point that Marable has tried to stress regarding the Durban conference.

What this book also suggests is that there are a number of lessons that have been learned from the dozens of conferences over the past several decades that, if applied, can enhance conference success and impact. Some of these are obvious and some less so. For example, it seems clear that holding conferences during election years in the USA is not a good idea. Pacing of conferences also seems to be an important consideration. It is not simply analysts who write of conference fatigue; it's a phenomenon commented upon by conference participants as well. In this context, however, it is probably worth remembering that Boutros-Ghali thought of conferences as being a way to break out of donor and other government and public opinion fatigue, including fatigue over the entire development effort.[8]

Conference success also seems to be affected by the quality of conference leadership (Stockholm versus Durban) as well as the venue in which the conference has been convened. What is important in terms of the latter is not simply whether the host is able to provide adequate funds and administrative support, but whether the environment is one that is likely to improve conference atmospherics (Johannesburg) or detract from them (Beijing). At a much more mundane level, the venue can significantly affect the degree and spontaneity of interaction between government and civil society attendees, demonstrated probably as much at Vancouver as anywhere else. It is also clear that while even specific financial commitments made to implement programs of action are often not realized (e.g. Rio), conferences concluding with vague or no financial commitments at all are likely to have even more limited long-term impacts (e.g. Least Developed Country conferences).

A little less obviously, it appears that too much emphasis has historically been placed on whether or not a conference results in new binding treaty commitments. While using that as a standard of conference success or failure surely makes it easy to pass judgment on conferences, it overlooks the evolution of norms and other "soft law" which can, at times and over time, have as binding an effect as so-called "treaty law" or become binding in the form of customary international law.[9] The Stockholm principles are probably most exemplary in this regard, but so are the evolving norms coming out of the small arms conference. "Soft law" has the added advantage of being easier to "negotiate" (i.e., articulate), especially important given the relatively short time from agreement on convening a conference until its conclusion, much less the very short time available for negotiations at the conference itself. Further, as the small arms and Beijing conferences attest to, "norm entrepreneurs" can be governments, intergovernmental organizations or NGOs.

Another consistent theme (and important factor in explaining how such conferences are perceived and thus the support they get or do not receive) relates to media coverage of the UN conferences. Not surprisingly, the coverage, especially in for-profit media, focuses on conflicts at the conferences rather than where consensus is reached. Since the most frequent and public conflicts are often in areas unrelated to or peripheral to the central theme of the conferences, the attentive and general publics in various countries learn little about the substance of the declarations, programs of action and much more about reservations, resolutions, boycotts and walkouts. They learned much more criticism of Israeli and US politics than about the demands of the G-77 or divisions within the EU. More was learned about the occupied territories than about over-fishing. More importantly perhaps, the media-savvy public learned much more about political backroom maneuverings than about the global challenges that led to the conferences being convened in the first place. While it is possible to explain these phenomena in terms of how the media gathers information for stories (i.e. limited numbers of foreign reporters, with limited foreign language skills and a tradition of turning to government sources for information rather than seeing "grass roots" organizations as equally legitimate or important), the role that the profit motive plays in what is presented (i.e. the need to emphasize the dramatic) and the role that ideology (dominant, elite and journalistic or occupational) plays in influencing how the stories are framed are also important.[10] While the media has been vital to the conferences' success at consciousness-raising, their potential for doing this has been lessened by their obvious focus on conferences' politicization rather than their reason for being. As the Habitat II conference suggests, there are things that conference secretariats can do to try and counteract this phenomenon.

The idea of holding sessions to encourage media coverage of the conference's substance is only one example among many of the institutional innovations that characterize UN global conferences. While the book began noting that a fairly common formula has been worked out for the convening, negotiating aspects and reporting on conferences, what the remaining chapters have recounted is the sort of experimentation which only *ad hoc* institutions, such as the conferences, are likely to try. Most of these experiments, of course, were a bit rough when they were first used. But, over time, they have the potential to add dramatically to the success of conferences in achieving their goals. At Vancouver, audio-visual presentations by governments were experimented with. The impact on those producing them, much less their dissemination, warrants empirical investigation. The same can be said for the global tribunals at Vienna, the conference commitments first tried in Beijing, NGOs' efforts at treaty-making in Rio, target-setting at Copenhagen, the 20/20 initiatives in Cairo, the involvement of local government officials in Istanbul and the Type 2 partnerships in Johannesburg.

And to continue a point alluded to earlier, while it is probably true that the earliest conferences rarely exposed "the root causes" of the problems on which they focused and thus many of the initiatives they proffered only offered "superficial or temporary relief,"[11] this seems less the case as we moved toward and into the twenty-first century. Conferees are no longer reluctant to speak out against market failures, the costs of the affluent living styles in the North or the human preoccupation with the present, oftentimes at the expense of future generations. Even in the ill-fated conference in Durban, there was a fairly open discussion of the fact that all contemporary societies are afflicted by racism and xenophobia and the challenges of anthropocentrism are widely discussed and not simply at women's conferences.[12] Such discussions, of course, underscore that the conferences are not only on topics preferred by the wealthy and powerful, as some earlier contended.

More controversial is a tentative conclusion that the broadening of conference agenda (from the 1970s to the 1990s and into the twenty-first century) has costs. While it is clear intellectually that issues such as those raised at the conferences in Cairo and Johannesburg are all interconnected, that more holistic conferences address the critics who claim that the conferences are duplicative, overlapping and a waste of a scarce human resources, and it is true that the cross-sectoral agendas were among the most intellectually significant consequences of such conferences (e.g., the need to integrate environmental consideration in all aspects of economic decision-making, the linking of population, food production and distribution and development and the necessity to include gender in just about every aspect of human activity), it is also true that such broad agendas make it difficult to reach consensus on specific agenda items. Moreover, there seems to be some evidence that the failure of some governments to fulfill the commitments in their part of cross-sectoral deals may be contributing to making other governments less forthcoming in proceeding with cross-sectoral discussions (e.g. developing countries' reluctance to engage in such discussions has been attributed to the perceived failure of developed countries to live up to their commitments in terms of financial aid, transfer of technology and debt rescheduling).[13] Perhaps the scope of such conferences needs to be narrowed to something that is "feasible" to make them more worthwhile.[14] Of course, as the Durban conference suggests, that in and of itself does not insure a successful conference. And, of course, as the Durban conference also evidences, there are often obvious topics that are not dealt with at UN conferences, often for "political" reasons, whether one is talking about the Dalit or the transfer of small arms to non-state actors.

There is also some contestation over the progression toward ever more specific target setting and bench-marking as contrasted to simply setting goals and making commitments, oftentimes left to NGOs to monitor. The challenge is that such targets need to be measurable—something taken quite seriously in terms of the MDGs—realistic and with a clear and meaningful commitment to monitor and follow up, something clearly exemplified by the Millennium Project, but also by the World Summit for Children. But there are other examples throughout this book of targets that were unrealistic when set and not even close to having been met. The worst culprit, of course, is the 0.7 percent ODA goal, and the growth targets at the conferences relating to the least developed countries. Setting targets and not meeting them results in them becoming symbolic rather than substantive. But it also has the tendency to undermine the legitimacy of the entire undertaking, in this instance not simply an individual global conference, but in some people's minds, UN conferences in general.

While one of the differences between the conferences in the 1970s and those in the post-Cold War era is that the latter were more likely to be attended by heads of state and government (i.e. summits and not just conferences), it is less clear whether this change has increased the effectiveness of such conferences. The advantage of having heads of state and government is that they have the capacity to make commitments that "mere ministers" cannot, that governments are likely to prepare well for them and do follow-up work, and that the media will focus on their statements and commitments. But there is no clear evidence that they have done that consistently (at the Millennium Summit, the UN Secretary-General *was* able to garner signatures to some of his priority treaties and protocols and a similar phenomenon was experienced with the convention on the rights of the child at the World Summit for Children), but heads of state also have the capacity to be "vetoers" (as with George H.W. Bush at Rio) and to dominate the press negatively, sometimes by merely not showing up (as with George Bush and Vladimir Putin at Johannesburg).

What this underscores is the key theme of this volume, one rarely attended to in works on global conferences. While the purpose of global conferences may be to shape the world order in particular directions, their ability to do so is significantly affected by institutional characteristics (including who attends the conference, where it is held, its timing, the quality of preparatory work, the quality of conference leadership, the existence of norm entrepreneurs promulgating or publicizing new ideas, etc.) but also by the world order in which they are operating, including the distribution of material and ideational power.

Indeed, one of the most important lessons of this volume—in addition to the need to be wary of generalizations based on one or two conferences, as is true of most of those cited in the book's first chapter—is that the fate of UN conferences is largely a consequence of the fact that they mirror the world order better than do most other institutions. That is a consequence of their *ad hoc* and thus porous nature. Not simply are they better able to experiment with new institutional arrangements than are fixed bureaucracies but they better reflect changes in the world order, including the rise of civil society (both forces favoring change and those resisting it), ideational trends (the rise and fall of the redistributive politics of the NIEO and the global spread of neo-liberal economic theories of development), changes in the global distribution of power (most notably the collapse of bi-polarity and the rise of a global hegemon), and conflicts within that order (including those in the Middle East). UN conferences are a better mirror of the world order than a UN Security Council dominated by the victors of WWII or the statist, one-country-one-vote UN General Assembly. Thus, while it is possible and desirable to identify the factors that will facilitate success in the future, as it has been to identify those from the past (effective transnational advocacy networks, politically savvy and respected conference Secretaries-General, sympathetic and comprehensive media coverage, meeting in the right venues at the right times in the business and electoral cycles, effective communication between parallel civil society meetings and the official ones, timely and informative NGO daily newspapers, creative norm entrepreneurs, etc.), it is foolhardy to think that conferences can succeed when they make demands at odds with the global distribution of ideational and material power. This observation is not meant to be a call for an end to global conferences. On the contrary: global issues like transnational migration, over-fishing, the scarcity of water and the pervasiveness of racism and xenophobia call out for global consciousness-raising and the sort of detailed study and national administrative expansion that have accompanied almost all global conferences in the past. But what it does suggest is that assessments of the success or failure of such conferences cannot be divorced from recognition of the structural parameters within which they operate.

Appendix I

Number of governments represented and chief officers at UN global conferences

Name of conference	Year	Governments represented	Principal officers
International Conference on Human Rights	1968	84	Ashraf Pahlavi (Iran)—President
United Nations Conference on the Human Environment	1972	113	Ingemund Bengtsson (Sweden)—President Maurice F. Strong (Canada)—Secretary-General
(Third) World Population Conference	1974	136	George Macovescu (Romania)—President Antonio Carrillo-Flores (Mexico)—Secretary-General P.B. Desair (India)—Rapporteur-General
World Food Conference	1974	133	Giuseppe Medici (Italy)—President Aftab Ahmad Khan (Pakistan)—Rapporteur-General
World Conference on Women	1975	133[1]	Pedro Ojeda Paullada (Mexico)—President Maria Groza (Romania)—Rapporteur-General

Name of conference	Year	Governments represented	Principal officers
United Nations Conference on Human Settlements (Habitat I)	1976	132	Barney Danson (Canada)—President Adolf Ciborowski (Poland)—Rapporteur-General
United Nations Water Conference	1977	116	Luis Urbano Jáuregui (Argentina)—President Yahia Abdel Mageed (Sudan)—Secretary-General Malin Falkenmark (Sweden)—Rapporteur-General
United Nations Conference on Desertification (UNCOD)	1977	95	Mostafa K. Tolba (Egypt)—Secretary-General
World Conference Against Racism	1978	125[2]	Mooki V. Molapo (Lesotho)—President C.V. Narasimhan (India)—Secretary-General R. Valdez (Ecuador)—Rapporteur-General
United Nations Conference on Science and Technology for Development	1979	142[3]	Hertha Firnberg (Austria)—President Miguel Rodríguez Mendoza (Venezuela)—Rapporteur-General
World Conference on the United Nations Decade for Women	1980	145	Lise Oster gaaard (Denmark)—President Lucille M. Mair (Jamaica)—Secretary-General

Name of conference	Year	Governments represented	Principal officers
United Nations Conference on New and Renewable Sources of Energy	1981	125	John Henry Okwanyo (Kenya)—President Enrique V. Iglesias (Uruguay)—Secretary-General Jan Witek (Poland)—Rapporteur-General
United Nations Conference on Least Developed Countries	1981	142	Jean-Pierre Cot (France)—President Gamini Corea (Sri Lanka)—Secretary-General Ibor Fabian (Hungary)—Rapporteur-General
World Assembly on Ageing	1982	124[4]	Hertha Firnberg (Austria)—President William M. Kerrigan (United States)—Secretary-General Lucien Johan Henar (Surinam)—Rapporteur-General
Second World Conference to Combat Racism and Racial Discrimination	1983	128[5]	Héctor Charry-Sampor (Colombia)—President James O.C. Jonah (Sierra Leone)—Secretary-General
International Conference on Population	1984	146	Manuel Bartlett Dias (Mexico)—President Rafael M. Salas (Philippines)—Secretary-General

Name of conference	Year	Governments represented	Principal officers
World Conference to Review and Appraise the Achievements of the United Nations Decade for Women: Equality, Development and Peace	1985	157[6]	Margaret Kenyatta (Kenya)—President Leticia Ramos Shahani (Philippines)—Secretary-General
(Second) United Nations Conference on Least Developed Countries	1990	149	Roland Dumas (France)—President Kenneth Kweku Sinaman Dadzie (Ghana)—Secretary-General
World Summit for Children	1990	153	Brian Mulroney (Canada)—Co-Chairman Mussa Traoré (Mali)—Co-Chairman
United Nations Conference on Human Environment and Development (UNCED)	1992	170[7]	Fernando Collor (Brazil)—President Maurice F. Strong (Canada)—Secretary-General
World Conference on Human Rights	1993	171	Alois Mock (Austria)—President Ibrahima Fall (Senegal)—Secretary-General Zdzislaw Kedzia (Poland)—Rapporteur-General
International Conference on Population and Development (ICPD)	1994	178[8]	Muhammad Hosni Mubarak (Egypt)—President Nafis I. Sadik (Pakistan)—Secretary-General

Name of conference	Year	Governments represented	Principal officers
World Summit for Social Development (WSSD)	1995	186[9]	Poul Nyrup Rasmussen (Denmark)—President Sadok Rabah (Tunisia)—Rapporteur-General
Fourth World Conference on Women	1995	189[10]	Chen Muhua (China)—President Gertrude Mongella (Tanzania)—Secretary-General
United Nations Conference on Human Settlements (Habitat II)	1996	171[11]	Süleyman Demirel (Turkey)—President Wally N'Dow (The Gambia)—Secretary-General
Millennium Summit	2000	189	Harri Holkeri (Finland)—President Kofi A. Annan (Ghana)—Secretary-General
Third United Nations Conference on the Least Developed Countries	2001	159[12]	Göran Persson (Sweden)—President Rubens Ricupero (Brazil)—Secretary-General
United Nations Conference on Illicit Trade in Small Arms and Light Weapons in All Its Aspects	2001	171[13]	Camilo Reyes Rodriguez (Colombia)—President
World Conference against Racism, Racial Discrimination, Xenophobia and Related Intolerance	2001	170[14]	Nkosazana Dlamini Zuman (South Africa)—President Mary Robinson (Ireland)—Secretary-General Edna María Santos Roland (Brazil)—Rapporteur-General

Name of conference	Year	Governments represented	Principal officers
International Conference on Financing for Development	2002	190[15]	Vincente Fox (Mexico)—President Hazem Fahmy (Egypt)—Rapporteur-General
Second World Assembly on Ageing	2002	188[16]	Thabo Mbeki (South Africa)—President Antoine Mifsud Bonnici (Malta)—Rapporteur-General
World Summit on Sustainable Development (WSSD)	2002	160[17]	José María Aznar (Spain)—President María Cecilia Rozas (Peru)–Rapporteur-General

Notes

1 The Netherlands Antilles, Papua New Guinea and Surinam were represented at the Conference as observers.
2 The United Nations Council for Namibia was a participant.
3 The Palestine Liberation Organization had observer status.
4 The United Nations Council for Namibia was a participant.
5 The United Nations Council for Namibia was represented as a participant.
6 The Special Committee against Apartheid and the United Nations Council for Namibia were also participants.
7 The EEC, Palestine and seven associate members of the regional commissions (American Samoa, Aruba, Hong Kong, Netherlands Antilles, Niue, Puerto Rico, and the United States Virgin Islands "attended the Conference."
8 The EEC participated and "the observer for Palestine" attended.
9 The European Community participated; Macau, the Netherlands Antilles and Palestine had observers.
10 Plus the European Community.
11 The "observer for Palestine" attended and three associate members of regional commissions.
12 Palestine had observer status.
13 Palestine had observer status.
14 Palestine was also represented at the Conference.
15 Puerto Rico and the United States Virgin Islands attended as observers (associate members of regional commissions).
16 American Samoa, British Virgin Island, Netherlands Antilles, Puerto Rico and the United States Virgin Islands (associate members of regional commissions) were represented as observers.
17 Netherlands Antilles and Puerto Rico attended as observers (associate members of regional commissions) as did Palestine.

Appendix II
Suggested further reading

Contextual studies

Müller, Joachim (ed.), *Reforming the United Nations: The Quiet Revolution.* Published in co-operation with the United Nations. The Hague: Kluwer Law International, 2001.

Simmons, P.J. and De Jonge Oudraa, Chantal (eds.), *Managing Global Issues: Lessons Learned.* Washington, DC: Carnegie Endowment for International Peace, 2001.

Country studies

Cooper, Andrew F., *Tests of Global Governance: Canadian Diplomacy and United Nations World Conferences.* New York: United Nations University Press, 2004.

Fues, Thomas and Hamm, Brigitte I. (eds.), *Die Weltkonferenzen der 90er Jahre: Baustellen für Global Governance.* Bonn: Verlag J.H.W. Dietz Nachf., 2001.

Riddell-Dixon, Elizabeth, *Canada and the Beijing Conference on Women: Governmental Politics and NGO Participation.* Vancouver: University of British Columbia Press, 2001.

Participants' insights and reflections

Boutros-Ghali, Boutros, *Unvanquished: A U.S.–U.N. Saga.* New York: Random House, 1999.

Somavia, Juan, *People's Security: Globalizing Social Progress.* Geneva: J. Somavia, 1999.

Strong, Maurice, *Where on Earth Are We Going?* Toronto: Viking Canada, 2001.

Policy-making processes

Emmerij, Louis, Jolly, Richard, and Weiss, Thomas G., *Ahead of the Curve? UN Ideas and Global Challenges*. Bloomington: Indiana University Press, 2001.

Knight, W. Andy (ed.), *Adapting the United Nations to a Postmodern Era: Lessons Learned*. New York: Palgrave, 2001.

Muldoon, James P., Jr. *et al.* (eds), *Multilateral Diplomacy and the United Nations Today*. Boulder, CO: Westview Press, 1999.

Schechter, Michael G. (ed.), *United Nations-Sponsored World Conferences: Focus on Impact and Follow-Up*. New York: United Nations University Press, 2001.

Weiss, Thomas G. and Gordenker, Leon (eds), *NGOs, the UN and Global Governance*. Boulder, CO: Lynne Rienner, 1996.

Wilkinson, Rorden and Hughes, Steve (eds.), *Global Governance: Critical Perspectives*. New York: Routledge, 2002.

Specific conferences

Black, Maggie, *Children First: The Story of UNICEF, Past and Present*. New York: Oxford University Press, 1996.

Graduate Institute of International Studies,. *Small Arms Survey 2003: Development Denied*. New York: Oxford University Press, 2003.

Johnson, Stanley, *The Politics of Population: The International Conference on Population and Development*. London: Earthscan, 1995.

Pietilä, Hilkka, *Engendering the Global Agenda: The Story of Women and the United Nations*. Geneva: UN Non-Governmental Liaison Service, 2002.

Pietilä, Hilkka and Vickers, Jeanne, *Making Women Matter: The Role of the United Nations*. London: Zed Books, 1990.

Singh, Jyoti Shankar, *Creating a New Consensus: The International Conference on Population and Development*. London: Earthscan, 1998.

Weiss, Thomas G. and Jennings, Anthony, *More for the Least?: Prospects for Poorest Countries in the Eighties*. Lexington, MA: Lexington Books, 1983.

Weiss, Thomas G. and Jordan, Robert S., *The World Food Conference and Global Problem Solving*. New York: Praeger, 1976.

Appendix III
Important electronic resources

Relevant UN websites

http://www.un.org/events/ref43.htm
http://www.un.org/events/conferences.htm
http://www.un.org/geninfo/bp/worconf.html
http://www.un.org/News/facts/confercs.htm

Other relevant websites

http://www.smallarmssurvey.org/
http://www.library.yale.edu/un/
http://www.acuns.wlu.ca/document-collection/
http://www.asil.org/resource/un1.htm

Notes

Foreword

1 See especially, Michael G. Schechter, *United Nations-Sponsored World Conferences: Focus on Impact and Follow-Up* (Tokyo: United Nations University Press, 2001).
2 Boutros Boutros-Ghali, "Secretary General Inaugurates UN Conference on Human Settlements (HABITAT II)," press release HAB/IST/3, June 3, 1996.

1 Introduction

1 "The World's Meeting Place," *The New York Times* (September 6, 2000), p. A26.
2 Leland M. Goodrich, "From League of Nations to United Nations," *International Organization*, vol. 1, no. 1 (1947): pp. 3–21. Stephen C. Schlesinger, *Act of Creation: The Founding of the United Nations, A Story of Superpowers, Secret Agents, Wartime Allies and Enemies and Their Quest for a Peaceful World* (Boulder, CO: Westview Press, 2003). Eric Helleiner, *States and the Reemergence of Global Finance: From Bretton Woods to the 1990s* (Ithaca, NY: Cornell University Press, 1994).
3 Michael G. Schechter, "International Institutions: Obstacles, Agents or Conduits of Global Structural Change?" in Michael G. Schechter (ed.), *Innovation in Multilateralism* (New York: United Nations University Press, 1999).
4 Allen reported "mutterings from bystanders" at the Habitat I conference in 1976 to the effect that Habitat might (appropriately) be the last of the so-called mega conferences, owing to conference fatigue and disappointments with the outcomes heretofore. As Allen observed: "Every UN Conference since Stockholm has begun with unreasonable optimism and ended with unreasonable gloom." He went on, however: "Then, on reflection, participants and commentators have agreed that perhaps the gathering was not

so futile after all." Robert Allen, "The Last of the Megaconferences?" *Development Forum* , vol. 4, July–August (1976): p. 2.

5 Frederick A.B. Meyerson, "Burning the Bridge to the 21st Century: The End of the Era of Integrated Conferences?" *ESCAP Report*, vol. 9 (2003): p. 6. It is worth noting that this is not the first time that there has been a call for a halt or at least slowing down of the convening of such conferences. For example, the 1963 Annual Report of the UN Secretary-General, noting the growing number of special conferences since 1958, strongly urged that no more than one major special conference of the UN be held in any one year. The General Assembly adopted this limit in 1965 [Resolution 2116 (XX)] and repeated it in resolutions in 1968 and 1969, but the number of special conferences, no matter how defined, has not been held to such a limit. Mark E. Allen *et al.*, *Report of the Joint Inspection Unit on Secretariat Organization and Procedures for the Preparation of United Nations Special Conferences*, JIU/REP/82/2 transmitted by A/37/112 (March 23, 1982), p. 1.

6 Shepard, for example, gives considerable credit to women's rights advocacy networks for the success in meeting the three main goals of the International Conference on Population and Development (ICPD): comprehensive sexual and productive health; women's empowerment; and respect for individuals' and couples' reproductive rights. But she gives the various UN women's conferences credit for the formation and legitimization of those advocacy networks. Bonnie L. Shepard, *NGO Advocacy Networks in Latin America: Lessons from Experience in Promoting Women's and Reproductive Rights* (*North–South Agenda Papers*, vol. 61) (Miami: Dante B. Fascell North–South Center, University of Miami, 2003), p. 6.

7 Michael H. Glantz, "The U.N. and Desertification: Dealing with a Global Problem," in Michael H. Glantz (ed.), *Desertification: Environmental Degradation in and around Arid Lands* (Boulder, CO: Westview Press, 1977), p. 1.

8 Koh, who was the widely lauded head of the Third Law of the Sea Conference, reflected on this point:

> I have said, only half in jest to *The New York Times* that the UN should learn not to hold a major international conference during a U.S. Presidential Election year. There was no doubt in my mind that his preoccupation with winning the election was a factor that caused President [George H.W.] Bush to adopt a defensive rather than a pro-active role [at the United Nations Conference on Environment and Development].
> (Tommy Koh, *The Quest for World Order: Perspectives of a Pragmatic Idealist*, Singapore: Institute of Policy Studies, 1998, p. 98)

9 Peter Willetts, "The Pattern of Conferences," in Paul Taylor and A.J.R. Groom (eds.), *Global Issues in the United Nations' Framework* (New York: St. Martin's Press, 1989), p. 46.

10 Interestingly, relatively early on in the evolution of such conferences, there seemed to be a consensus that institutional learning, at least in terms of the preparatory phases of such conferences, was not occurring. Allen *et al.*, *Report*, p. 25.

11 For a useful discussion of the meaning and evolution of global conference diplomacy, see Volker Rittberger, "Global Conference Diplomacy and International Policy-Making: The Case of UN-Sponsored World Conferences," *European Journal of Political Research*, vol. 11, no. 2 (1983): pp. 167–182.

12 Jacques Fomerand's listing of UN conferences begins with the 1947–1948 [which really met beginning in 1946] Havana Conference on Trade and Employment. "UN Conferences: Media Events or Genuine Diplomacy?" *Global Governance*, vol. 2, September–December (1996): Appendix. The UN Joint Inspection Unit (JIU) dates the conferences from the 1950s. Allen *et al.*, *Report*, p. 1.

13 The UN JIU made this same observation and suggests that it might be why the UN General Assembly called upon the Secretary-General to draft standard procedures for such conferences. The Secretary-General's report, however, lacked any clear definition. Allen *et al.*, *Report*, p. 1.

14 Italics in the original. Willetts, "Pattern of Conferences," p. 37. As this work will show, there are even exceptions to this "bottom line" definition. Not all countries were eligible to attend the Stockholm conference, in many ways the paradigmatic UN global conference.

15 Allen *et al.*, *Report*, p. 1.

16 The Secretary-General/JIU's definition includes Special Sessions of the United Nations: the Millennium Summit and the World Summit for Children are included here, but all other special sessions are omitted. The reasons for including these two should become clear.

17 United Nations, Economic Commission for Latin America and the Caribbean (ECLAC), "United Nations Summits and Conferences," www.eclac.cl/cumbres/listado_cumbres.asp?idioma+IN (accessed June 7, 2004). Interestingly, ECLAC's very comprehensive listing omits the United Nations Conference on Illegal Trade in Small Arms and Light Weapons.

18 But there are obvious and important exceptions, not least of all the United Nations Conference on Illegal Trade in Small Arms and Light Weapons and the World Summit, although all conferences obviously have some relevance to the development process. Many of the issues of relevance to economically less developed countries are also very impor-

tant to affluent countries, such as the destruction of biodiversity, over-fishing of the oceans, and pollution of rivers.

19 Willetts, "Pattern of Conferences," p. 35.

20 Gill Seyfang, "Environmental Mega-Conferences: From Stockholm to Johannesburg and Beyond," *Global Environmental Change: Human and Policy Dimensions*, vol. 13 (2003): p. 224.

21 Willetts notes, for example, that the Swedish initiative for the UN Conference on the Human Environment (UNCHE) was credited to the Maltese delegate to the UN General Assembly, whereas the US call for the World Food Conference was really pursuant to a decision by the 1973 Non-Aligned Summit. "Pattern of Conferences," p. 46.

22 Specialized agencies are autonomous organizations working within the UN through ECOSOC's coordinating machinery and through the Chief Executives Board for Coordination (CEB). The specialized agencies are: International Labour Organization (ILO); Food and Agriculture Organization of the United Nations (FAO); United Nations Educational, Scientific and Cultural Organization (UNESCO); World Health Organization (WHO); International Bank for Reconstruction and Development (IBRD); International Development Association (IDA); International Finance Corporation (IFC); Multilateral Investment Guarantee Agency (MIGA); International Centre for Settlement of Investment Disputes (ICSID); International Monetary Fund (IMF); International Civil Aviation Organization (ICAO); International Maritime Organization (IMO); Universal Postal Union (UPU); World Meteorological Organization (WMO); World Intellectual Property Organization (WIPO); International Fund for Agricultural Development (IFAD); United Nations Industrial Development Organization (UNIDO); World Tourism Organization (WTO).

23 Economic Commission for Africa (ECA); Economic Commission for Europe (ECE); Economic Commission for Latin America and the Caribbean (ECLAC); Economic and Social Commission for Asia and the Pacific (ESCAP); Economic and Social Commission for Western Asia (ESCWA).

24 Commission on Human Rights; Commission on Narcotic Drugs; Commission on Crime Prevention and Criminal Justice; Commission on Science and Technology for Development; Commission on Sustainable Development (CSD); Commission on the Status of Women; Commission on Population and Development; Commission for Social Development; and the Statistical Commission.

25 Paul Taylor, "The Origins and Institutional Setting of the UN Special Conferences," in Taylor and Groom, *Global Issues*, pp. 9–22. United Nations, *The World Conferences: Developing Priorities for the 21st Century*

(*UN Briefing Papers*) (New York: United Nations Department of Public Information, 1997), p. 3.

26 United Nations, *World Conferences*, p. 3.

27 Willets, "Pattern of Conferences," p. 41.

28 The major UN funders' support is important because the general pattern of funding is for the UN to provide the secretariat, organize the documentation and service the proceedings, including the Preparatory Committees (PrepComs), including with translators and security personnel. These costs are seen to range between $1.8 million and $3.4 million, with the exception of the Rio Conference, which cost the UN $10 million. When the conference is not held at the UN's facilities—which is frequent—the costs of the conference facilities themselves, as well as the local staff, travel and hotels for UN staff, are generally covered by the host government. Given this division of costs, it's hard to get a firm grasp on the total cost of the various conferences. Recently, in order to save the host money, much translation has been done remotely. United Nations, *World Conferences*, p. 7. On the difficulty of getting a firm figure on such conferences, in part because of "in kind" contributions by various UN agencies, see Allen *et al..*, *Report*, p. 13.

29 United Nations, *World Conferences*, p. 1.

30 Elisabeth Correll, *The Negotiable Desert: Expert Knowledge in the Negotiations of the Convention to Combat Desertification* (Linköping: Department of Water and Environmental Studies, Linköping University, 1999), pp. 67–68.

31 Taylor "Origins and Institutional Setting," p. 8.

32 Rittberger "Global Conference Diplomacy," p. 171.

33 Thomas G. Weiss and Robert S. Jordan, *The World Food Conference and Global Problem Solving* (Praeger Special Studies in International Economics and Development) (New York: Praeger, 1976), pp. 2 and 2n.

34 Bernstein makes this point in reference to the UN CHE:

> The Stockholm conference's significance lies in its articulation of a nascent set of norms that would become the basis for international environmental law and practice. Earlier conferences and activities of regional or functional organizations possibly did as much to promote specific actions to protect the environment, but Stockholm began, or at least made explicit, the process of a global response to care for the Earth's ecosystems under a common framework.
> (Steven Bernstein, *The Compromise of Liberal Environmentalism*, New York: Columbia University Press, 2001, p. 31)

The same point, however, can be made about water security, racism, desertification, etc.

35 Seyfang, "Environmental Mega-Conferences," p. 225. Weiss and Jordan, *World Food Conference*, pp. 2–4. Robert S. Jordan with Clive Archer, Gregory P. Granger and Kerry Ordes, *International Organizations: A Comparative Approach to the Management of Cooperation*, 4th edn. (Westport, CT: Praeger, 2001), p. 212.

36 Keck and Sikkink conclude that:

> international conferences did not create women's networks, but they legitimized the issues and brought together unprecedented numbers of women from around the world. Such face-to-face encounters generated the trust, information sharing, and discovery of common concerns that gives impetus to network formation.
>
> (Margaret E. Keck and Kathryn Sikkink, *Activists Beyond Borders: Advocacy Networks in International Politics*, Ithaca, NY: Cornell University Press, 1988, p. 169)

While noting the legitimating role of women's conferences for regional and global networks, Shepard notes that: "In Latin America, as in other regions, new national advocacy networks were formed as part of national consultation processes leading up to UN conferences." Shepard, *NGO Advocacy Networks*, p. 6.

37 The UN General Assembly decided by Resolution 35/5 in 1980 that preparatory work for special conferences should henceforth be carried out by existing organs.

38 The host state's responsibilities normally include assisting with accommodations, medical facilities, local transportation, security, personnel, supplies and equipment, conference media and communications and working out arrangements for representatives' privileges and immunities. Allen *et al.*, *Report*, p. 20.

39 Ibid., p. 20.

40 Some of the "failures" of early conferences were blamed on members of the secretariat staffs "who were more concerned with securing permanent jobs [in whatever institutions were set up following the conferences] than with making expert contributions to conference preparation." Ibid., p. 20.

41 Björn-Ola Linnèr and Henrik Selin, "The Road to Rio: Early Efforts on Environment and Development," Paper Presented at the Joint Annual Conference of the American Society for Environmental History and the National Council of Public History (Victoria, British Columbia, April 2004), p. 3.

42 Weiss and Jordan, *World Food Conference*, p. 51.

43 Willetts, "Pattern of Conferences," pp. 54–56.

44 Taylor, "Origins and Institutional Setting," p. 8.
45 Michael G. Schechter, "Making Meaningful UN-sponsored World Conferences of the 1990s: NGOs to the Rescue?" in Michael G. Schechter (ed.), *United Nations-Sponsored World Conferences: Focus on Impact and Follow-Up* (Tokyo: United Nations University Press, 2001), pp. 192–193.
46 Meyerson, "Burning the Bridge," p. 6.
47 Ibid.

2 Setting the pattern, 1968–1972

1 Diplomatically, the UN Secretary-General in his address at the conference (on April 22, 1968) spoke of the fact that it was fitting to celebrate the anniversary of the Universal Declaration of Human Rights "in a land whose culture and civilization are among the oldest in the world," sidestepping the Shah of Iran's checkered record of human rights. U Thant, "Address at the International Conference on Human Rights," in Andrew W. Cordier and Max Harrelson (eds.), *Public Papers of the Secretary-General of the United Nations*, vol. VIII: *U Thant 1968–1971* (New York: Columbia University Press, 1977), p. 61.
2 U Thant's opening address also alluded to a provision of the Universal Declaration of Human Rights that has been highly contentious in the twenty-first century: "Everywhere in the world, the family constitutes a natural and fundamental unit." "Address," p. 68. The same provision was repeated in Conference Resolution XVIII. On the contentious nature of this provision and arguments about the UN's policy since then, see, for example: Maria Sophia Aguirre and Ann Wolfgram, "United Nations Policy and the Family—Redefining the Ties that Bind: A Study of History, Forces and Trends," *Brigham Young University Journal of Public Law*, vol. 16, no. 2 (2002): pp. 113–178, and Thalif Deen, "Rights: U.N. Deeply Split over Same-Sex Marriage," *Global Information Network* (New York, March 16, 2004), p. 1 (available as ProQuest Document ID 580067891).
3 The UN had celebrated its tenth and fifteenth anniversaries in a number of ways, including convening special meetings of the UN General Assembly. They were more celebratory than substantive in nature. United Nations, *United Nations Action in the Field of Human Rights* (New York: United Nations, 1980), ST/HR2/Rev.1, pp. 375–376.
4 Richard Falk, "Interpreting the Interaction of Global Markets and Human Rights," in Alison Brysk (ed.), *Globalization and Human Rights* (Berkeley: University of California Press, 2002), p. 70. Marina Svensson, *Debating Human Rights in China: A Conceptual and Political History* (Lanham, MD: Rowman & Littlefield, 2002), p. 35.

5 Henry J. Steiner and Philip Alston, *International Human Rights: Law, Politics, Morals*, 2nd edn. (New York: Oxford University Press, 2000), p. 143.

6 United Nations, *United Nations Action*, p. 303.

7 U Thant, "Address," p. 66.

8 M.J. Peterson, *The General Assembly in World Politics* (Boston: Allen & Unwin, 1986), p. 40.

9 United Nations, *United Nations Action*, p. 303.

10 U Thant, "Address," p. 66.

11 Kathleen Teltsch, "U.N. Opens Year on Human Rights: Assembly President Issues Worldwide Peace Appeal," *The New York Times* (December 30, 1967).

12 Ann Marie Clark, *Diplomacy of Conscience: Amnesty International and Changing Human Rights Norms* (Princeton, NJ: Princeton University Press, 2001), p. 7. Howard Tolley, *The International Commission of Jurists* (Philadelphia: University of Pennsylvania Press, 1994), pp. 107–108.

13 Drew Middleton, "Israel is Accused at Rights Parley: Her Participation in it is Challenged by Arabs," *The New York Times* (April 22, 1968).

14 Arthur W. Rovine, *The First Fifty Years: The Secretary-General in World Politics 1920–1970* (Leyden: A.W. Sijthoff, 1970), p. 417.

15 Ibid., p. 444.

16 Drew Middleton, "Thant Issues Plea on Race Conflict: At Iran Parlay, He Asks End of Bias 'In Our Generation,'" *The New York Times* (April 21, 1968).

17 "Apartheid Assailed by U.N. Conference," *The New York Times* (May 4, 1968)

18 Resolution I Adopted by the Conference, "Respect for and Implementation of Human Rights in Occupied Territories," reproduced in *American Journal of International Law*, vol. 63, no. 3 (1969); p. 678.

19 "U.N. Group Calls on Israel to Respect Arabs' Rights," *The New York Times* (May 10, 1968).

20 United Nations, *Yearbook of the United Nations, 1968* (vol. 22) (New York: United Nations, 1971), p. 543. It wasn't until 1980 that Rhodesia's white minority consented to hold multiracial elections. Robert Mugabe won a landslide victory and the country achieved independence on April 17, 1980, under the name Zimbabwe.

21 "Amnesty in Human Rights Year," *Amnesty International Annual Report 1st June 1967–31st May 1968* (London: International Secretariat, 1968), pp. 3–4.

22 UN Document A/CONF.32/41. Reproduced in *American Journal of International Law*, vol. 63, no. 3 (1969): p. 675. Although certainly not phrases that were supported by all the Western powers at the time, they were more moderate and explicit than those contained in specific resolutions passed at the conference (wherein apartheid was called a "crime

against humanity punishable in accordance with the provisions of relevant international instruments dealing with such crimes," a declaration of "emphatic recognition and vigorous support of the legitimacy of the struggles of the people and patriotic liberal movements in southern Africa," and a call for the UN Security Council to take "appropriate action against the Republic of South Africa under Chapter VII, and in particular under Article 41, of the [UN] Charter, including strong economic sanctions"). United Nations, *Yearbook of the United Nations, 1968*, p. 541. The Council only imposed mandatory sanctions on South Africa in 1977 and only because of "increasing public pressure and the intransigence of the white leadership" there. Gregory H. Fox, "Democracy," in David M. Malone (ed.), *The UN Security Council: From the Cold War to the 21st Century* (Boulder, CO: Lynne Rienner, 2004), p. 71.

23 According to Cox and Jacobson:

> Developmentalism can be defined as the promotion of economic growth in poor countries by methods consistent with the expansion of a liberal world economy. In practice, this meant creating conditions propitious to the flow of private direct investment, or, in other words, encouraging dependent capitalism.
>
> (Robert W. Cox and Harold K. Jacobson, "Decision Making," in Robert W. Cox with Timothy J. Sinclair, *Approaches to World Order*, Cambridge: Cambridge University Press, 1996, p. 362.)

24 UN Document A/CONF.32/41, p. 676.

25 UN Document A/CONF.32/41, pp. 675–676.

26 Resolution XVIII, "Human Rights Aspects of Family Planning," adopted on the report of the Second Committee, reproduced in *American Journal of International Law*, vol. 63, no. 3 (1969); p. 679.

27 United Nations, *Yearbook of the United Nations, 1969* (vol. 23) (New York: United Nations, 1972), p. 528.

28 The Spring 1967 suggestion by the Czech government to convene an ECE meeting of government experts to examine environmental problems "in a comprehensive and long-term perspective" has been characterized as a precursor to the Swedish proposal for the UNCHE. Yves Berthelot and Paul Rayment, "The ECE," in Yves Berthelot (ed.), *Unity and Diversity in Development Ideas: Perspectives from the Regional Commissions* (Bloomington, IN: Indiana University Press, 2004), p. 107.

29 Robert Wade, "Greening the Bank: The Struggle over the Environment, 1970–1995," in Devesh Kapur, John P. Lewis and Richard Webb (eds.), *The World Bank: Its First Half Century*, vol. 2: *Perspectives* (Washington, DC: Brookings Institution Press, 1997), pp. 618–619.

30 Unlike most pesticides, whose effectiveness is limited to destroying one or two types of insects, DDT was capable of killing hundreds of different kinds at once. DDT was developed in 1939 and was used in WWII to clear South Pacific islands of malaria-causing insects for the benefit of US troops; in Europe it was used as an effective de-lousing powder. In 1948, its inventor, Paul Müller, was awarded the Nobel Prize in Physiology or Medicine.

31 U Thant, "Statement at Opening of the Preparatory Committee for the United Nations Conference on the Human Environment," New York, March 9, 1970, reproduced in Cordier and Harrelson, *Public Papers: U Thant*, p. 346.

32 As quoted in: Sally Morphet, "NGOs and the Environment," in Peter Willetts (ed.), *"The Conscience of the World": The Influence of Non-Governmental Organisations in the U.N. System* (Washington, DC: Brookings Institution, 1996), p. 123.

33 Ibid., p. 124.

34 Ibid., pp. 124–125.

35 Ibid., p. 126.

36 Branislav Gosóvic, *The Quest for World Environmental Cooperation: The Case of the UN Global Environment Monitoring System* (New York: Routledge, 1992), p. 5.

37 Ibid., pp. 5–6, 12–13.

38 Björn-Ola Linnér and Henrik Selin, "The Road to Rio: Early Efforts on Environment and Development," paper presented at the Joint Annual Meeting of the American Society for Environmental History and the National Council of Public History (Victoria, British Columbia, April 2004), p. 3.

39 On UNCTAD's role as the Group of 77's secretariat, see Thomas George Weiss, *International Bureaucracy: An Analysis of the Operation of Functional and Global International Secretariats* (Lexington, MA: Lexington Books, 1975), pp. 98–100.

40 Wade, "Greening the Bank," pp. 622–623.

41 Linnér and Selin, "Road to Rio," p. 3.

42 Mick Hamer, "The Filthy Rich: How Developed Nations Plotted to Undermine Global Pollution Controls," *New Scientist* (January 5, 2002), p. 7.

43 The formula arose out of the question as to how the UN Secretary-General was to determine which entities were states when a treaty is open only to "states." If they are UN members or parties to the Statute of the International Court of Justice, there is no ambiguity. However, a difficulty occurs as to possible participation in treaties when entities which appeared otherwise to be states could not be admitted to the United Nations, nor become parties to the statute owing to the opposition, for political reasons,

of a permanent member of the Security Council. Since that difficulty did not arise as concerns membership in the specialized agencies, where there is no "veto" procedure, a number of those states became members of specialized agencies, and as such were in essence recognized as states by the international community. Accordingly, and in order to allow for as wide a participation as possible, a number of conventions then provided that they were also open for participation to states members of specialized agencies. For example, the Vienna Convention on the Law of Treaties was opened for signature by all states members of the United Nations or of any of the specialized agencies or of the International Atomic Energy Agency (IAEA) or Parties to the Statute of the International Court of Justice, and by any other state invited by the General Assembly of the United Nations to become a party to the Convention. This type of entry-into-force clause was called the "Vienna formula." United Nations, Treaty Section, Office of Legal Affairs, *Summary of Practice of the Secretary-General as Depository of Multilateral Treaties*, ST/LEG/7/Rev.1 (New York: United Nations, 1999).

44 Rumki Basu, *The Global Environment and the United Nations with Special Reference to India's Environmental Policy* (New Delhi: National Publishing House, 1998), p. 32.

45 Ibid., p. 31.

46 Gosóvic, *Quest for World Environmental Cooperation*, pp. 7–8.

47 John McCormick, "The Role of Environmental NGOs in International Regimes," in Norma J. Vig and Regina S. Axelrod (eds.), *The Global Environment: Institutions, Law, and Policy* (Washington, DC: CQ Press, 1999), p. 59.

48 Gosóvic, *Quest for World Environmental Cooperation*, pp. 7–8.

49 Ibid., pp. 10–11.

50 Ibid., p. 9.

51 Wade, "Greening the Bank," pp. 620–621.

52 Frederick A.B. Meyerson, "Burning the Bridge to the 21st Century: The End of the Era of Integrated Conferences?" *ESCAP Report*, vol. 9 (2003); p. 9.

53 Gert Rosenthal, "ECLAC," in Berthelot, *Unity and Diversity in Development Ideas*, p. 207.

54 Lynton Keith Caldwell, with Paul Stanley Weiland, *International Environmental Policy: From the Twentieth to the Twenty-First Century*, 3rd edn. rev. (Durham, NC: Duke University Press, 1996), pp. 65–66.

55 McCormick, "Role of Environmental NGOs," p. 58.

56 Louis Emmerij, Richard Jolly and Thomas G. Weiss, *Ahead of the Curve? UN Ideas and Global Challenges* (Bloomington, IN: Indiana University Press, 2001), p. 81.

57 Caldwell, *International Environmental Policy*, pp. 66–67. Basu, *Global Environment*, p. 29.

58 Bas Arts, *The Political Influence of Global NGOs: Case Studies on the Climate and Biodiversity Conventions* (Utrecht: International Books, 1998), p. 20.

59 Wade, "Greening the Bank," pp. 623–624.

60 Kevin Danaher (ed.), *50 Years is Enough: The Case against the World Bank and the International Monetary Fund* (Boston: South End Press, 1994).

61 Wade, "Greening the Bank," pp. 623–627.

3   The first rush of UN global conferences, 1974–1979

1 Joachim Müller (ed.), *Reforming the United Nations: The Quiet Revolution*, published in co-operation with the United Nations (The Hague: Kluwer Law International, 2001), p. 12.

2 Jason L. Finkle and C. Alison McIntosh, "United Nations Population Conferences: Shaping the Policy Agenda for the Twenty-First Century," *Studies in Family Planning*, vol. 33, March (2002); p. 12.

3 Stanley Johnson, *The Politics of Population: The International Conference on Population and Development, Cairo 1994* (London: Earthscan, 1995), p. 18.

4 Finkle and McIntosh, "United Nations," pp. 12–13.

5 W. Parker Mauldin *et al.*, "A Report on Bucharest: The World Population Conference and the Population Tribune, August 1974," *Studies in Family Planning*, vol. 5, December (1974); p. 358.

6 For a good discussion of the NIEO, see Craig N. Murphy, "What the Third World Wants: An Interpretation of the Development and Meaning of the New International Economic Order Ideology," *International Studies Quarterly*, vol. 27, no. 1 (1983).

7 Mauldin *et al.*, "Report," p. 358.

8 Ibid., p. 361.

9 As of 1995, the Population Commission was renamed the Commission on Population and Development.

10 Hilkka Pietilä and Jeanne Vickers, *Making Women Matter: The Role of the United Nations*, updated and expanded edn. (London: Zed Books, 1994), p. 77.

11 Objections were raised about the credentials of the Republic of Vietnam and the Khmer Republic. United Nations, *Yearbook of the United Nations, 1974* (vol. 28) (New York: United Nations, 1977), p. 551.

12 Finkle and McIntosh, "United Nations," p.13.

13 Mauldin *et al.*, "Report," p. 362.

14 Ibid., p. 376.

15 Ibid., p. 372.
16 Paul Taylor, "Population: Coming to Terms with People," in Paul Taylor and A.J.R. Groom (eds.), *Global Issues in the United Nations' Framework* (New York: St. Martin's Press, 1989), p. 161. See also: Paul Demeny, "Bucharest, Mexico City and Beyond," *Population and Development Review*, vol. 11 March (1985): p. 99.
17 Jyoti Shankar Singh, *Creating a New Consensus: The International Conference on Population and Development* (London: Earthscan, 1998), pp. 10–11..
18 Mauldin *et al.*, "Report," p. 377.
19 Ibid., pp. 378–379.
20 In light of the frequent reoccurrence of emergency food aid—often resulting from either drought or civil war or both—situations that faced many economically less developed countries, the UN General Assembly and the FAO established the WFP in 1961. The WFP, which began operations on a trial basis in 1963 and a permanent basis in 1965, is charged with providing food on an emergency basis to areas experiencing disaster or famine.
21 Thomas G. Weiss and Robert S. Jordan, *The World Food Conference and Global Problem Solving* (Praeger Special Studies in International Economics and Development) (New York: Praeger, 1976), pp. 10–11. Michael Watts and David Goodman, "Agrarian Questions: Global Appetite, Local Metabolism; Nature, Culture, and Industry in *Fin-de-Siècle* Agro-Food Systems," in David Goodman and Michael J. Watts (eds.), *Globalising Food: Agrarian Questions and Global Restructuring* (New York: Routledge, 1997), p. 1.
22 Kissinger notes that during his US Senate confirmation hearings for US Secretary of State (September 7–21, 1973), a number of Senators asked "questions about particular concerns." Among those was Senator Hubert Humphrey who asked about

> a more comprehensive and humane use of our food assistance abroad. I [Kissinger] promised Humphrey I would put forward a new American policy to combat world hunger—a promise I fulfilled the following year at a United Nations World Food Conference in Rome held at American initiative and at which I unveiled a comprehensive new program ... I promised that the United States stood ready to define its responsibilities in the dialogue between rich and poor nations in a humane and cooperative spirit.
>
> (Henry Kissinger, *Years of Upheaval*, Boston: Little, Brown, 1982, pp. 429, 447)

Of course, the initiative wasn't entirely that of the USA or, apparently, Kissinger's, who got much credit for it.

23 Weiss and Jordan, *World Food Conference*, pp. 104–105.

24 Reportedly, the USSR first declined membership in the FAO because of the Soviet Union's poor performance in food production and unwillingness to have that widely publicized. It continued to avoid the FAO because it was "considered a Western stronghold." Moreover, the Soviets did not want to contribute support to yet another international forum presumably, in part at least, because of its long-standing position that only states are actors under international law. Ibid, p. 104. Gerhard von Glahn, *Law among Nations: An Introduction to Public International Law*, 6th edn. (New York: Macmillan, 1992), pp. 34–35.

25 Weiss and Jordan, *World Food Conference*, pp. 12–14.

26 Churches exerted pressure within the USA to get the USA to take something more than a noncommittal position at the conference and the Canadian NGOs appeared to have been the most organized, which might explain why the Canadians committed themselves to doubling their food aid. Ibid, pp. 131–133.

27 Hilkka Pietilä, *Engendering the Global Agenda: The Story of Women and the United Nations* (Development Dossier) (Geneva: UN Non-Governmental Liaison Service, 2002), pp. 32–33.

28 The USSR ensured that this time they included the Democratic Republic of Germany, which attended. On the other hand, there was considerable controversy about the participation of Vietnam at the conference. The Soviets insisted that the South Vietnamese government could not participate because the government of the Democratic Republic of Vietnam had not been issued an invitation. The Chinese also objected to the participation of the Lon Nol regime as representatives of the Khmer Republic. United Nations, *Yearbook of the United Nations, 1974*, p. 489.

29 Weiss and Jordan, *World Food Conference*, p. 137.

30 Ibid., pp. 25–26.

31 Ibid., p. 77.

32 Gaspar contends that while the WFC's first priority was nutrition, it made no serious attempt to look at how food is marketed. He uses this as an example of how the conferences, and institutions and programs they spun off, do not challenge the existing global structure (in this instance, capitalism) and thus are either doomed to failure or at least are only marginally helpful in addressing the problems for which they were convened or set up. Diego de Gaspar, "Beyond Conference Ritual," *Development Forum*, vol. 4, July–August (1976); p. 2.

33 Weiss and Jordan, *World Food Conference*, pp. 65, 67, 77.

34 Universal Declaration on the Eradication of Hunger and Malnutrition, adopted on November 16, 1974, by the World Food Conference Convened

Under General Assembly Resolution 3180 (XXVIII) of December 17, 1973 and endorsed by General Assembly Resolution 3348 (XXIX) of December 17, 1974.

35 Hazzard contends that the rights of women, like human rights in general, stagnated during Hammarskjöld's time as Secretary-General. As noted earlier, human rights did gain prominence during his successor's time at the UN, but women's rights were not the focus in U Thant's administration. Shirley Hazzard, *Countenance of Truth: The United Nations and the Waldheim Case* (New York: Viking, 1990), p. 44.

36 Pietilä, *Engendering the Global Agenda*, pp. 29–30.

37 Pietilä and Vickers, *Making Women Matter*, p. 73.

38 Ibid.

39 Ibid., p. 76.

40 Ibid., pp. 75–76.

41 Ibid., pp. 78–79.

42 Martha Alter Chen, "Engendering World Conferences: The International Women's Movement and the UN," in Thomas G. Weiss and Leon Gordenker (eds.), *NGOs, The UN, and Global Governance* (Boulder, CO: Lynne Rienner, 1996), p. 140.

43 Pietilä and Vickers, *Making Women Matter*, p. 79.

44 Hilary Charlesworth, "Women as Sherpas: Are Global Summits Useful for Women?" *Feminist Studies*, vol. 22, Fall (1996): pp. 537–547.

45 Chen, "Engendering World Conferences," p. 140.

46 Pietilä, *Engendering the Global Agenda*, pp. 34–35.

47 As quoted in US Department of State, "Habitat: United Nations Conference on Human Settlements, Vancouver, BC, Canada, May 31 to June 11, 1976," Department of State Publication 8844, International Organization and Conference Series 121 (Washington: US Department of State, Office of Media Services, Bureau of Public Affairs, 1976), p. 1.

48 R.J. Crooks, "Preface," in *Human Settlements: The Environmental Challenge, A Compendium of United Nations Papers Prepared for the Stockholm Conference on the Human Environment 1972* (London: Macmillan for the Centre for Housing, Building and Planning, United Nations Department of Economic and Social Affairs, 1974), pp. xiii–xiv.

49 United States, Department of Housing and Urban Development, Habitat National Center, "United Nations Conference on Human Settlements: Habitat '76" (Washington: US Department of Housing and Urban Development, Habitat National Center, 1976), p. 1.

50 Jon Tinker, "Let Vancouver Be Remembered," *Development Forum*, vol. 4, July–August (1976); p. 3.

51 United Nations, *Yearbook of the United Nations, 1976* (vol. 30) (New York: Office of Public Information, United Nations, 1979), p. 441.

52 Principle 4 of the Declaration stated that it was

> the duty of all people and Governments to join the struggle against any form of colonialism, foreign aggression and occupation, domination, apartheid and all forms of racism and racial discrimination referred to in the resolutions as adopted by the General Assembly of the United Nations.

53 Two years after the Conference, the UN Center for Human Settlements (UNCHS, or Habitat) was established and located in Nairobi. It became the lead agency within the UN for coordinating activities in the field of human settlements.
54 Robert Allen, "The Last of the Megaconferences?" *Development Forum*, vol. 4, July–August (1976); p. 3.
55 Ibid.
56 Boyce Rensberger, "Water Crisis Caused by Man and Nature to be Explored at U.N. Conference," *The New York Times* (March 14, 1977), p. 12.
57 Paul Hofmann, "U.N. Says World Water Supply is Not as Reliable as It Appears," *The New York Times* (July 22, 1976), p. 2.
58 Ibid.
59 Kathleen Teltsch, "Politics Unlikely at Water Parley," *The New York Times* (March 14, 1977), p. 12.
60 Maryanne Dulansey, *Water Resource Development: The Experience of U.S. Non-Profit Organizations: Programs, Issues and Recommendations* (New York: American Council of Voluntary Agencies for Foreign Service, Inc., Technical Assistance Information Clearing House, 1976), pp. 1–2.
61 United Nations, *Yearbook of the United Nations, 1977* (vol. 31) (New York: Office of Public Information, United Nations, 1980), p. 553.
62 Anthony D'Amato and Kirsten Engle (eds.), *International Environmental Law Anthology* (Cincinnati, OH: Anderson, 1996), p. 299.
63 According to D'Amato and Engle:

> For six years, the countries of the Sahel—Mauritania, Senegal, Mali, Upper Volta, Niger, and Chad—were devastated by uninterrupted droughts and resultant famine. The natural and human consequences were tragically catastrophic: Lake Chad shrunk to only one-third of its normal size; the Niger and Senegal river systems failed to flood, thus leaving barren much of the most productive croplands in the region; shallow wells dried up, seriously restricting the grazing range of pastoralists; vegetation was denuded as starving animals stripped the land; and splotches of new desert appeared to the north.

Reasonable rainfall did return to the Sahel in 1974, but not before drought, famine, and disease had killed an estimated 250,000 people and millions of domestic animals.

(International Environmental Law), p. 297

64 Richard Samson Odingo, "Review of UNEP's Definition of Desertification and its Programmatic Implications," in R.S. Odingo (ed.), *Desertification Revisited: Proceedings of an Ad Hoc Consultative Meeting on the Assessment of Desertification UNEP/DC/PAC, Nairobi, February 1990* (Nairobi: Desertification Control Programme Activity Centre, United Nations Environment Programme, 1977), p. 8.
65 Michael H. Glantz, "The U.N. and Desertification: Dealing with a Global Problem," in Michael H. Glantz (ed.), *Desertification: Environmental Degradation in and around Arid Lands* (Boulder, CO: Westview Press, 1977), p. 3.
66 Elisabeth Correll, *The Negotiable Desert: Expert Knowledge in the Negotiations of the Convention to Combat Desertification* (Linköping Studies in Arts and Science) (Linköping: Department of Water and Environmental Studies, Linköping University, 1999), pp. 67–68.
67 Glantz, "The U.N. and Desertification," p. 9.
68 Correll, *Negotiable Desert*, p. 68.
69 Odingo, "Definition of Desertification," p. 9.
70 Philippe Cullet, "Desertification," in "Institutional and Infrastructure Resource Issues II: Conventions, Treaties and Other Responses to Global Issues," in *Encyclopedia of Life Support Systems*, developed under the Auspices of UNESCO (Oxford: Eolss Publishers, 2002). http://www.eolss.net
71 Ibid.
72 Wangu Mwangi, "The Desertification Convention: 'Not Just Another Document.'" December 1, 1997. International Development Research Centre. http://archive.idrc.ca/books/reports/v222/convent.html (accessed June 13, 2004).
73 United Nations, *Yearbook of the United Nations, 1977*, pp. 510–511.
74 Representatives from the European Economic Community rejected the characterization of apartheid as a crime against humanity; the German and British delegations took exception to the notion of mandatory sanctions on South Africa and the Swedish delegate took exception to the notion that apartheid was a threat to international peace and security. United Nations, *Report of the World Conference to Combat Racism and Racial Discrimination, Geneva, 14–24 August 1978*, A/CONF.92/40 (New York: United Nations, 1979), pp. 1–2, 5, 9–14, 10, 15–26, 65–66, and 74.

75 The Xinhua General Overseas New Service (August 27, 1978), accessed through Lexis-Nexim™ Academic.

76 *The New York Times* (August 16, 1978). Reproduced by Information Bank Abstracts.

77 The Xinhua General Overseas News Service (August 25, 1978), accessed through Lexis-Nexim™ Academic. In 1977, the Somalis had switched sides in the Cold War from the East to the West and Ethiopia had switched from being pro-West to being pro-Soviet.

78 The Xinhua General Overseas New Service (August 20, 1978), accessed through Lexis-Nexis™ Academic. For a discussion of China's relations with the "third world," see Samuel S. Kim, "China and the Third World in the Changing World Order," in Samuel S. Kim (ed.), *China and the World: Chinese Foreign Relations in the Post-Cold War Era*, 3rd edn. (Boulder, CO: Westview Press, 1994), p. 128.

79 Christopher N. Camponovo, "Disaster in Durban: The United Nations World Conference Against Racism, Racial Discrimination, Xenophobia, and Related Intolerance," 34 *George Washington International Law Review*, vol. 34, no. 4 (2003); pp. 663–664 and 664n.

80 Quoted in Andrew Warshaw, Associated Press, Dateline, Geneva, August 27, 1978. Accessible from http://web.lexis-nexis.com/univers/ (accessed June 15, 2004).

81 Peter M. Haas, "UN Conferences and Constructivist Governance of the Environment," *Global Governance* , vol. 8 (2002); p. 79.

82 Ward Morehouse, "The Vienna Syndrome," *The New York Times* (September 6, 1979), p. A21.

83 United Nations, *Yearbook of the United Nations, 1979* (vol. 33) (New York: Office of Public Information, United Nations, 1982), pp. 633–642.

84 Morehouse, "Vienna Syndrome," p. A21.

4 Conferences during a period of crisis and distraction, 1980–1989

1 While most commentators write of a crisis of multilateralism that was brought on by the US decision to go to war in Iraq in 2003, even without the sanction of the UN Security Council, underscoring another lapse into unilateralist policies by the USA, Cox and some others point to a different sort of crisis that arose at the time of the Gulf War of 1991 and the subsequent Security Council endorsed military action. While many saw this as the re-emergence of the United Nations as its founders had intended it, a kind of Concert of Great Powers, Cox sees it as posing a different problem for multilateralism, moving from the problem of whether the UN "could survive without the political and financial support of the United States" to

whether the UN "could function as a world organization if it came to be perceived as the instrument of its most powerful member." Robert W. Cox, "Multilateralism and World Order," in Robert W. Cox with Timothy J. Sinclair, *Approaches to World Order* (Cambridge: Cambridge University Press, 1996), p. 499.

2 Ibid., p. 498.

3 Mohammed Ayoob, *The Third World Security Predicament: State Making, Regional Conflict, and the International System* (Boulder, CO: Lynne Rienner, 1995), pp. 115–137, 178.

4 Joachim Müller (ed.), *Reforming the United Nations: The Quiet Revolution*, published in co-operation with the United Nations (The Hague: Kluwer Law International, 2001), pp. 16–17.

5 Judith P. Zinsser, "From Mexico to Copenhagen to Nairobi: The United Nations Decade for Women, 1975–1985," *Journal of World History*, vol. 13, no. 1 (2002): pp. 151–152.

6 United Nations, *Yearbook of the United Nations, 1980* (vol. 34) (New York: Office of Public Information, United Nations, 1983), pp. 885–886.

7 Ibid., pp. 891–892.

8 Elizabeth Riddell-Dixon, *Canada and the Beijing Conference on Women: Governmental Politics and NGO Participation* (Vancouver: University of British Columbia Press, 2001), p. 16.

9 Zinsser, "From Mexico," p. 153.

10 Ibid.

11 Ibid., p.157.

12 Martin Soroos, *Beyond Sovereignty: The Challenge of Global Policy* (Columbia: University of South Carolina Press, 1986), p. 24.

13 Hilkka Pietilä, *Engendering the Global Agenda: The Story of Women and the United Nations* (Geneva: UN Non-Governmental Liaison Service, 2002), pp. 24–26.

14 United Nations. Economic and Social Council. Commission on Science and Technology for Development. "Action Arising from the Second Session: Scientific and Technological Aspects of Sustainable Energy Systems, Note by the UNCTAD Secretariat." E/CN.16/1997/3, March 19, 1997, p. 4.

15 Cox writes of "functionalism" as the UN's organizational ideology of the 1940s through the 1960s. Basically it "sought to base international organization upon interests inherent in society rather than making them dependent upon the goodwill of states." That is, the functionalists' hope was that enhanced social and economic integration, led by experts rather than politicians making decisions, would overcome the objection to the loss of state sovereignty that was necessary for supranational decision-making to evolve. "Decision Making," in Cox with Sinclair, *Approaches*, p. 362. For

a more elaborate discussion of functionalism and administrative ideologies, see Ernst B. Haas, *Beyond the Nation-State: Functionalism and International Organization* (Stanford, CA: Stanford University Press, 1964), chap. 4.

16 United Nations General Assembly, "United Nations Conference on New and Renewable Sources of Energy," Article 2 of Resolution 33/148.

17 United Nations General Assembly, "United Nations Conference on New and Renewable Sources of Energy," Article 3 of Resolution 33/148.

18 Catherine Gwin, "U.S. Relations with the World Bank, 1945–1992," in Devesh Kapur, John P. Lewis and Richard Webb (eds.), *The World Bank: Its First Half Century*, vol. 2: *Perspectives* (Washington, DC: Brookings Institution Press, 1997), pp. 261–262.

19 Steven Ferrey, "A Crisis in Energy of Wood," *The New York Times* (August 15, 1981), p. A15.

20 Although rejecting any intergovernmental plan or firm commitments, the USA agreed to double its energy aid in fiscal year 1982 to $70 million. "U.N. Energy Talks End with Plea for Money," *The New York Times* (August 23, 1981), p. 4.

21 "World Bank's Energy Loans," *The New York Times* (August 18, 1981), p. D16. "U.N. Energy Parley Seeks a Compromise," *The New York Times* (August 21, 1981), p. A5. "Fundless Energy Fund," *The New York Times* (August 23, 1981), p. E3.

22 "World Bank's Energy Loans," p. D16.

23 "Arabs Quit U.N. Parley as Israeli Starts to Speak," *The New York Times* (August 20, 1981), p. A5.

24 United Nations, *Yearbook of the United Nations, 1981* (vol. 35) (New York: Office of Public Information, United Nations, 1984), p. 690.

25 Accessed on June 20, 2004 from http://www.g8usa.gov/24695pf.htm

26 "U.N. Energy Talks End with Plea for Money," p. 4.

27 Soroos, *Beyond Sovereignty*, pp. 107–108.

28 United Nations, *Yearbook of the United Nations, 1982* (vol. 36) (New York: Office of Public Information, United Nations, 1985), p. 898.

29 United Nations, *Yearbook of the United Nations, 1971* (vol. 25) (New York: Office of Public Information, United Nations, 1974), p. 232.

30 Muchkund Dubey, "A Third-World Perspective," in Jagdish N. Bhagwati and John Gerard Ruggie (eds.), *Power, Passions and Purpose: Prospects for North–South Negotiations* (Cambridge, MA: MIT Press, 1984), pp. 65–66. While no single factor explains the collapse of the North–South dialogue, most give some credit to the refusal of the North to enter into serious negotiations and the related disparity in power between the North and South, and to the fragmentation of the "third world" coalition. Robert O. Brien and Marc Williams, *Global Political Economy: Evolution and Dynamics* (New York: Palgrave Macmillan, 2004), p. 284.

31 By the time the conference was convened, however, Giscard d'Estaing had been replaced as French President by François Mitterrand and it was less clear how excited he was with France footing the bill for the conference, especially as earlier conferences on the same topic had not been successful. "Mitterrand Urges Aid to the Poorest Nations," *The New York Times* (August 31, 1981).

32 United Nations, *Yearbook of the United Nations, 1981*, p. 407.

33 Thomas G. Weiss and Anthony Jennings, *More for the Least? Prospects for Poorest Countries in the Eighties* (Lexington, MA: Lexington Books, 1983), p. 155.

34 Jean-Pierre Cot, "Foreword," in Weiss and Jennings, *More for the Least?*, p. xi.

35 A.h.B. de Bono, MD, Director of the International Institute on Ageing – Malta, accessed on June 20, 2004 at http://aging.senate.gov/events/hr19ab.htm

36 United States, House of Representatives, Select Committee on Aging, *U.S. Perspectives: International Action on Aging* (January 1985) Y4.Ag4/2:Un3, pp. viii and 25–26.

37 United Nations, *Yearbook of the United Nations, 1982*, pp 1182–1186.

38 United States, House Select Committee on Aging, *U.S. Perspectives*, pp. 13–16 and 27.

39 Gertrude Dubrovky, "Parley Warned on Aged," *The New York Times* (August 8, 1982), p. 1.

40 "Interview with the Secretary-General of the Second World Conference to Combat Racism and Racial Discrimination" (transcript of an interview with James O.C. Jonah prepared for "World Chronicle," United Nations Radio and Visual Services Division), *Objective: Justice*, vol. 15, June (1983): p. 25.

41 Ibid., pp. 20, 24–25, 30–31.

42 United Nations, *Report of the Second World Conference to Combat Racism and Racial Discrimination, Geneva (1–12 August 1983)*, A/CONF.119/26 (New York: United Nations, 1983), p. 13.

43 Ibid., p. 15.

44 Ibid., p. 31.

45 Jyoti Shankar Singh, *Creating a New Consensus: The International Conference on Population and Development* (London: Earthscan, 1998), p. 12

46 Ibid., p. 13.

47 The 1984 Mexican debates were not closely monitored by the international women's movement; still feminists present at the conference managed to ensure that women's issues received this sort of high priority. Sonia Corrêa in collaboration with Rebecca Reichmann, *Population and Reproductive Rights: Feminist Perspectives from the South* (London: Zed Books, 1994), p. 59.

48 United Nations, *Yearbook of the United Nations, 1984* (vol. 38) (New York: Office of Public Information, United Nations, 1987), p. 715.

49 Jason L. Finkle and C. Alison McIntosh, "United Nations Population Conferences: Shaping the Policy Agenda for the Twenty-First Century," *Studies in Family Planning*, vol. 33, March (2002); p. 13.

50 Corrêa, *Population and Reproductive Rights*, p. 12.

51 Paul Demeny, 'Bucharest, Mexico City and Beyond," *Population and Development Review*, vol. 11, March (1985); pp. 100–102.

52 Richard J. Meislin, "Population Parley to Open in Mexico Today," *The New York Times* (August 4, 1985).

53 Stanley Johnson, *The Politics of Population: The International Conference on Population and Development* (London: Earthscan, 1995).

54 "U.N. Parley Urges Bank on Promoting Use of Abortion," *The New York Times* (August 10, 1985), p. 1.

55 "Family Planning Global Aid Urged," *The New York Times* (August 4, 1984): p. A6. "Free Market as Contraceptive," *The New York Tines* (June 2, 1984): p. A22. Richard J. Meislin, "U.S. Asserts Key to Curbing Births is a Free Economy," *The New York Times* (August 8, 1984): p. A8.

56 The US delegation tried to change the conference's main working document to include several short phrases favoring free enterprise and the sentence "The benefits of such a policy tend ultimately to lower fertility rates." "Family Planning Global Aid Urged," *The New York Times* (August 6, 1985).

57 Demeny, "Bucharest" pp. 100–102.

58 Richard J. Meislin, "Delegate to Mexico Meeting Says U.S. Still Backs Family Planning," *The New York Times* (August 9, 1985).

59 For an elaboration on these challenges, see Demeny, "Bucharest," pp. 102–105.

60 Reportedly, Buckley wanted the USA to abstain in the vote on the conference final declaration because of what he saw as an anti-Israeli package, but the State Department insisted that he stick with the original plan of accepting the conference's actions by consensus. "Buckley and State Dept. in Clash," *The New York Times* (August 15, 1985).

61 Richard J. Meislin, "Population Parley Approves a Resolution Aimed at Israel," *The New York Times* (August 12, 1985). See also Richard J. Meislin, "U.N. Population Conference Adopts 88 Proposals on Global Growth," *The New York Times* (August 13, 1985).

62 Richard J. Meislin, "Political Issues Snarled U.N. Population Talks," *The New York Times* (August 14, 1985).

63 Charlotte G. Patton, "Women and Power: The Nairobi Conference, 1985," in Anne Winslow (ed.), *Women, Politics, and the United Nations* (Westport, CT: Greenwood Press, 1995), pp. 65–66. On the other hand, fourteen of the delegations were headed by men; a US delegate, Alan L. Keyes, who seemed never more than a few feet from Maureen Reagan, the head of the US delegation, took a leading role in the conference by demanding points

of order; men on the Egyptian, Syrian and PLO delegations dominated the proceedings at times and engaged in most debates; most of the interpreters were men, as was the official UN legal advisor to the Conference, who was often called on to aid the Conference President. "U.S. Delegate Protests Conference on Women," *The New York Times* (July 27, 1985).

64 Patton, "Women," p. 62.

65 Elaine Sciolino, "As Their 'Decade' Ends, Women Take Stock," *The New York Times* (July 8, 1985), p. C10. "President Addresses Delegates to Nairobi," *The New York Times* (July 9, 1985). Sheila Rule, "At Nairobi Women's Parley, Old Wounds Still Fester," *The New York Times* (July 13, 1985).

66 Elaine Sciolino, "U.N. Women's Parley Opens in Kenya after Rules Fight is Settled," *The New York Times* (July 14, 1985).

67 Hikka Pietilä, *Engendering the Global Agenda: The Story of Women and the United Nations* (Geneva: UN Non-Governmental Liaison Service, 2002), pp. 35–36.

68 The US delegate Alan Keyes was booed when he requested a vote on apartheid. The final vote on a paragraph calling for UN sanctions against South Africa and giving support to national liberation movements was 122–1 (United States)–12. Patton, "Women," p. 70.

69 "Women," pp. 71–72. Elaine Sciolino, "East–West Rivalries Dominate Women's Meeting," *The New York Times* (July 19, 1985). Elaine Sciolino, "Arabs in Walkout at Women's Talks," *The New York Times* (July 21, 1985).

70 "U.S. Blamed at Women's Parley," *The New York Times* (July 17, 1985).

71 Bonnie L. Shepard, *NGO Advocacy Networks in Latin America: Lessons from Experience in Promoting Women's and Reproductive Rights* (North–South Agenda Papers, vol. 61) (Miami: Dante B. Fascell North–South Center, University of Miami, 2003), p. 6.

72 Patton, "Women," p. 65.

73 Elaine Sciolino, "In Nairobi, Consensus," *The New York Times* (July 28, 1985).

74 Elaine Sciolino, "U.S. Women Split with Delegates in Kenya," *The New York Times* (July 18, 1985).

75 "U.S. Delegate Protests."

76 Nadine Brozan, "Maureen Reagan Assesses Nairobi," *The New York Times* (August 1, 1985).

77 Patton, "Women," p. 71.

78 Ibid., p. 74.

79 Elaine Sciolino, "U.N. Urged to Promote Women," *The New York Times* (November 4, 1985).

80 Riddell-Dixon, *Canada*, pp. 23–24.

5 United Nations global conferences in the post-Cold War era, 1990–1999

1 United States, Congress, 90th Congress, 1st Session, 1985, *U.S. Statutes at Large, Public Laws*, vol. 99, part 1 (Washington, DC: Government Printing Office, 1987), p. 1134.

2 For details, see, for example, Thomas W. Weiss, David P. Forsythe and Roger A. Coate, *The United Nations and Changing World Politics*, 4th edn. (Boulder, CO: Westview Press, 2004), chap. 3. David M. Malone (ed.), *The UN Security Council: From the Cold War to the 21st Century* (Boulder, CO: Lynne Rienner, 2004), especially part 4.

3 Maggie Black, *Children First: The Story of UNICEF, Past and Present*, published for UNICEF (New York: Oxford University Press, 1996), p. 25.

4 United Nations, *Yearbook of the United Nations, 1990* (vol. 44) (New York: Office of Public Information, United Nations, 1993), p. 369.

5 Paul Lewis, "Poorest Countries Seek Increases in Aid," *The New York Times* (July 1, 1990).

6 United Nations, *Report of the Second United Nations Conference on the Least Developed Countries, Paris 3–14 September 1990*, A/CONF.147/18 (New York: United Nations, 1991), pp. 11–13.

7 United Nations, *Yearbook of the United Nations, 1990*, pp. 372–373.

8 Steven Greenhouse, "Poor Nations Get Unspecified Pledge of Aid," *The New York Times* (September 14, 1990).

9 Black, *Children First*, p. 25.

10 Ibid., p. 26.

11 Yves Beigbeder, *New Challenges for UNICEF: Children, Women and Human Rights*, (London: Palgrave, 2001) p. 35.

12 Black, *Children First*, pp. 25–31 and 140–141. Beigbeder, *New Challenges for UNICEF*, pp. 33–35.

13 Kofi A. Annan, *We the Children: Meeting the Promises of the World Summit for Children* (New York: United Nations, 2001), p. 3.

14 Peter M. Haas, "UN Conferences and Constructivist Governance of the Environment," *Global Governance*, vol. 8 (2002); p. 79.

15 Duncan Brack, Fanny Calder and Müge Dolun, *From Rio to Johannesburg: The Earth Summit and Rio+10* (London: Royal Institute of International Affairs, Energy and Environment Programme, 2001), p. 2.

16 Gill Seyfang and Andrew Jordan, "The Johannesburg Summit and Sustainable Development: How Effective are Environmental Mega-Conferences?" in Ollav Schram Stokke and Øystein B. Thommessen (eds.), *Yearbook of International Co-operation on Environment and Development 2002/2003* (London: Earthscan, 2002), p. 21.

17 Chris Mensah, "The United Nations Commission on Sustainable Development," in Jacob Werksman (ed.), *Greening International Institutions* (London: Earthscan, 1996), p. 22.
18 United Nations, *Yearbook of the United Nations, 1992* (vol. 46) (New York: Office of Public Information, United Nations, 1993), p. 670.
19 For a review of a number of the most prominent of these commissions, see Joachim Müller (ed.), *Reforming the United Nations: The Quiet Revolution*, published in co-operation with the United Nations (The Hague: Kluwer Law International, 2001), part 1.
20 "It is of interest that the term 'sustainable development,' though widely used, [was] not defined either in Agenda 21 or in any of other texts emerging from UNCED." Rumki Basu, *The Global Environment and the United Nations with Special Reference to India's Environmental Policy* (New Delhi: National Publishing House, 1998), p. 95.
21 According to Lamont Hempel:

> What he and his staff could not foresee, however, was how quickly the political vacuum left by the breakup of the Soviet Union would be filled with ethnic strife, recessionary pressures, and an inability or unwillingness to redirect the so-called "peace dividend" to matters of social and environmental security.
> Lamont C. Hempel, *Environmental Governance: The Global Challenge*, (Washington, DC: Island Press, 1996), p. 31

22 Seyfang and Jordan, "Johannesburg Summit," p. 21.
23 Peter M. Haas, Marc A. Levy and Edward A. Parson, "Appraising the Earth Summit: How Should We Judge UNCED's Success?" *Environment*, vol. 34, no. 8 (1991); pp. 29–30.
24 According to Tommy Koh:

> The New York-based diplomats, who were the most politicized, wanted all of the sessions to be held in New York. The Geneva-based diplomats argued that they should be held in Geneva, the home of the UNCED Secretariat. The supporters of UNEP, which is based in Nairobi, argued that they should be held in Nairobi.
> Tommy Koh, *The Quest for World Order: Perspectives of a Pragmatic Idealist*, (Singapore: Institute of Policy Studies, 1998), p. 98

25 Haas *et al.*, "Appraising the Earth Summit," p. 32.
26 Michael Grubb *et al.*, *The "Earth Summit" Agreements: A Guide and Assessment: An Analysis of the Rio '92 UN Conference on Trade and Development* (London: Earthscan, 1993), p. 51.

27 For the Forum's genealogy, see Ronnie D. Lipschutz, *Global Environmental Politics: Power, Perspectives, and Practice* (Washington, DC: CQ Press, 2004), p. 200.

28 Lipschutz, *Global Environmental Politics*, pp. 200–201.

29 Ibid.

30 Grubb *et al.*, *"Earth Summit,"* pp. 51–52.

31 Charlesworth notes that this resulted from extensive lobbying by international women's groups during the conference. "Women as Sherpas: Are Global Summits Useful for Women?" *Feminist Studies*, vol. 22 (1996): pp. 537–547. The inclusion of such provisions in the Rio documents was a change from Stockholm. Ranee K.L. Panjabi, *The Earth Summit at Rio: Politics, Economics, and the Environment* (Boston: Northeastern University Press, 1997), pp. 77–79.

32 Mensah, "United Nations Commission," pp. 25–32.

33 Felix Dodds, "The Context: Multi-Stakeholder Processes and Global Governance," in Minu Hemmati (ed.), *Multi-Stakeholder Processes for Governance and Sustainability: Beyond Deadlock and Conflict* (London: Earthscan, 2002), pp. 31–33.

34 Alexander Timoshenko and Mark Berman, "The United Nations Environment Programme and the United Nations Development Programme," in Jacob Werksman (ed.), *Greening International Institutions* (London: Earthscan, 1996), pp. 39–49.

35 Indeed, it was only "after considerable pressure from the rest of the OECD" that the USA agreed to widespread references to the need for "new and additional resources," always unspecified as to amount however. Grubb *et al.*, *"Earth Summit,"* p. 29.

36 William A. Lafferty and James Meadowcroft, "Patterns of Governmental Engagement," in William M. Lafferty and James Meadowcroft (eds), *Implementing Sustainable Development: Strategies and Initiatives in High Consumption Societies* (Oxford: Oxford University Press, 2000), pp. 347–349.

37 Zoe Young, *A New Green Order? The World Bank and the Politics of the Global Environmental Facility* (London: Pluto Press, 2002), p. 6.

38 Ibid., p. 7

39 Ibid.

40 Young, *A New Green Order?* pp. 6–15.

41 Grubb *et al.*, *"Earth Summit,"* pp. 53–54.

42 UN Secretary-General Boutros Boutros-Ghali gives himself some of the credit for convincing President Bush to attend. He says that the US President seemed reluctant to go, "fearing it would stir up domestic 'anti-green' opposition to him in a presidential election year." Boutros-Ghali, who admits that the environment wasn't one of his own priorities when he

took over as Secretary-General, credits Al Gore, Tommy Koh and Maurice Strong with convincing him of its importance. Boutros Boutros-Ghali, *Unvanquished: A U.S.–U.N. Saga* (New York: Random House, 1999), pp. 163–164.

43 Brack, Calder and Dolun, *From Rio to Johannesburg*, p. 2.

44 Grubb *et al.*, *"Earth Summit,"* p. 34.

45 President Bush's successor, President Clinton, signed the Convention on Biological Diversity (CBD), but it has not received Senatorial approval or been ratified by the US President. Members of Congress seem concerned that it "might impede the sovereignty and economic free range of America." Since its "birth" at Rio, there have been more than fifteen major meetings under its aegis, but little progress has been made toward either measuring biological diversity or slowing the extinction of species. Frederick A.B. Meyerson, "Burning the Bridge to the 21st Century: The End of the Era of Integrated Conferences?" *ESCAP Report*, vol. 9 (2003): p. 7.

46 Hempel, *Environmental Governance*, p. 34.

47 Panjabi, *Earth Summit*, p. 134.

48 James Brooke, "U.S. Has a Starring Role at Rio Summit as Villain," *The New York Times* (June 2, 1992), p. A10; Keith Schneider, "White House Snubs U.S. Envoy's Plea to Sign Rio Treaty," *The New York Times* (June 5, 1992), p. A1; James Brooke, "President, in Rio, Defends His Stand on Environment," *The New York Times* (June 13, 1992), p. 1; Michael Wines, "Bush Leaves Rio with Shots at Critics, U.S. and Foreign," *The New York Times* (June 14, 1992), p. 11.

49 Hempel, *Environmental Governance*, p. 35.

50 Haas *et al.*, "Appraising the Earth Summit," p. 26.

51 Hempel, *Environmental Governance*, p. 44.

52 Notable in this regard is the Cocoyoc [Mexico] Declaration that was issued in October 1974 at a UNEP and UNCTAD sponsored symposium on Patterns of Resource Use, Environment and Development Strategies. The purpose of the symposium was to discuss implications of the use of technologies that were destructive to the physical environment in light of the need for economic and social development. The Declaration noted "the evils that flow from excessive reliance on the market system," suggesting that unequal distribution between industrialized and economically less developed countries contributed to environmental pressure and degradation. The Declaration called for aggressive action. United Nations, General Assembly, Second Committee, Twenty-Ninth Session, Agenda Item 46, *United Nations Environment Programme*, November 1, 1974, A/C.2.292.

53 Seyfang and Jordan, "Johannesburg Summit," p. 21.

54 Grubb *et al.*, *"Earth Summit,"* pp. 55–56.

55 Ibid., pp. 55–57.

56 Panjabi, *Earth Summit*, pp. 12–13.

57 Grubb *et al.*, "*Earth Summit*," p. 24.

58 Hempel, *Environmental Governance*, pp. 42–43.

59 Grubb *et al.*, "*Earth Summit*," p. 24.

60 Ken Conca, "Beyond the Earth Summit Framework," *Politics and the Life Sciences*, vol. 21 (2002); p. 2.

61 See, for example, Daniel C. Thomas, *The Helsinki Effect: International Norms, Human Rights, and the Demise of Communism* (Princeton, NJ: Princeton University Press, 2001).

62 Boutros-Ghali, *Unvanquished*, p. 170.

63 Linda Gail Arrigo, "A View of the United Nations Conference on Human Rights, Vienna, June 1993: From among the Throng at the Non-Governmental Organization Forum," *Bulletin of Concerned Asian Scholars*, vol. 25, no. 3 (1993); pp. 69–70.

64 Elisabeth L. Larson, "Comment: United Nations Fourth World Conference on Women: Action for Equality, Development, and Peace (Beijing, China: September 1995)," *Emory International Law Review*, vol. 10 (1996).

65 Florence Butegwa (ed.), *The World Conference on Human Rights: The WiLDAF Experience* (Harare: Women in Law and Development in Africa, 1993), p. 24.

66 Susan Marks, "Nightmare and Noble Dream: The 1993 World Conference on Human Rights," *Cambridge Law Journal*, vol. 53 (1994): p. 61.

67 Arrigo, "View," p. 71.

68 United Nations, General Assembly, World Conference on Human Rights; Report of the Regional Meeting for Asia of the World Conference on Human Rights; Bangkok, 29 March–2 April 1993 (April 7, 1993). A/CONF.157/ASRM8. A/CONF.157/PC/59.

69 Marks, "Nightmare and Noble Dream," p. 56.

70 Larson, "Comment," p. 712.

71 Boutros-Ghali, *Unvanquished*, p. 167.

72 United Nations, General Assembly, Fifty-Third Session, Item 113(d) of the Provisional Agenda, Human Rights Questions: Comprehensive Implementation of and Follow-up to the Vienna Declaration and Programme of Action, *Follow-up to the World Conference on Human Rights: Note by the Secretary-General* (September 11, 1998), A/53/372, Section I.8.

73 Felice D. Gaer, book review of *The United Nations High Commission for Human Rights: The Challenge of International Protection* by Bertrand G. Ramcharan, *American Journal of International Law*, vol. 98, no. 2 (2004); p. 393.

74 Ibid., p, 392–395

75 Marks, "Nightmare and Noble Dream," p. 60.

76 Thomas G. Weiss, David P. Forsythe and Roger A. Coate, *The United Nations and Changing World Politics*, 4th edn. (Boulder, CO: Westview Press, 2004), p. 198.

77 Panjabi, *Earth Summit*, pp. 32–33.

78 The idea of convening another conference dealing with population issues long predated the conclusion of the Rio Conference. For example, the Economic and Social Council (ECOSOC), on July 26, 1989 (Resolution 1989/91) decided, in principle, to convene a UN meeting on population sometime in 1994 and agreed on July 26, 1991 (Resolution 1991/92) that it should be called the International Conference on Population and Development.

79 Jason L. Finkle and C. Alison McIntosh, "United Nations Population Conferences: Shaping the Policy Agenda for the Twenty-First Century," *Studies in Family Planning*, vol. 33, no. 1 (2002), p. 14.

80 C. Alison McIntosh and Jason L. Finkle, "The Cairo Conference on Population and Development: A New Paradigm?" *Population and Development Review*, vol. 21, no. 2 (1995), pp. 232–233..

81 Finkle and McIntosh, "United Nations", pp. 230–231.

82 Finkle and McIntosh, "United Nations," p. 18.

83 Paige Whaley Eager, "From Population Control to Reproductive Rights: Understanding Normative Change in Global Population Policy (1965–1994)," *Global Society*, vol. 18, no. 2 (2004), p. 146.

84 Finkle and McIntosh, "United Nations," p. 19. See also Adrienne Germain and Rachel Kyte, *The Cairo Consensus: The Right Agenda for the Right Time*, 2nd edn. (New York: International Women's Health Coalition, 1995), p. 1.

85 McIntosh and Finkle, "Cairo Conference," p. 14.

86 Janet Gottschalk, "Cairo to Beijing: Disaster Averted," *Social Justice*, vol. 22, no. 4 (1995), p. 91.

87 McIntosh and Finkle suggest that Clinton's election and his reversal of the "Mexico City policy" immediately after taking office "sent a signal to feminists that the political climate had changed dramatically and would be more hospitable to women's issues." They continue: "More than this, however, the Clinton policy change also heartened the population community, including the US Agency for International Development (USAID), UNFPA, US foundations and NGOs, and their counterparts in other countries." McIntosh and Finkle, "Cairo Conference," p. 236.

88 Eager, "From Population Control," pp. 159–162.

89 Charlesworth, "Women as Sherpas," vol. 22 (1996), pp. 537–547.

90 Kathrin Day Lassila, "Cairo: The Real Story," *Amicus Journal*, vol. 16, no. 3 (1994).

91 United Nations, "Report of the International Conference on Population and Development, Cairo, 5–13 September 1994," A/CONF/171/13/Rev.1 (New York: United Nations, 1995), paragraphs 4.18, 8.16, 8.21, 7.6.

92 Stanley Johnson, *The Politics of Population: The International Conference on Population and Development* (London: Earthscan, 1995), p. 202.

93 Finkle and McIntosh, "United Nations," p. 20.

94 Jyoti Shankar Singh, *Creating a New Consensus: The International Conference on Population and Development* (London: Earthscan, 1998), p.161.

95 "Opening Statement by Kofi Annan, Secretary-General of the United Nations at the Twenty-First Special Session of the General Assembly, 30 June–2 July 1999," in *Review and Appraisal of the Progress Made in Achieving the Goals and Objectives of the Programme of Action of the International Conference on Population and Development, 1999 Report*, ST/ESA/SER.A/182 (New York: Department of Economic and Social Affairs, Population Division, 1999), p. 2.

96 Louis Emmerij, Richard Jolly and Thomas G. Weiss, *Ahead of the Curve? UN Ideas and Global Challenges* (Bloomington, IN: Indiana University Press, 2001), p. 114.

97 Boutros-Ghali, *Unvanquished*, p. 171.

98 United Nations, *The World Conferences: Developing Priorities for the 21st Century* (UN Briefing Papers) (New York: United Nations, Department of Public Information, 1997).

99 Barbara Crossette, "Talks in Denmark to Discuss All the Ways the World Hurts," *The New York Times* (March 6, 1995).

100 "The Gift Relationship," *The Economist* (March 18, 1995).

101 Eveline Herfkens, "Foreword: 'Juan Somavia: Citizen Diplomat,'" in Juan Somavia, *People's Security: Globalizing Social Progress* (Geneva: J. Somavia, 1999), pp. iv–vi.

102 United Nations, World Summit for Social Development, *Report of the World Summit for Social Development (Copenhagen, 6–12 March 1995)*, April 19, 1995, A/CONF.166/9.(New York: United Nations, 1995).

103 Boutros-Ghali, *Unvanquished*, p. 171.

104 Johnson, *Politics of Population*. Singh, *Creating a New Consensus*.

105 United Nations, *Report of the World Summit for Social Development*.

106 Barbara Crossette, "Once a Sideshow, Private Organizations Star at U.N. Meetings," *The New York Times* (March 12, 1995).

107 Tahlif Deen, "Rich Nations Decline to Increase Their Aid," *India Abroad*, vol. 25 (1995).

108 Peter Henriot, "Forward Steps at the Social Summit," *America*, vol. 172, no. 14 (1995).

109 United Nations, *World Conferences*, pp. 52–53.

110 Carol Ann Traut, "Policy Implementation in an International Setting: A Case Study of China and the 1995 United Nations Conference on Women," *International Journal of Public Administration*, vol. 22, no. 2 (1999).

111 Ibid., pp. 290–297.

112 Ibid., p. 287.

113 Roya Akhavan-Majid and Jyotika Ramaprasad, "Framing Beijing: Dominant Ideological Influences on the American Press Coverage of the Fourth UN Conference on Women and the NGO Forum," *Gazette*, vol. 62, no. 1 (2000).

114 Hilkka Pietilä, *Engendering the Global Agenda: The Story of Women and the United Nations* (Geneva: UN Non-Governmental Liaison Service, 2002), p. 58.

115 Riddell-Dixon gives the Canadian delegation considerable credit for the precedent-setting definition of rape as a war crime and crime against humanity. Elizabeth Riddell-Dixon, *Canada and the Beijing Conference on Women: Governmental Politics and NGO Participation* (Vancouver: University of British Columbia Press, 2001).

116 Joan Dunlop, Rachel Kyte and Mia MacDonald, "Women Redrawing the Map: The World after the Beijing and Cairo Conferences," *SAIS Review*, vol. 16, no. 1 (1996).

117 Charlesworth, "Women as Sherpas."

118 Pietilä notes that the concept of gender did not appear in the Nairobi Forward-Looking Strategies and only began to appear in UN documents after Nairobi. *Engendering the Global Agenda*, p. 63.

119 Emmerij *et al.*, *Ahead of the Curve?*, p. 106.

120 Dunlop *et al.*, "Women," pp. 161–164.

121 Charlesworth, "Women as Sherpas."

122 Dunlop *et al.*, "Women," pp. 157–161. In negotiations, the US delegation played a low-key role, remaining "[s]ilent at critical moments due to fear of domestic lobbies of the Christian right." However the US delegation fought to defend the language from the 1993 Vienna conference.

123 Bonnie L. Shepard, *NGO Advocacy Networks in Latin America: Lessons from Experience in Promoting Women's and Reproductive Rights* (North–South Agenda Papers, no. 61) (Miami: Dante B. Fascell North–South Center, University of Miami, 2003), p. 6.

124 Charlesworth, "Women as Sherpas."

125 *Beijing+5 Process and Beyond* (New York: United Nations, Division for the Advancement of Women, 2000). Available at http://www.un.org/womenwatch/daw/followup/bfbeyond.htm (accessed on December 31, 2002).

126 United Nations, General Assembly, Twenty-Third Special Session, Agenda Item 10, "Further Actions and Initiatives to Implement the

Beijing Declaration and Platform for Action," (New York: United Nations, 16 November 2000).

127 Odil Tunali, "Habitat II; Not Just Another Doomed Global Conference," *World Watch*, vol. 9 (1996), p. 34.

128 Although not as highly politicized as earlier conferences, it is worth noting that the PrepCom asked the General Assembly to authorize ECOSOC to decide on the accreditation of three NGOs that it had recommended not be accredited to Habitat II: Taiwan International Alliance, Canada Tibet Committee and Tibetan Rights Campaign. ECOSOC did not accredit them to the conference. United Nations, *Yearbook of the United Nations, 1996* (vol. 50) (New York: Office of Public Information, United Nations, 1998), p. 992.

129 Joan M. Veon, transcription of interview with Dr. Waly N'Bow and Dr. Noel Brown, 1996. Available at www.womensgroup.org/NDOW.html (accessed on July 4, 2004).

130 Tim Honey, "The Habitat Agenda: Local Governments are Critical in Sustainable Urban Development," *Public Management*, vol. 78 (1996), p. 23.

131 Axumite Gebre-Egziabher and Wandia Seaforth, "Countdown to Istanbul+5: Second and Final Prepcom for Istanbul+5 Concludes Successfully Despite Initial Set-Back," *Habitat Debate*, vol. 7, no. 1 (2001).

132 Dodds, "The Context."

133 United Nations, *Yearbook of the United Nations, 1996*, p. 993.

134 This was in spite of the fact that the conferees had wrestled with such contentious issues as "housing as a human right." Honey, "Habitat Agenda," p. 23.

135 Margaret R. Biwas, "The United Nations Conference on Human Settlements (Habitat II)," *Environmental Conservation*, vol. 23, no. 4 (1996), p. 374.

136 United Nations General Assembly, Fifty-First Session, Agenda Item 96(3), "Sustainable Development and International Economic Cooperation: Human Settlements, Implementation of and Follow-up to the Outcome of the United Nations Conference on Human Settlements (Habitat II)," *Report of the Secretary-General* (September 20, 1996).

137 Axumite Gebre-Egziabher, "Five Years after Habitat II: Successes and Set-Backs," *Habitat Debate*, vol. 7, no. 1 (2001). Gebre-Egziabher and Seaforth, "Countdown to Istanbul+5."

6 The twenty-first-century UN global conferences

1 Mearsheimer is an important exception, as he doesn't believe any country can become a global hegemon. John J. Mearsheimer, *The Tragedy of Great Powers* (New York: W.W. Norton, 2001).

2 See, for example, Nial Ferguson, *Colossus: The Price of America's Empire* (New York: Penguin Press, 2004).

3 John Gerard Ruggie, "global_governance.net: The Global Compact as Learning Network," *Global Governance*, vol. 7, October–December (2001): pp. 371–372. Available at http://www.unglobalcompact.org/content/AboutTheGC/Overview_About.htm?ViewID=253 (accessed on October 3, 2004).

4 Fergus Watt, "What Did the Millennium Summit Do?" *Mondial*, November (2000), p. 16.

5 Ibid., p. 16.

6 Lilana B. Andonova and Marc A. Levy, "Franchising Global Governance: Making Sense of the Johannesburg Type II Partnerships," in Olva Schram Stokke and Øystein B. Thommessen (eds.), *Yearbook of International Co-operation on Environment and Development 2003/2004* (London: Earthscan, 2003).

7 Quaker United Nations Office Staff, "The State of the UN 2002," *A Quaker Perspective*, vol. 1 (2000), p. 1.

8 United Nations, Department of Economic and Social Affairs, Statistics Division, *Millennium Indicators Database*, 2004. Available at: http://milleniumindicators.un.org/unsd/mi/mi_goals.asp (accessed on July 4, 2004).

9 Lloyd Axworthy, *Navigating a New World: Canada's Global Future* (Toronto: Alfred A. Knopf Canada, 2003), p. 408.

10 United Nations Non-Governmental Liaison Service, "NGOs Assess the Millennium Development Goals," *NGLS Roundup*, vol. 105 (2003).

11 United Nations Non-Governmental Liaison Service, "MDGs: Moving Forward on Millennium Development Goals," *NGLS Roundup*, vol. 98 (2002).

12 Mark Baird and Sudhir Shetty, "Getting There: How to Accelerate Progress toward the Millennium Development Goals," *Finance and Development*, vol. 4, 4 (2003), p. 14.

13 United Nations Non-Governmental Liaison Service, "MDGs: Taking Root at the National Level?" *NGLS Roundup*, vol. 106 (2003), p. 1.

14 Annan's speech was reproduced in full in the *The New York Times* (September 23, 2003).

15 United Nations, General Assembly, Third Conference on the Least Developed Countries, Brussels, Belgium, 14–20 May 2001, *Brussels Declaration*, A/CONF.191/12 (July 2, 2001).

16 United Nations, General Assembly, Third Conference on the Least Developed Countries, Brussels, Belgium, 14–20 May 2001, *Programme of Action for the Least Developed Countries; Adopted by the Third Conference on the Least Developed Countries in Brussels on 20 May 2001*, A/CONF.191/11 (June 8, 2001), p. 24.

17 Vasantha Arora, "Wolfensohn Urges Rich, Poor Nations to Fight Poverty," *India Abroad* (May 25, 2001) p. 24.

18 Krause contends that the odd phrase "in all its aspects" in the conference title, in principle, opened the way to a wide-ranging examination of all aspects of the production, stockpiling, and trade in small arms and light weapons. Keith Krause, "Multilateral Diplomacy, Norm Building and UN Conferences: The Case of Small Arms and Light Weapons," *Global Governance*, vol. 8 (2002): p. 249.

19 Khatchik Derghoukassian, "U.S. Hegemony and the Global Rifle Association: Small Arms and Light Weapons on the International Security Agenda," paper presented at the Annual Meeting of the International Studies Association (Montreal, 2004).

20 Peter Batchelor and Keith Krause (eds.), *Small Arms Survey 2003: Development Denied* (Oxford: Oxford University Press, 2003), p. 222.

21 Edward Laurence and Rachel Stohl, *Making Global Public Policy: The Case of Small Arms and Light Weapons* (Geneva: Small Arms Survey, Graduate Institute of International Studies, 2002), p. 3.

22 Aaron Karp, "Laudable Failure," *SAIS Review*, vol. 221, no. 1 (2002): pp. 179–180.

23 United Nations General Assembly, "General and Complete Disarmament" (December 12, 1995).

24 United Nations General Assembly, "General and Complete Disarmament: Small Arms," A/52/298 (August 27, 1997).

25 Laurence and Stohl, *Making Global Public Policy*.

26 Peter Batchelor and Keith Krause (eds.), *Small Arms Survey 2002: Counting the Human Cost* (Oxford: Oxford University Press, 2002).

27 Ibid., p. 205.

28 Laurence and Stohl, *Making Global Public Policy*.

29 Peter Batchelor, "NGOs as Partners: Assessing the Impact," *Disarmament Forum*, vol. 1, no. 1 (2002), pp. 37–38.

30 Batchelor, "NGOs as Partners," pp. 38–39.

31 Karp, "Laudable Failure," pp. 178–179, 189.

32 Ibid.

33 The financial value of the small arms business is estimated at $21 billion per year, exclusive of the black market, which is estimated to be another $10 billion per year. The Permanent five members of the UN Security Council account for 88 per cent of the authorized arms exports. The USA is the largest exporter of small arms, selling approximately $1.2 billion per year. Lyndon Jeffels, "Small Arms: The Real Weapons of Mass Deaths, Destruction," *Daily Mirror* (October 16, 2003). Sean D. Murphy, "UN Conference on Illicit Trade in Small Arms," *American Journal of International Law*, vol. 95, no. 4 (2001), p. 90.

34 Derghoukassian, "U.S. Hegemony," pp. 9–13.

35 Krause, "Multilateral Diplomacy," p. 247.

36 Batchelor and Krause, *Small Arms Survey 2002*, p. 204.

37 As is often the case, regional groups are sometimes able to reach consensus on a higher level than the global tendency to go to the "lowest common denominator." The OAU's Bamako [Mali] Declaration on an African Common Position on the Illicit Proliferation, Circulation and Trafficking of Small Arms and Light Weapons (of December 1, 2000) represents this, i.e. it includes a commitment to "accept trade in small arms" as being limited to governments and authorized registered licensed traders, while the UN conferees could not limit sale to non-state actors. The point, here, of course, is that the Bamako Declaration remains just that, a declaration and not legally binding.

38 Tamar Gabelnick, "U.S., 'Rogues' Hold Out," *Bulletin of the Atomic Scientists*, vol. 57, no. 5 (2001), p. 18.

39 Murphy suggests that many governments—contrary to the US position—believed that controlling illicit trade could not be accomplished without first better regulating the legitimate trade in arms. But "most states acknowledged that any agreement would be ineffective without U.S. participation." Murphy, "UN Conference," p. 903.

40 Batchelor and Krause, *Small Arms Survey 2003*, p. 223.

41 Owen Greene, "The 2001 UN Conference: A Useful Step Forward?" *SAIS Review*, vol. 22, no. 1 (2002).

42 Laurence and Stohl, *Making Global Public Policy*, pp. 25–26; Derghoukassian, "U.S. Hegemony," pp. 17–18; Biting the Bullet, *Implementing the Programme of Action 2003: Action by States and Civil Society*, 2003, International Action Network on Small Arms. Available at www.reliefweb.int/w/lib.nsf/WebPubDocs/619C8C1EF823D072C1256DD C003DC059OpenDocument, p. 6 (accessed on May 8, 2004).

43 Peter Batchelor, "The First Biennial Meeting of States on Small Arms: Building Momentum for Global Action," *Disarmament Diplomacy*, vol. 72 (2003).

44 Laurence and Stohl, *Making Global Public Policy*, pp. viii, 1, 10–16.

45 Biting the Bullet, *Implementing*, p. 6.

46 Ibid., p. 5.

47 Israel had made revocation of the resolution a condition of their participation in the Madrid Peace Conference in progress in the last quarter of 1991. The culmination of the long struggle came on December 16, 1991 when the UN General Assembly revoked Resolution 3379, with a vote of 111 to 25 (with 13 abstentions). On September 23, 1991, in a speech at the General Assembly, US President George H.W. Bush stated that "to equate Zionism with the intolerable sin of racism is to twist history and forget

the terrible plight of Jews in World War II and indeed throughout history."

48 Rita Maran, "A Report from the United Nations Conference against Racism, Racial Discrimination, Xenophobia, and Related Intolerance, Durban, South Africa, 2001," *Social Justice: A Journal of Crime, Conflict and World Order*, vol. 29, no. 1 (2002), p. 180.

49 William B. Wood, "The UN World Conference against Racism," *U.S. Congress, House International Relations Committee, Subcommittee on International Operations and Human Rights* (US Department of State, July 31, 2001), p. 1.

50 United Nations General Assembly, "Third Decade to Combat Racism and Racial Discrimination and the Convening of a World Conference against Racism, Racial Discrimination, Xenophobia and Related Intolerance," A/RES/52/111 (December 12, 1997), February 18, 1998.

51 Makani Themba-Nixon, "Race in the 'Post Third World,'" *ColorLines: Race, Culture, Action*, vol. 4, no. 3 (2001), pp. 3–4.

52 "World Conference against Racism, Racial Discrimination, Xenophobia and Related Intolerance, Durban, South Africa, 31 August–7 September 2001," (New York: United Nations, 2001).

53 "The fact that a South Asian living in London is Black and a South Asian living in Los Angeles is definitely not demonstrates how local permutations of race and racism shape both racial consciousness and racial conflict." Themba-Nixon, "Race," pp. 1, 3.

54 Wood, "UN World Conference."

55 Christopher N. Camponovo, "Disaster in Durban: The United Nations World Conference against Racism, Racial Discrimination, Xenophobia and Related Intolerance," *George Washington International Law Review*, vol. 34, no. 4 (2003), p. 660.

56 Wood, "UN World Conference."

57 Steven Erlander, "America's Close Allies Decide to Stick It Out in Durban to Save the Meeting," *The New York Times* (September 4, 2001), p. A8.

58 John H. Cushman, "U.S. Delegates in Durban Practiced Minimalism," *The New York Times* (September 4, 2001).

59 Manning Marable, "Structural Racism and American Democracy," *Souls; A Critical Journal of Black Politics, Culture, and Society*, vol. 3, no. 1 (2001), p. 8.

60 Rachel L. Swarns, "After the Race Conference: Relief, and Doubt over Whether It Will Matter," *The New York Times* (September 10, 2001), p. A8.

61 The Canadian delegation explained that it had stayed on

[in order to] have our voice decry the attempts at this Conference to delegitimize the State of Israel and to dishonour the history and suffering of the Jewish people. We believe, and we have said it in the clearest possible terms, that it was inappropriate—wrong—to address the Palestinian–Israel conflict in this forum.

(United Nations, Report of the World Conference against Racism, Racial Discrimination, Xenophobia and Related Intolerance, Durban 31 August–8 September 2001, A/CONF.189/12, United Nations, 2001)

62 Camponovo, "Disaster in Durban," p. 696.
63 Erlander, "America's Close Allies," p. A8.
64 Rachel L. Swarns, "At Race Talks, Delegates Cite Early Mistrust," *The New York Times* (September 5, 2001). Reportedly the French were pretty much alone of the colonial powers in calling the slave trade a crime against humanity. Erlander, "America's Close Allies," p. A8.
65 Fakir Hassen, "World Conference on Racism: Dalit Issue Finds No Mention in Declaration," *News India-Times* (September 14, 2001).
66 Swarns, "After the Race Conference," p. A10.
67 Manning Marable, "Structural Racism and American Democracy" vol. 6 (Winter 2001): 8.
68 United Nations Non-Governmental Liaison Service, "World Conference against Racism: United to Combat Racism," *NGLS Roundup*, vol. 82 (2001).
69 Jonathan L. Watkins, "The Monterrey Consensus: Will Developing Countries Benefit from the Financing for Development Conference with Greater Sustainable Economic Growth?" (University of Missouri, Kansas City, Department of Economics Working Paper, April 2002).
70 United Nations, Report of the International Conference on Financing and Development, Monterrey, Mexico, 18–22 March 2002, A/CONF.198/11 (2002).
71 United Nations, General Assembly, Fifty-Seventh Session, Item 95 of the provisional agenda, High-level international intergovernmental consideration of financing for development, "Follow-Up Efforts to the International Conference on Financing for Development; Report of the Secretary-General," A/57/319 (August 8, 2002).
72 United Nations, *Report of the Second World Assembly on Ageing, Madrid, 8–12 April 2002*, A/CONF.197/9 (New York: United Nations, 2002), p. 1.
73 Ibid.
74 Ibid., p. 2.
75 Ibid., pp. 3–4.
76 Ibid., pp. 7–8.
77 "U.N. Offers Action Plan for a World Aging Rapidly," *The New York Times* (April 14, 2002).

78 Steven van Krimpen, "Population: Ageing Poses Challenges Worldwide," *Global Information Network* (New York, March 4, 2002), p. 1.
79 Hillel Landes, "Israel-Bashing Overshadows U.N. Conference on the Elderly," *Jewish Telegraphic Agency* (New York, April 15, 2002), p. 10.
80 Quoted in "U.N. Offers Action Plan."
81 Ken Conca, "Beyond the Earth Summit Framework," *Politics and Life Sciences*, vol. 21, no. 2 (2002), p. 53.
82 Jericho Burg, "The World Summit on Sustainable Development: Empty Talk or Call to Action?" *Journal of Environment and Development*, vol. 12, no. 1 (2003).
83 Ibid., p. 111.
84 Ibid., p. 116.
85 Pablo Gutman, "What Did WSSD Accomplish? An NGO Perspective," *Environment* vol. 45, no. 2(2003), p. 22.
86 Burg, "World Summit," p. 112.
87 UN Non-Governmental Liaison Service, "World Summit on Sustainable Development," *NGLS Roundup*, vol. 96, November (2002).
88 Andonova and Levy, "Franchising Global Governance."
89 Antonio G.M. La Viña, Gretchen Hoff and Ann Marie DeRose, "The Outcomes of Johannesburg: Assessing the World Summit on Sustainable Development," *SAIS Review*, vol. 23, no. 1 (2003).
90 Ibid., p. 60.
91 Gutman, "What Did WSSD Accomplish?", p.24.
92 Viña *et al.*, "Outcomes," p. 67.
93 United Nations Non-Governmental Liaison Service, "CSD-11 Builds Implementation Track for Johannesburg Outcomes," *NGLS Roundup*, vol. 102 (2003).

7 Conclusion

1 Quoted in Louis Emmerij, Richard Jolly and Thomas G. Weiss, *Ahead of the Curve? UN Ideas and Global Challenges* (Bloomington: Indiana University Press, 2001), p. 116.
2 Juan Somavia, *People's Security: Globalizing Social Progress* (Geneva: J. Somavia, 1999), p. 176.
3 Peter Henriot, "Forward Steps at the Social Summit," *America*, vol. 172, no. 14 (1995), p. 4.
4 Hilary Charlesworth, "Women as Sherpas: Are Global Summits Useful for Women?" *Feminist Studies,* vol. 22 (Fall 1996): pp. 537–547..
5 Emmerij *et al.*, *Ahead of the Curve?,* p. 89.
6 Ibid., p. 89.
7 Ibid., p. 117.

8 Ibid., p. 88.
9 Philip Allott, "The Concept of International Law," in Michael Byers (ed.), *The Role of Law in International Politics: Essays in International Relations and International Law* (Oxford: Oxford University Press, 2000).
10 Roya Akhavan-Majid and Jyotika Ramaprasad, "Framing Beijing: Dominant Ideological Influences on the American Press Coverage of the Fourth UN Conference on Women and the NGO Forum," *Gazette*, vol. 62, no. 1 (2000).
11 Lamont C. Hempel, *Environmental Governance: The Global Challenge* (Washington, DC: Island Press, 1996).
12 These recent developments seem in some tension with Hempel's earlier most pessimistic assessment. Hempel, *Environmental Governance*.
13 Jacques Fomerand, "The Politics of Norm Setting at the United Nations: The Case of Sustainable Human Development," in Dennis Dijkzeul and Yves Beigbeder (eds.), *Rethinking International Organizations: Pathology and Promise* (New York: Berghahn Books, 2003).
14 Paul Wapner, "World Summit on Sustainable Development: Toward a Post-Jo'burg Environmentalism," *Global Environmental Politics*, vol. 3, no. 1 (2003), p. 9.

Index